LIQUID LIFE

A "Let's See E.T." button is placed on a Jizō, a protector of deceased children and fetuses in Japanese Buddhism. Thousands of Jizō can be found in Japanese cemeteries specially dedicated to memorializing such children. (Kamakura.) (Photo courtesy of Christopher McCooey.)

LIQUID LIFE

ABORTION AND BUDDHISM IN JAPAN

William R. LaFleur

PRINCETON UNIVERSITY PRESS

PRINCETON, NEW JERSEY

Library of Congress Cataloging-in-Publication Data

LeFleur, William R.
Liquid life : abortion and Buddhism in Japan / William R. LaFleur.
p.   cm.
Includes bibliographical references and index.
ISBN 0-691-07405-4
ISBN 0-691-02965-2 (pbk.)
1. Abortion—Religious aspects—Buddhism. 2. Abortion—Japan.
I. Title.

HQ767.38.B83L34 1992 294.3'56976'0952-–dc20 92-13258

This book has been composed in Linotron Sabon

Princeton University Press books are printed
on acid-free paper and meet the guidelines
for permanence and durability of the Committee
on Production Guidelines for Book Longevity
of the Council on Library Resources

First Princeton paperback printing, 1994

Printed in the United States of America

10 9 8 7 6

To Yoshimitsu and Sumiko Nishi

In our kind of world
Some ask heaven for children;
Others dispose of them in earth.

(Anonymous Senryū, eighteenth century)

CONTENTS

LIST OF ILLUSTRATIONS   xi

PREFACE   xiii

ACKNOWLEDGMENTS   xvii

PART ONE: ORIGINAL CONCEPTS

CHAPTER 1
Behind the Great Buddha   3

CHAPTER 2
A World of Water and Words   14

CHAPTER 3
Social Death, Social Birth   30

CHAPTER 4
Jizō at the Crossroads   44

PART TWO: HISTORICAL PROCESSES

CHAPTER 5
Edo: An Era in View   69

CHAPTER 6
Edo: Population   89

CHAPTER 7
Edo: Polemics   103

CHAPTER 8
Sex, War, and Peace   119

PART THREE: CONTEMPORARY ISSUES

CHAPTER 9
Apology   143

CHAPTER 10
Moral Swamps   160

CHAPTER 11
A Rational, National Family   177

CHAPTER 12
Crossovers   198

Conclusion   214

APPENDIX
"The Way to Memorialize One's Mizuko"   221

NOTES   225

BIBLIOGRAPHY   243

INDEX   253

ILLUSTRATIONS

All photographs are by the author, unless otherwise indicated.

A "Let's See E.T." button is placed on a Jizō, a protector of deceased children and fetuses in Japanese Buddhism. Thousands of Jizōs can be found in Japanese cemeteries specially dedicated to memorializing such children. (Kamakura.) (Photo courtesy of Christopher McCooey.) *Frontispiece*

Weather-exposed images are often covered with knitted garments and festooned with inexpensive jewelry. (Chichibu.)   7

Images are protected too by umbrellas; pinwheels are children's toys and also replicas of the Wheel of the Dharma, a Buddhist symbol. (Chichibu.)   8

The kokeshi dolls originated in the famine-beleaguered northeast and appear to be a folk art related to the mizuko.   52

A site of Sai-no-kawara, where the sea meets the land on the northern tip of Sado Island.   60

Miniature Jizō images are placed throughout the rocky terrain of the Sado Sai-no-kawara site.   60

Dolls on site dedicated to mizuko express the emotions of children as well as the relations of parents to their children.   61

The center of Sado's Sai-no-kawara is a cave with images; no priest is in attendance.   61

Dolls at sites such as that on Sado Island include traditional as well as modern, robot-like types.   62

The Jizō at Ueno in Tokyo is a caped man when seen from the front and a phallus when seen from behind. (Photo reproduced from Manabe Kōsai, *Jizō bosatsu no kenkyū* [Kyoto: Sanmitsudō Shoten, 1960].)   125

A woman prays before inchoate, fetoid images in a portion of a traditional temple posted as dedicated to mizuko Jizō rites. (Tokyo.)   137

A Tokyo newspaper includes this advertisement, in which a temple claims to be unexcelled in northeastern Japan in its mizuko rites and ability to exorcize malign influences. (Tokyo, 1968.)   139

Wood pallets on which parents write out apologies to their mizuko. (Asakusa, Tokyo.)   153

PREFACE

IN 1975 I WAS IN JAPAN for studies that had nothing directly to do with abortion. But since the *Roe v. Wade* decision was already beginning to kick up a storm back home in the United States and since during that year I was already spending a lot of time talking with Japanese Buddhist monks and scholars, I sometimes casually dropped the question, "What, by the way, do you Buddhists think of abortion? Have the Buddhist denominations in Japan taken up this problem and made any kind of pronouncement on it?"

My second question was, I will admit, a bit disingenuous, since I already knew it is not the practice of Buddhist organizations, at least in Japan, to state public "positions" on social issues. In response to my first question, a certain pattern emerged in the answers:

> Oh, of course, Buddhism teaches that we are not to take the lives of others! The scriptures are very clear about that—as well as that babies in wombs are life. But, yes, if it's the question of abortion in today's society, we are really in a dilemma. It's really a problem, isn't it? We cannot say it is absolutely wrong. Women who have to get abortions go through a tremendous amount of pain and stress. We have to show compassion for them in that, don't we? Still, we also need to feel sorry for the aborted infants, too.

This struck me as a waffling kind of answer, an uneasy forcing together of the orthodox proscription against the taking of life and sympathy for the plight of women who are pregnant although they do not wish to be.

Japan's abortion rate had begun to soar. I noted discussions of that fact in the major Japanese papers. Then on recreational walks through the cemeteries on the hills around Kyoto, I began to observe what I learned—through questions about the matter—were the "parents" of aborted fetuses going to the cemeteries for simple rituals. Wondering about that, I inquired into what it meant. I talked to people, took notes, found things in scattered books, and bit by bit tried to work out an approach to this study.

I found that in Japan, although some aspects of the religion and abortion problem are similar to what they are in the West, in other important ways they are also very different. It is those differences, I believe, that help explain why in today's Japan, in spite of problems, the abortion issue does not polarize the society into two opposing camps as it does in ours. Over time one of my questions had become, "How have the Japanese managed to deal with abortion so that it has *not* become a matter over which the society tears itself apart?" The answer fascinates me. It is my core concern here.

This book examines the whole abortion and religion problem from an eccentric angle. It is about abortion in a culture that, while strikingly modern, is also decidedly not Western. Japan is a civilization that is in many ways inextricably intertwined with our own—in business, the arts, scientific exchanges, and world philanthropy—but its intellectual and religious traditions have made it significantly different from the West.

"Different," however, need not mean unintelligible. Nor should it mean that Westerners dare let that "difference" lie enveloped in some kind of romantic haze. I began this book with the assumption that we ought to be making a greater mental effort to understand Japan and that, if we could do so, we might possibly break out of the nasty pattern whereby we oscillate between romanticizing Japan and cursing it for doing things we do not expect or like. There are reasons why we are often caught up short by Japanese actions.

Although there are areas of wide consensus within Japanese society, I am reluctant to believe there is something we can peg as the uniform "Japanese mind." Within Japanese thinking there are differences and debates. A Japanese "debate" on religion and abortion took place, I found, before our own, and it was carried out in a very different way. What continues of it today touches on some issues that are not exactly like our own. Those differences are themselves, I suggest, good entry-points into current strains of Japanese thought.

Even when not being debated with similar intensity in the public arena, abortion—perhaps because it touches so many basic life-and-death issues—elicits powerful moves of the mind and heart. These emotions become apparent in these pages, where I often let the representatives of various Japanese viewpoints speak for themselves.

I am not inclined to write of a Japanese "mask" or to suggest that the Japanese intentionally create a "wall of secrecy" behind which things are done. Privacy is not secrecy. Even more important, it is not deception. Most of the things we need and want to know about the Japanese are quite available in Japanese books, archives, newspapers, television, and conversations we can carry on with Japanese people. I did not need to be a Western ninja jumping over bizarre intellectual or cultural walls to do the research in this book. It was a matter of reading Japanese books and essays and of talking to people. It was also a matter of thinking about how the whole religion and abortion problem might be viewed from a rather different—and importantly different—angle.

There has been a noticeable, although certainly not large, increase in the number of persons in both Europe and America who think of themselves as "Buddhist," some by ethnic links and others by choice. There is an even larger number of persons with a passing interest in knowing what Buddhism is—either for personal reasons or because our culture's deepening involvment with Asian societies requires more and more contact with persons there who are in some sense Buddhist.

Books on basic Buddhist teaching and guides to meditation are now fairly accessible. Yet we in the West know next to nothing about what might go into decisions about ethical questions in communities informed by Buddhism. This book deals with only one example, and there are Buddhists who may object very much to the way in which the Japanese seem to have handled the question of abortion. The Japanese, to be sure, do not represent *all* Buddhists. Yet they stand within that tradition, and how they happen to think about sexuality, reproductivity, the family, and abortion are therefore things we do well to know.

Clearly I could not write about this topic without reference to the nature of the debates that are raging within our own society. I make no apologies for doing that, since I have on a number of occasions found it necessary to make explicit and implicit comparisons. Moreover, if some of the ideas presented here could be used as a heuristic tool for looking at—and trying to solve—our own abortion dilemma, I would be doubly pleased. At the same time I will not be surprised if some readers object strongly to parts of this book—or prejudge it as belonging to an inappropriate "learning from Japan" genre. But perhaps that kind of prejudgment is part of our problem today or, at least, an index to it.

Part 1, called "Original Concepts," shows how the Japanese took motifs and symbols found in many cultures but, due to the specificity of history, molded them in ways that seem surprisingly different from what others have done with them. Medieval views of the life cycle and its significance for how people dealt with the death of children and fetuses is given special attention. At the end of this section, I look at how the religious imagination, informed by a Buddhism mixed with folk ideas, portrayed the fate of the unborn and the newly born.

The central chapters, drawn together as "Historical Processes," are about the painful course and social troubles that brought Japan its current relatively benign solution to the abortion problem. These chapters deal with the periods called early modern and modern—that is, from approximately 1600 to 1945. In Japan conflict in religious and philosophical ideas was sharp during much of that time—and abortion was drawn into the struggle. I suggest some ideas about why certain issues, seemingly at the basis of Japan's early modern development, were so different from the West's—and from China's.

Contemporary issues are the focus of the final third of this book. The gamut of Japanese opinion on abortion is presented—as well as an analysis of these views. Here I try to connect Japanese thinking about abortion with what is often said about the "strong family" in Japan. This, in turn, leads into a discussion of what I have dubbed "fecundism" and its related problems. I also suggest where my position fits into some current discussions by philosophers and ethicists, but that is really only a way of trying to show how these Japanese materials might be incorporated into such discussions. Two of my deepest concerns—about how we study Japan and about the world's population—are brought together in the Conclusion.

Unless otherwise indicated, all translations are my own.

ACKNOWLEDGMENTS

T HIS BOOK has been greatly benefited by individuals who gave informed comment when portions of it were presented as lectures and at seminars at various places. These included the Association for Asian Studies, the UCLA Center for the Study of Women, the Southern California Japan seminar, the Reischauer Institute at Harvard University, the Buddhist studies seminar at the University of Chicago, Williams College, Swarthmore College, the Matsushita seminar at the University of Puget Sound, the University of Washington, and the Japan studies seminar at California State University in San Diego. The Academic Senate of UCLA provided grants for research in Japan, and an endowment from Joseph B. Glossberg assisted me in the final writing at the University of Pennsylvania. The excellent scholars and library of the Kokubungaku Shiryōkan in Tokyo were of great use to me during the spring and summer of 1990, even though I was primarily at work there on a different topic. The group of superb graduate students with whom I was privileged to work at UCLA provided valuable reactions to my work—as did the participants in a National Endowment for the Humanities Summer Seminar for College Teachers held at UCLA during 1989.

Individuals who have been especially helpful have been Kozy K. Amemiya, whose emerging research on Japanese women and the problem of abortion will prove of great importance; Herman Ooms and Emily Ooms, who themselves had inquired into this topic and raised probing questions in our discussions; Barbara Ruch, who has drawn Americans into being interested in the otherwise concealed role of women in Japanese Buddhism; Emiko Ohnuki-Tierney, whose own research and perspective on Japan has been very valuable to me; and Lynne Katsukake, who directed me to some materials on mizuko in contemporary fiction. Others with whom I have had profitable conversations have been June O'Connor, Robert Kirsner, Masayo Kaneko, Herbert Morris, Buzzy Teiser, Henry D. Smith, Robert Wargo, Christopher McCooey, Gananath Obeyesekere, and Kazumitsu Katoh. Farrell Graves and Devin Whatley were of great help with bibliographical matters—as was Meike Hoffmeister with the preparation of the index.

I am grateful to Margaret Case of Princeton University Press for giving this manuscript the expert, professional care for which she has become so widely respected. Jennifer Matthews, her assistant, also helped in many ways. Carol Roberts edited the text with care and in such a way that the whole is now much more readable than it otherwise would have been.

Princeton's outside readers gave suggestions from their expertise, and I have incorporated many of them.

The dedication suggests how much I owe to Yoshimitsu and Sumiko Nishi, parents-in-law whose home has been a venue for my research in various ways. Mariko, my wife, has helped me immeasurably, especially in terms of day-to-day conversation about the topics of this book. Because she cares deeply that I not make egregious mistakes about either women or her home-land, she monitored this project in a way I deeply appreciate. Needless to say, whatever errors remain are all my own.

PART ONE

ORIGINAL CONCEPTS

Chapter 1

BEHIND THE GREAT BUDDHA

> When kitsch becomes this grand, it becomes art.
> (Donald Richie, *The Inland Sea*)

THE CROWD OUT BACK

THE QUIET, hill-nestled, seaside city of Kamakura, only two hours from Tokyo by train, is a natural stop for tourists. It combines beauty with history. During the thirteenth and much of the fourteenth centuries, it served as the de facto headquarters of the Japanese government, precisely at a time when a new wave of Buddhist influence from China was having a profound religious, aesthetic, and architectural impact on Japan. The beautiful temples of Kamakura are well maintained and remarkably intact. They, as well as a number of important Shinto shrines in Kamakura, can be reached on a walking tour—although most tourists nowadays make their visits by piling in and out of buses that make the temple rounds.

Tourists in Kamakura, both Japanese and foreign, are virtually certain to stop to see what is commonly referred to as the "Great Buddha" at Kōtokuin, a 37.7-foot high cast-iron image of Amida Buddha seated outdoors in a pose of tranquil contemplation. A good number of people are invariably found there—strolling the enclosed plaza to admire the image, squeezing through a narrow door into the interior of the icon for an inside view, and taking snapshots of individuals or groups in front of the very photogenic, always accommodating, giant figure in seated meditation. The Great Buddha of Kamakura is, many would claim, one of the "wonders" of East Asia, and for that reason it is on the itinerary of most Europeans and Americans touring Japan.

Only two blocks away, however, is a Buddhist site that relatively few non-Japanese will include on their guided tours. Having once seen the Great Buddha, you must follow a back street to find it, a temple named Hase-dera. Like much in Kamakura, it has a history reaching back to the medieval period. Japanese with a special interest in medieval history or art go there to see the wooden image of Kannon, the figure who is considered by Buddhists to be a cosmic source of compassion.[1] The wooden Kannon at Hase-dera Temple is an image about which a good deal of lore has accumulated over the centuries, much of it of historical interest to some tourists.

If you are not Japanese, you will probably never get beyond the Great Buddha, and in the event you do go down the side street to see Hase-dera, you will more than likely return after a quick view of its Kannon. But that is unfortunate because, as a matter of fact, one of the most interesting and revealing scenes in today's Japan consists of what is taking place in the cemetery that is "out back," behind the Kannon of Hase-dera. The Buddhist cemetery there stretches in tiers up the slope of the hill behind the temple. And the careful observer will note that it is to that cemetery, not the Kannon image, that the majority of Japanese visitors to Hase-dera now throng. Many of them will spend more time there than anywhere else in Kamakura—in spite of the fact that tour books and guides make only a passing reference to the cemetery.

Today one can obtain a small leaflet of information about the Hase-dera in English. Bearing a 1983 date, it tells about the Kannon image, tries to correct the impression—easily gained from the image itself—that Kannon is female, and gives a fair amount of legendary detail about its history. Then, in what is little more than a note appended at the end, there is reference to activities taking place in the temple's cemetery. It reads:

> MIZUKO JIZŌ
>
> The Kannon is a Buddhist deity whose special task is to help raise healthy children. Many people come and set up small statues, representing their children, so that he can watch over them. More recently, parents have set up statues for miscarried, aborted or dead-born babies, for the Kannon to protect. These are called Mizuko-jizō and in the Hase-dera there are about 50,000 such Jizōs. Mothers and fathers often visit the Mizuko-jizō to pray for the souls of the children they have lost.

It is this casual, almost passing, reference to "aborted babies" that tells why there is a constant stream of people to the cemetery tucked behind a temple that is itself much less well-known than the nearby Great Buddha.

At one time, what was remembered here were mostly miscarried or stillborn infants; now, however, it is certain that the vast majority are the results of intentionally terminated pregnancies. At Hase-dera in 1983 the tally of the miscarried, stillborn, and aborted was already about fifty thousand; since then it has risen much higher.

Hase-dera, however, is only one of a growing number of Buddhist temples in Japan that offer such services. Many of these temples began by offering other kinds of services to their parishioners. In recent years, with the rise in the number of abortions, their priests found that more and more people were looking for some kind of religious service specifically attuned to the needs of parents who had had abortions, such religious service being a rite through which such people obviously seek to assuage the guilt or alleviate the distress they are feeling about abortion. These temples have responded with the provision of *mizuko kuyō*, the now-common name for such rituals, which have recently shown phenomenal numerical growth. For temples such as Hase-dera, it appears that the provision of rites for aborted fetuses was an additional service that was at least initially subordinate to the more traditional rituals of the temple. In recent years, however, this augmentation has progressively become a major service of the temple, and people come from all over the greater Tokyo metropolitan area to Hase-dera because they feel somehow compelled, rightly or wrongly, to "do something" about the abortions they have had. The mizuko kuyō of Hase-dera meet a certain public demand.

PURPLE CLOUD TEMPLE

There is another kind of temple, however, for which the mizuko kuyō is the original and only reason for the temple's existence. Such temples are relative newcomers to the scene and have been the object of most of the public criticism of mizuko kuyō in Japan—for reasons described in a later chapter. There are some striking differences. Unlike Hase-dera, the place described below began its existence as a memorial park to provide rites almost exclusively for deliberately aborted fetuses. It occupies ground dedicated for that purpose, advertises itself as such in the public media, and provides no other observable public service.

A good example of this kind of institution is a place named Shiun-zan Jizō-ji, on the outskirts of the city of Chichibu in Saitama Prefecture, approximately two hours from Tokyo by train. Its name rendered into English is "The Temple of Jizō on the Mountain of the Purple Cloud." This institution also has a branch office in the city of Tokyo. The main temple in the Chichibu mountains—here abbreviated to "Purple Cloud Temple"—can best be understood if I describe what I saw on my own visit there.

Although a bus passes by it, the temple is most easily reached from the city of Chichibu by car or taxi—approximately a thirty- or forty-minute drive. There is no mistaking the place once it has been reached. It occupies a sequence of adjacent hillsides, all of which are carefully tiered and set with narrow walking paths and row upon row of nearly identical, small, stone images—statues of Jizō. These are very similar to the ones seen in the cemetery at Hase-dera, except that virtually all those at Purple Cloud Temple are newly chiseled and carefully installed. Their gray granite is still precise in outline and shiny on the surface, not worn down by the elements—that is, they do not have the Buddhist image's famed reputation for showing the attractive signs of great age or antiquity.

There is something very striking about the scene—but also perplexing, perhaps even disturbing, to someone who does not know exactly what is going on there. Unlike most Buddhist institutions which have a prominent, architecturally impressive temple building as the center of focus, the "temple" on this site is a diminutive, modern building and almost insignificant in the midst of the carefully honed hills with their multitude of Jizō images. Inasmuch as the images constitute a "cemetery," it is clear that here the ordinary pattern for temples has been reversed. That is, although in most Buddhist institutions—Hase-dera, for instance—the temple building itself stands forth prominently and has a cemetery "out back," Purple Cloud Temple immediately presents itself as in fact a cemetery, and its "temple," by contrast, serves much more as a kind of business and promotion office. Although it calls itself a "temple," in layout and architecture it is really what the Japanese call a mountain *bochi*—a cemetery or memorial park.

Also striking to the first-time visitor is the uniformity of the stone Jizō images on this site. Row upon row upon row—they are the same in basic shape. They differ only very slightly in size; most are approximately two feet in height. The stone is cut so as to suggest that each image wears the foot-length robes of a Buddhist monk, who is also tonsured. There is no cut in the stone to suggest even a hint of a hairline or hair; these figures are perfectly bald. Their eyes are almost completely shut, in the manner found in most Buddhist images, a manner that denotes the meditation and tranquillity into which the figure has become absorbed. To anyone able to recognize the signs, there can be no doubt that these figures are, at least in some sense, monks who are aspirants to the highest goals of Buddhism. The robes, the tonsure, and the eyes closed in meditation all combine to make this clear.

At the same time, however, something else comes quickly to mind. These are diminutive figures—child-sized. The visage they present, while that of tranquillity, could also be seen as one of perfect innocence. And even their lack of hair connotes something of childhood, if not infancy. The statue, which on first sight may have suggested a monk, now prompts something of a double take; the monk is really a child. More precisely, it is *also* a child.[2]

The figure's accoutrements make this certain. Virtually every one of the stone Jizō images wears a large red bib—of the type usually worn by an infant or a young child. Then, as if to push the identification with childhood beyond doubt, Jizō images are frequently provided with toys. Whole rows of them at Purple Cloud Temple are provided with pinwheels, whose brightly colored spokes spin audibly in the wind. But individual statues are given individual toys as well—for instance, the kind of miniature piano a child might play with. For some of the images, sweaters or even more elaborately knitted garments and hats are provided. And, of course, flowers are placed by each one.

Weather-exposed images are often covered with knitted garments and festooned with inexpensive jewelry. (Chichibu.)

Images are protected too by umbrellas; pinwheels are children's toys and also replicas of the Wheel of the Dharma, a Buddhist symbol. (Chichibu.)

The double-take effect—seeing in the figures both monk and child simultaneously—is important, because the image is meant to represent two realities at the same time. For the visitor to Purple Cloud Temple who does not understand such things, there is a readily available guide sheet, which says:

> A Jizō image can do double service. On the one hand it can represent the soul of the mizuko [deceased child or fetus] for parents who are doing rites of apology to it. At the same time, however, the Jizō is also the one to whom can be made an appeal or prayer to guide the child or fetus through the realm of departed souls. [See Appendix for translation of entire document.]

Jizō is quite remarkable in that it is a stand-in for *both* the dead infant and the savior figure who supposedly takes care of it in its otherworld journey. The double-take effect—one moment a child and the next a Buddhist savior in monkish robes—is intentional.

Visits to places such as the temple at Purple Cloud are in no way limited to adults. In fact, one finds there a surprisingly large number of children. They join their mothers—and sometimes fathers or grandmothers—in putting flowers in front of the Jizō images, in washing down the granite stone with water carried over from a nearby faucet, and in saying simple prayers before the sculptured stones. At Purple Cloud Temple there is even a small playground in the middle of the cemetery where children can be seen enjoying themselves.

To note the presence and play of these children is also to call attention to the relatively "happy" mood in this kind of place. The atmosphere is far from lugubrious. The red-bibbed images on the hills, the gentle whirring sound and bright appearance of the thousands of upright pinwheels, the presence and play of well-dressed children—all these combine to provide a lightness of feeling that would probably be totally unknown, even incongruous, in the cemeteries of Europe and America. In the garb provided for some of the images, in the toys they are given, and in the pins and medallions attached to them there is a playfulness—even a gentle levity. In fact, the notion that Jizō is a savior who very much enjoys playing with children goes back some centuries in Japan's religious history.[3]

The non-Japanese who might chance to visit such a place would probably at first have their perplexity compounded with the feeling that all of this is a type of religious kitsch or, at least, is rather "inappropriate" for a place dedicated to memorializing the departed dead. An hour spent walking around the stones and carefully observing the Japanese and their activities might, however, bring the visitor to quite different conclusions—especially if the intent of the activities were explained.

The sense of kitsch arises because two things are conflated here that we in the West usually want to separate as much as possible—that is, the cemetery and the nursery. But such temples are, after all, cemeteries not for adults but for children—children who, even though dead, are assumed to be, in ways explained below, still "alive" and related to this place. Consequently, a sense of play is deemed entirely appropriate, as are the toys that make that possible. These cemeteries are the concrete embodiment of human imagination directing its attention to beings who, while no longer in the same world with us as they once were, still are present in our memories and projections. In the minds of most Japanese, the cemetery is the place par excellence that links this world with the "other" world; it is the node of contact between the metaphysical and the physical. And when it is the departed children or aborted fetuses that are being remembered, it is the Jizō image and cemeteries such as these that provide such a tangible, empirical contact point with the "other" world in which they are thought to reside.

Levity, it is worth noting, is not altogether absent from the cemeteries of the West. The inscriptions on occasional tombstones and even the designs of some memorial architecture show that clearly. However, what reinforces the tendency of the Japanese to make their Jizō cemeteries places of lightness and play is the sense that the deceased children "on the other side" are, if anything, eager to enjoy a few happy moments with the family members who come out from their otherwise busy lives to visit them. The promotional literature provided by Purple Cloud Temple makes it clear that most of the time spent by such children in the "other world" is far from happy; since they are quite miserable there, the visit from their families is especially appreciated. Thus, the whole experience is modeled after that of reunion rather than separation and, as such, the proper thing is to demonstrate the joy rather than the sorrow of the occasion. Loving attention to the dead is shown by washing down the memorial image—an ancient Buddhist practice—providing fresh flowers, and bringing the occasional new toy or garment. These activities and the recitation of simple prayers are expected. But beyond these there is the sense of an active *communication*, emotional if not verbal, between the living family and the departed child.

"Child" is the term used, but there can be no doubt that the overwhelming majority of children memorialized at Purple Cloud Temple are fetuses whose progress in the womb was terminated. The assumption throughout, however, is that in the other world such fetuses are fully formed; they are not so much infants as children and are able to react as a child of at least a year or two might to the attention they receive from parents and siblings in this world.

THE FIRST PRECEPT

All this is not to say that places like this, even in Japan, are free of controversy. Purple Cloud Temple, as I will show, has been the object of considerable public suspicion.

It is first necessary, however, to pay attention to more general criticisms of Japanese Buddhists for what some see as their failure to level a stern condemnation of the abortion practices now widely accepted in their society. Not only observers from the West but also a good number of non-Japanese Asians—Buddhists among them—tend, at least at first sight, to find something terribly odd and incongruous in the Japanese Buddhist temples' practice of providing guilt-relieving rituals for persons who have had abortions.

Isn't it, such observers will ask, the responsibility of a religious body to bring abortion itself under control? What possible justification could there be for lending abortion what is all but a religious seal of approval? Isn't there something fundamentally unscrupulous about a religious organization that collects monies from people for providing a mass, Buddhist in this case, for an aborted fetus?

Some Buddhists, especially if they are not Japanese or have no acquaintance with the cultural factors involved in this way of handling abortion, are likely to find a flat contradiction beween abortion and what is universally called the "First Precept" of Buddhism—a vow of moral behavior that states, "I will not willingly take the life of a living thing." This committment to not killing is not found somewhere at the end of the Buddhist equivalent of the Ten Commandments but at the very top of the list. Its priority in the Buddhist moral code is certain; Buddhist teaching includes a very strong statement against the taking of life. In the rules of the early Buddhists, this proscription had clear implications: "As far as the human being is concerned, even the abortion of an embryo which was just conceived is regarded as a crime."[4]

One way around this, at least in theory, would be to define the unborn fetus as "nonlife," as some kind of mere stuff or relatively inert matter. If that were so, we can imagine how the Japanese Buddhist might conceivably find a way out of his or her dilemma. As a matter of fact, however, Japanese are for the most part much less ready than persons in the West to refer to an unborn fetus in terms that suggest it is something less than human or even less than sentient. The Japanese tend to avoid terms like "unwanted pregnancy" or "fetal tissue." That which develops in the uterus is often referred to as a "child"—even when there are plans to abort it. Many Japanese Buddhists, committed by their religion to refrain from taking life, will nonetheless have an abortion and in doing so refer to the aborted fetus as a child, one that clearly has been alive.

Perplexed as to how this could possibly be, we rightly wonder what prevents such persons from feeling they have been split in two by the gap between their religious principles and their real practice? How are the two reconciled? One answer to these questions, of course, would be to claim that these Japanese—or at least those morally compromised in the above fashion—are not, in fact, Buddhists at all. This would be to judge that they carry the name without a real right to do so; it would be to see the conflict beween principle and reality as simply too great. This judgment that Japanese Buddhism is inauthentic, we should note, is quite often made both inside and outside of Japan, by both non-Buddhists and Buddhists alike. It is tantamount to saying that Japanese "Buddhism" is really a thin veneer over a mind-set or religious view that is, in fact, non-Buddhist, perhaps even anti-Buddhist.[5]

Clearly, to move to that judgment closes the whole discussion from the outset. As a matter of fact, however, most of the religions of the world would fare miserably if measured against the emphatic demands and commands of their founders. Few are the Christians who take the command of Jesus literally when he requires that they sell all their possessions in order to follow him. Likewise, both Jews and Christians have felt the necessity of "interpreting" the command in the Decalogue that they not kill; everything from allowances made for capital punishment to theories of the "just war" have turned up as ways, for better or worse, in which religious persons and communities in the West have accommodated the proscription against killing to what they see as clear, realistic needs. Lay Buddhists in Southeast Asia as well have found their way clear to serve in armies. Likewise Buddhist kings and presidents have dispatched armed troops into battle. The "interpretation" of seemingly unambiguous commands and precepts goes on all the time in religion.

There are, in fact, a lot of adjustments between the strict ethical axioms that are laid down at the base of a tradition and the moral realities of everyday life in the present. There have to be. And these adjustments that take place "in between" *are*, in fact, the tradition. It is from within this tradition that today's person takes what is needed to put together for himself or herself a script for making moral decisions.

Our moral lives and our moral reasoning are, in fact, very much as Jeffrey Stout describes in his *Ethics after Babel*; that is, in finding our way through moral dilemmas—especially relatively new ones—we have no alternative but to "draw on a collection of assorted odds and ends available for use and kept on hand on the chance that they might someday prove useful." Stout's important study takes Claude Lévi-Strauss's notion of the *bricoleur*, an odd-job expert who can create something impressive and eminently useful out of leftover bits and pieces, and goes on to show how what we call "ethical thought" is almost invariably just that— namely, moral *bricolage*.[6]

With respect to how most Japanese Buddhists today think about abortion, this book will attempt to show that Stout's notion of doing ethics by putting together bits and pieces into an acceptable—and *useful*— assemblage describes the process exactly. An effort will be made to fill in what those bits and pieces are and explain why many Japanese today take them to be "traditional." It is this that allows them the freedom to avoid being hemmed in by Buddhism's early prosriptions against abortion and, at the same time, to act responsibly still *as Buddhists* in key ways. The intention is to describe the intellectual and cultural bridgework between early Buddhism's precept against killing and the conscience of the contemporary Japanese woman who has an abortion and still wishes, in spite of that, to think of herself as a "good" Buddhist.

Stout's claim, one that seems clearly right, is that "great works of ethical thought" are often brought into being when people "start off by taking stock of problems that need solving and available conceptual resources for solving them [and] proceed by taking apart, putting together, reordering, weighting, weeding out, and filling in."[7]

In much of their history, the Japanese have, it seems almost as if by a clear preference, carried out moral reasoning in this fashion. In ethics they have long been bricoleurs, very skilled ones in fact. This, then, is why a close look at how their thinking about abortion took shape is likely to reveal an aperture through which to take a deeper look into Japanese society as well.

Chapter 2

A WORLD OF WATER AND WORDS

> The life-force of the world . . . is water, and the Nummo Pair
> are present in all water; they *are* water, the water of the seas, of
> coasts, of torrents, of storms, and of the spoonfuls we drink.
> (From a myth of the Dogon of Africa,
> in Marcel Griaule, *Conversations with Ogotemmeli*)

LIFE'S DEFINITION

IF ONLY we could *define* "life"; then most things, we often feel,
would begin to fall into place. Our ethical dilemmas in so many areas,
we believe, would begin to dissolve. Ours is a society that seems to
have long cherished the belief that through adequate definitions it might
achieve some salvation from its most troubling problems. There has been,
in both private and public talk, a great fondness for the phrase "merely a
matter of semantics"—as if matters of substantive difference do not exist
and the only problem we have is the relatively easy one of clarifying a few
key terms. We put a lot of stock in what can be accomplished by merely
clearing away certain terminological mists.

Our hope of finding agreement through commonly accepted definitions
is not unconnected with another belief common within our part of the
world: if only we could pass the "right" laws or repeal certain other laws,
our society would be on the road to solving its deepest social problems.

I do not wish to demean clear definitions or make light of the importance of good laws. Yet our total *reliance* upon such devices deserves
scrutiny. And this is because such a dependence obscures the fact that
really large concepts will never be boxed within precise definitions, and in
hoping they will we are chasing phantoms. Likewise, our habituated belief that the only way to get social improvement is by changing the laws
narrows our society's vision of the possible. The society that comes to
think it can help itself only through legal means is in danger of slipping
into a kind of social schlerosis. Its options have become narrowed.

How we tend to conceive of the problem of abortion is an obvious case
in point. Because what is sometimes called America's new "civil war"
over abortion divides us so deeply, we look to the courts or future changes
in the courts to either retain or alter our laws. Just as we hope someone
somewhere—probably a medic or a judge—will be able tell us exactly

what makes a person "dead," so we hope to be told at what "point" in time life begins. By locating that exact moment we will, we think, be able to distinguish acts that are innocuous and even charitable from ones that are murderous and cruel. Thus we try to pull off moral miracles with words and definitions.

The alternative to precise definition is not irrationality. It is not irrational to recognize that some concepts simply do not lend themselves to easy definition: "life," "humanness," even "mind" may simply be fish too large to be caught by our definitions. They always slip off the word hooks we fashion to try to snag them.

It is in such contexts that we turn to metaphor and poetry.[1] Poetry, many people seem instinctively to know, often "works" better vis-à-vis such matters because it opens up to their largeness rather than closing them down by tight delimitation and the chopping of logic.

So too the alternative to total dependence upon laws is not necessarily social chaos. In many societies it has been ritual. In some ways ritual is poetry that human beings have taken up with their bodies and turned into a special kind of social practice. And ritual, we do well to realize, "defines" important concepts by presenting them as connected rather than cut off from one another. Instead of logic chopping and the unconnected neat boxes produced by definitionism, ritual provides activities that fuse a wide variety of things that seem otherwise unrelated. Whole ganglia of semantic units are present in ritual—and allowed to seem coordinated on a deep level. Ritual, then, can operate with considerable effect and power in the realm of morals. It can, much more than we usually realize, be one of the odd but important pieces we can pick up and fit into that piece of bricolage that is our moral posture in the world.

I want to argue that ritual operates so—and rather brilliantly so—in the way Japanese Buddhists deal with abortion. An instance of what I mean can be observed at a temple called Nembutsu-ji, in the Adashino area of western Kyoto. Claimed as having a history going back to the ninth century, this temple includes a famous site where eight thousand stone Buddhas, originally markers on graves scattered widely for centuries, have been gathered—in fact, packed tightly—into an enclosed space, where they sit like eight thousand stone adherents listening to the preaching of Amida Buddha, who is represented in an image much larger and more imposing than any of the rest. A thousand candles placed on these stones one night in late August of each year makes for one of the most memorable festive events in Kyoto.

However, this temple too has an "out back" section to which a lot of people—including a fair number of young couples now—make their way. The temple's shrine dedicated to mizuko is impressive not only for the tangible emotion shown by persons entering there but also for the large number of dolls, both traditional Japanese ones and those of the more "Western" type, that are assembled there. Here again are playthings of this world intended to be freely enjoyed by dead children and aborted fetuses in their own world.

Beyond the cemetery is a grove, which has a rather striking icon at its center. Actually the icon is hexagonal, each of its six sides showing in relief a figure of Jizō, the savior-figure associated closely with children, in six different realms of being. According to the Buddhist cosmology adopted in early medieval times by the Japanese, Jizō is present in each of the six realms that comprise the universe. He is in painful realms such as hell not because he is being punished but voluntarily in order to rescue creatures caught in such places.[2]

At the base of this hexagonal sculpture and encircling it is a water-filled trough. Those who step up to pay their respects immediately realize what they are to do: they gather up water in the small wooden ladles lying in the water-trough and pour the liquid over the six relief images on the sides of the icon, walking around it clockwise in order to accomplish this. Jizō in all the six realms of suffering is, by this ritual, symbolically cleaned, cooled, and refreshed.

The offering of water is, it should be noted, for the relief of other-world sufferers, aborted fetuses in most cases. And the term "mizuko," applied exclusively to fetuses and to children who die early, literally means "children of the waters."

Why, we do well to ask, is the use of water symbolism so dominant? My suggestion is that it is surely not an irrational piling up and doubling of symbols but, rather, an especially potent way in which modern Japanese Buddhists can say what they want to say—and do what they want to do—concerning abortion and the fate of fetuses. Rituals are packed with meaning, and this one is no exception. But to grasp the thinking here we need to take the parts out of the ritual package and look at them. And in doing so, it is hoped, we can get closer to what is going on here.

ORIGINAL FIRE

One aspect of the action at Nembutsu-ji Temple—ablution—is easily accounted for. It has deep roots in Asian Buddhist ways of doing things. Going back to Buddhist origins in India, we find that the practice of pouring water over the images of Buddhas and other revered figures was known as *argha*. The ritual, simple and basic, was widely accepted in lands into which Buddhism penetrated. The Japanese took up the practice eagerly, calling it *aka*, and we see multiple references to it in early art and literature. For instance, in the "Lavender" chapter of *The Tale of Genji*, we read of a group of young girls pouring water on the Buddha shelf and offering cut flowers as well.[3]

That is easy and straightforward. But what must be noted next is surprising. Within *early* Buddhism as it developed in India, at least aside from ablutions, there was apparently not very much of a role for water and water symbolism. Hiro Sachiya, who has written extensively about Buddhism, has astutely pointed out that unlike in Christianity, in which water rituals—for example, baptism—are of great importance, in the early stage of Buddhism, water had almost no symbolic role to play.[4]

What was far more important at that stage was the image of fire. According to early Buddhism, people's movement towards spiritual emancipation requires that they slake the fires of their passions. Hiro contrasts this with the New Testament message of the Gospel according to John 4:1–15 in order to note that the early Buddhist message to suffering humankind, significantly, was not the presence of some kind of divinely given Water of Life but, rather, of the need for people themselves to undertake the disciplines needed to deprive such fires of the fuels that keep them raging. A lecture attributed to Shakyamuni Buddha and often regarded as an encapsulation of his teaching—one referred to by T. S. Eliot as "Buddhism's Sermon on the Mount"—is called by Buddhists the great "Fire Sermon."[5]

In early Buddhism, at least, the focus was not upon some external source that—like a god—would do something to douse the fire of passions or satisfy the consuming desires of human beings. It was, rather, upon our own potential, through the practice of virtues and the mastery of "self," to remove what was fueling such passions and threatening to consume life.

There was, I wish to suggest, another level of significance in the absence of water symbolism in early Buddhism—and this point is crucial for understanding what shaped some of the later Buddhist thinking about even such issues as abortion. Insufficient attention has, to date at least, been paid to the fact that Buddhists originally almost totally ignored the power of water symbolism—other than to refer to it as a purifying agent. This means that a common human mental association between water and the "source of life," present in many of the world's religions, was something the early Buddhists decided not to make a part of the religious path they articulated.

There was, I believe, something quietly revolutionary in this. In the language of religious systems, the silent dropping of a major symbol is often as important as the formation of a new one. And in erasing the symbol of fertile waters the Buddhists were letting go of a large and powerful one. They were diverging sharply from a major theme in Indian spirituality—one expressed, for instance, in the *Bhavisyottara-purana*, where the ocean is addressed as follows:

> Water, thou art the source of all
> things and of all existence.[6]

My point is that for the early Buddhists the notion of primordial waters had become totally unimportant, because for them fertility and fecundity were not part of religion rightly conceived. They were simply not interested in cosmogonic myths, in tales about life emerging from muddy seas, or in motifs of fecund waters—all of which have been part and parcel of man's religious imagination, both Eastern and Western, for a very long time.

This lack of interest was because the early Buddhists viewed the reproductive instincts of men and women as *simply there*, not needing whole religious constructs to support, glorify, and urge them on. If anything, because it tends to entrap us in a cycle of passions and of attachments to sexual pleasures, our reproductivity adds to our sufferings. The early Buddhists took a man or a woman's urge to have sex and reproduce as a given; what was needed, in their view, was to break *out* of the reproductive pattern—that is, for men and women to get free of the pattern whereby they beget karma that causes them to be reborn again and again in misery. Fertility and fecundity, for these Buddhists, were not "blessings" of a deity or concrete evidence of "faith"; because of their hold on our emotions, they were, if anything, roadblocks to the peace of nirvana.

When the ancient Buddhists differed from most other religions on this point, they did so emphatically. Just as they showed no interest in water-based myths of cosmic or human origin, so their rites and account of things had no place for the phallic lingam and vulviform yoni so common in Indian religion. This was not so much from puritan prurience about sex but because, on a more fundamental level, Buddhists held that religion—or at least the religious path as they understood it—was *unconnected to fecundity and reproductivity*.

This disengagement of religion from reproductivity was a large step. Two and a half millennia ago in India it was one of the things that gave a definite but somewhat unusual shape to Buddhism. As we shall note below, this disengagement was a position that later caused considerable problems for Buddhists in China and Japan—when they were pressed by others to show their religion was not "world-rejecting." On the other hand, as we shall see, even this degree of diffidence about reproductivity was something that, for better or worse, entered into Japanese history—with an impact on the development of thinking about issues like abortion.

The Return of the Waters

It is worth recalling just what the Buddhists were throwing away when they rejected the symbol of the fecund waters. It was a risky move, for few things seem more pervasive in humankind's religions and philosophies than the use of water as a potent symbol. The connection between fecund waters and initial appearances of life runs throughout the mythologies and literatures of the archaic world. For the ancient Jews, the connection was made as follows: "And God said, Let the waters bring forth swarms of living creatures, and let the birds fly above the earth across the firmament of the heavens. So God created the great sea monsters and every living creature that moves, with which the waters swarm. . . . [A]nd God blessed them saying, Be fruitful and multiply and fill the waters in the seas and let the birds multiply on the earth."[7] The ancient Indians had been less concerned to make a distinction between an ultimate and a proximate source but, as already noted, they addressed water as "the source of all things and all existence." So too did Thales (fl. 585 B.C.E.) who, according to Aristotle, made the first declaration in the entire history of Greek philosophy: "The first principle and basic nature of all things is water." Among the ancient Chinese, the *Tao Te Ching* not only prized the waters as the great source of things but even turned the lowliness of such waters into something to be imitated for its unsurpassed wisdom: "The reason why the River and the Sea are able to be king of the hundred valleys is that they excel in taking the lower position."[8] Water was even the perfect model of goodness. "Highest good is like water," writes the author of this classic.[9]

Interesting in all of these and other classic texts is the fact that, in spite of cultural differences exhibited, the waters are again and again hailed as that from which "life" and other things of surpassing value emerge. The range of use of such symbolism is broad: simple peasants saw in the waters the source of fertility they wanted in their crops and sexual unions. But even humankind's grander myths made powerful use of the ocean imagery and, beyond that, philosophers had seen in water a prized metaphor for some of the most important points they wanted to establish.

To cut themselves off from the tradition of using water symbolically was something which, in fact, the Buddhists were not able to do in a total way. Fire sermons, a distaste for myths about fecund waters, a dissociation of "right" religion from anything having to do with sexuality and reproductivity—these were all constitutive of the Buddhism that is often thought to have been "original" or, at least, constitutive of the early stage.

But things did not stop there. Buddhism, as it moved through time and across cultural borders, grew beyond this early form. Most people who were Buddhist adherents were not monks. Life without sexual activity and reproduction may have been a goal pursued by an elite cadre of monks, but it was neither acceptable nor viable for the larger community of Buddhist laypersons who supported them, people who held the hope that in some future life they might personally make the crucial ritual step of household departure and entry into monkhood. For the present, however, the piety of laypersons could not go that far, and they went on living in families, having sexual relations, getting pregnant, bearing children, and seeing generativity and the perpetuation of a "house" as, at least in some sense, good.

Such people were also farmers, and in much of South, Southeast, and East Asia their diet was based on rice. This meant that the timely arrival and dispersion of the rains was a matter of great importance to them. They supported the celibate monks in their monasteries but were themselves often very anxious about the need to have abundant and timely water for their crops. And water symbolism, as we know from the rich documentary evidence from that part of the world, was soon enough bound in deeply with the cultic life of such lay Buddhists. Productivity, reproductivity, the fecundity associated with the waters—all these were deeply connected in the peasant mind. Communities of monks might profess that such things had nothing to do with "real" religion, but laypersons had to have religion that was connected to the needs of their own lives.

Throughout Asia wherever Buddhism moved northward and eastward, we find evidence of monks countenancing and even lending their blessings to peasant rituals meant to ensure well-behaved rains, excellent harvests, and well-born progeny. These could be rituals in which monks might participate only as an accommodation to public demand—but, as anthropologists have shown, the spiritual "power" of these disciplined monks was thought to have a communicative effect.[10]

In such developments, of course, the Buddhist tradition was getting progressively more complex, more ambiguous, and more messy. But that is to say also that the resources available for *moral bricolage* were becoming increasingly rich and varied. The tradition was no longer univocal. It now contained an early posture of being skittish about cosmological myths, fertile waters, and human reproductivity—but it was also bending to accommodate something of the natural human interest in such things. It is doubtful that Buddhism could ever have become one of the so-called "world" religions without such a development.

Pragmatic accommodation goes on all the time—in tension with the oldest part of the tradition. For instance, Richard Gombrich and Gananath Obeyesekere have recently documented what, at least for the conservative Buddhism of Sri Lanka, is quite a remarkable recent development, namely an "attempt to Buddhicize the marriage ceremony." It is important to realize that until very recently marriage in Sri Lanka was totally secular and that only with the arrival of European Christians—with their concept of the wedding as a religious sacrament—did such a notion even take root there. But, according to Gombrich and Obeyesekere, Buddhist tradition has been enlarged also by the fact that in recent decades some Sinhalese monks have resided abroad: "These monks have a Western lay following whose members *want* to sacramentalize their marriages. In the United States monks must sign marriage licences and consequently must perform some kind of ritual, especially for those whom they call *hippi bauddhayo* ('hippie Buddhists')."[11] The fact of the matter is that Buddhist monks have been drawn more and more into direct and indirect participation in weddings in Sri Lanka, too. That makes necessary some strange twists and innovative uses of old texts and ritual elements. Some of these elements, paradoxically, were originally connected to the *renunciation*, not the affirmation, of marriage, home life, and procreation.[12]

My point is that the Buddhist "position" on these things is mixed. In early Buddhism there was a decisive turning away from the sanctioning of fertility. In that sense the Buddhists were not natalist and could be called a-natalist and in some instances even anti-natalist. They opposed the taking of life, but they also opposed anything that would declare human reproduction an unqualified "good." For those seeking the highest path of virtue, sex, fertility, and children were clearly "impediments"—exactly the name Shakyamuni gave to his son, who was born at a time when Shakyamuni wanted to take up the religious path. In some instances, this perspective seems to fall almost like a plumb line down through time—as for instance, when Yoshida Kenkō, a quasi-Buddhist recluse of fourteenth-century Japan, writes in his classic work *Tsurezuregusa*, "A man should never marry; I am charmed when I hear a man say, 'I am living alone'" and again, "Even members of the nobility, let alone persons of no consequence, would do well not to have children."[13]

But over the centuries the power of the water and fertility symbolism came back, either directly or in some subtle, indirect form. Sometimes it was kept at arm's length, in the form of alternative religious systems in the same culture, neither blessed nor cursed by the Buddhists. The old fertility cults of Southeast Asia are like that, and in Japan, at least to some extent, much of Shinto represents such a system. But at other times, especially when Buddhists were afraid of losing the allegiance of laypersons or wanted to seem less "other-worldly," they moved even further to bring the power of water back into their own systems of belief and practice. The whole Buddhist tradition is constituted by such adjustments—and such tension.

MIZUKO

If water serves as a source of life, it can also, by a symbolic extension, serve as that to which the dead can be returned. This is quite natural. And there is a logic in it, too: if the recently deceased are literally sent into a realm widely taken to be the source of life, they can be expected to have a good chance of finding renewed life there. Resurrection, rebirth, reincarnation—the waters can be expected to facilitate whatever is desired.

This life-giving quality of water is something the Indian religious mind knew about and still expresses powerfully. Anyone who has visited the holy city of Benares knows that the entire city physically focuses on the river that runs through it; all beings go down into the waters of the Ganges, the holiest of rivers, which courses for more than fifteen hundred miles, from the Himalayas to the Bay of Bengal. This river is hailed as a mother (*Ganga Mata*), and the myths and legends connected with it clearly show it as *both* the receiver of the dead and the fecund source of all new life. So it is wholly to be expected that pious Hindus not only bathe therein but also deposit in its waters the ashes of their cremated dead and corpses of those unburned.

Westerners are usually unprepared for how vividly present all this is in Benares. It is a memorable experience to walk down to the great ghats, to enter a boat and float on the Ganges' waters, and then to see the corpses of infants and young children bobbing in the river next to the boat. Many of those whose bodies go into the river whole are so dispatched because the bereaved are too poor to afford the firewood needed for cremation. In such cases the importance of having a dead relative make a successful entry into the river completely overshadows any concern about the physical state of the corpse: induction into the *waters* is what counts, not the pyre and its fire. To return the dead to the maternal river and perhaps from there to the the great sea—this is what has overwhelming importance.

It is important to recall that however different actual religious practices may be in different cultures, the ways in which symbols cohere are often the same. Christians, for instance, readily take advantage of the waters-of-death theme combined with the waters-of-new-life theme when they practice the rite of baptism. "Dying to the old life" and "being raised to a new one in Christ" are themes clearly combined and graphically demonstrated, especially when the rite involves actual immersion.

Such similarities of religious practice across cultures bear out the claims made by Mircea Eliade in his comprehensive study of water and water symbolism, a study that encompasses a vast number of cultures:

> To state the case in brief, water symbolizes the whole of potentiality; it is *fons et origo*, the source of all possible existence. . . . Principle of what is formless and potential, basis of every cosmic manifestation, container of all seeds, water symbolizes the primal substance from which all forms come and to which they will return either by their own regression or in a cataclysm. . . . Immersion in water symbolizes a return to the pre-formal, a total regeneration, a new birth.[14]

Gaston Bachelard also noted: "Water, the substance of life, is also the substance of death for ambivalent reverie."[15]

Japan, of course, is very different from India. The notion of corpses floating down a sacred river will strike the Japanese, as it does most persons of the West, as culturally foreign.

Nevertheless, since water can symbolize both birth and death concepts for virtually all peoples, it is not surprising that the Japanese made their own creative use of it. And, in my view, one of their most powerful usages of water symbolism has been as a "language" for expressing whole congeries of ideas and images connected not only with the death of children but also with the disposal of fetuses. It is not an accident that the child who dies in infancy or a fetus jettisoned from the womb is commonly referred to as a *mizuko,* a word that, as noted above, literally means "water-child" or "child of the waters." For generations the term has to many people seemed just right. It straddles and holds together both worlds; it is an acknowledgment of death and at the same time an expression of faith in some kind of rebirth.

Mizuko is, in fact, a very subtle word and, because understanding it is crucial for grasping how even Japanese of today view abortion, it deserves a close look. Although there is a rare usage of the term to refer to a live newborn, the predominant usage is to refer to a dead infant, a stillborn, or a fetus that has been aborted.[16] In his important studies of Japan's demographic history, Takahashi Bonsen sees the term—and the concept it suggests—as traceable to the accounts of what is called the "leech-child" in the *Kojiki* and the *Nihonshoki,* early Japanese cosmogonic myths written down in the eighth century.[17] The *Kojiki*, for instance, narrates that Izanagi and Izanami, the primal couple, while in a progency-producing phase, happened to make a ritual mistake: "Nevertheless, they commenced procreation and gave birth to a leech-child. They placed this child into a boat made of reeds and floated it away."[18] Although the emphasis on ritual propriety in early Japan is itself fascinating, the item of compelling importance here is "hiru no ko," the term translated as "leech-child."

Takahashi Bonsen points out that the *Shiojiri*, a work written around 1697 by Amano Sadakage, notes that the way in which sericulturalists in the countryside discarded unusable silkworms—by putting them into the river in straw vessels—and the way people reduced the number of their children were both interpreted as being like the way the mythical primal couple disposed of their leech-child.[19] We cannot know whether this was new or old usage, but it at least suggests an attempt to relate the reduction of children to the actions of a primal couple in the national myths.

In a sense, then, the leech-child became the prototype for all children sent either literally or figuratively back into "the waters"—all mizuko. Although the term "liquidate" in our language has rather horrible connotations, in Japanese the phrase "to make into liquid" is philosophically and ethically much more acceptable. In an interesting essay on the role of water in Japanese psychology and philosophy, Iwai Hiroshi stresses that the Japanese tend to have very positive, relatively fear-free attitudes vis-à-vis water, rivers, oceans, and the like. He also believes that in the Japanese psyche water tends to connote things maternal and is powerfully linked to the watery but comfortable environment of the womb.[20]

If Iwai is right, we can see the structure of meanings embraced by the term "mizuko" and also why as a piece of language it connotes something approachable and comfort-bringing rather than awful and frightening. The child who has become a mizuko has gone quickly from the warm waters of the womb to another state of liquidity. Life that has remained liquid simply has never become solidified. The term suggests that a newborn, something just in the process of taking on "form," can also rather quickly revert to a relatively formless state.

In that sense the term tells of a death. But simultaneously it appeals to the *fons et origo* function of the waters and the sea; it suggests with great power that the child or fetus in question will come to life again. That is, it straddles and embraces both truths. Of course, to the eye of strict reason only one of these truths is allowed: the child or fetus that has become "liquid" has become dead. But to the eye that allows the symbol to be ambivalent, the second truth is also a reality: the water-child has reverted to a former state but only as preparation for later rebirth in this world. And in Japan the acceptance of *both* truths was wide, having deep roots in cultural history. There both the most archaic stratum of religious belief and Buddhism, something introduced later from abroad, maintained that in some sense the dead "return" to this world.

To regard the water-child as in some way suspended in water is to say that willy-nilly a fetus is a still-unformed child, a child still in the "becoming" stage rather than emphatically existing as a discrete entity or "being." A water-child is a child who has only just begun to emerge from the great watery unknown; it could just as easily be said to be water that has only just begun to take shape as a human-being-to-be.

It is important to see how emphatically the Japanese, living on islands encircled by ocean waters, envisioned the origin of human life as the congealing of a loosely formed, watery substance. The *Kojiki* tells of a whole congregation of heavenly gods giving Izanagi and Izanami exactly such a mandate:

> "Complete and solidify this drifting land!" Giving them the Heavenly Jeweled Spear, they entrusted the mission to them. Thereupon, the two deities stood on the Heavenly Floating Bridge and, lowering the jeweled spear, stirred with it. They stirred the brine with a churning-churning sound; and when they lifted up [the spear] again, the brine dripping down from the tip of the spear piled up and became an island.[21]

Thus the land, the world—and as such, the formedness of reality for humankind—came to be.

If the sea is the source of life, it can also be its *receptacle*. The myths are clear that when there are children who for some reason or other cannot be accepted to live with gods, humans, or god-like humans, such children are properly returned to the sea. The great paradigm for this, of course, is the leech-child, one who according to some accounts was recognized as unfit for continued life because three years after being born it still could not walk. In the *Nihonshoki* [*Nihongi*], a mythological cycle also written down in the eighth century, there is an episode in which a male god known as Hiko-hoko-demi breaks a strict taboo against males being present when women are in childbirth. He spies on a goddess, Toyo-tama-hime, as she is delivering a child. Because this goddess, so the story goes, turns into a sea dragon during parturition, the consequences of being spied on are dire:

> [Toyo-tama-hime] was greatly ashamed, and said, "Hadst thou not disgraced me, I would have made the sea and land communicate with each other, and forever prevented them from being sundered. But now that thou hast disgraced me, wherewithal shall friendly feelings be knit together?" So she wrapped the [newborn] infant in rushes, and abandoned it on the sea-shore. Then she barred the sea-path, and passed away.[22]

In the *Kojiki* and *Nihonshoki* we have clear instances where, either because of physical imperfection or a breach of ritual purity, the just-born child is not just abandoned but relinquished to the wind and waves. The implication is that having come from the sea, life-forms most naturally return there as well.

Of course, in some ways things happen much more easily in the world of myths than in the harder, empirically painful world of human beings. No one likes to visualize details of disposing of an unwanted fetus—the mechanics of surgical instruments, the raw physicality of a bloody mixture of tissues and fluids, the receptacles for disposal.

There is evidence to suggest that through much of Japanese history a mizuko that was no longer alive was usually placed under the floorboards of houses in rural areas; there it was believed to mix with the waters of natural springs and make its way to larger bodies or reservoirs of water, the greater receptacle of life under the earth. Outdoor burial near running waters was also probably common.[23]

FLEXIBLE RETURN

Although the physical facts of abortion may be startling and crude, the language humans use to describe them is clearly meant to soften and humanize them. This is exactly what is shown by the terminology used by Japanese who have, either by natural death or human agency, had a mizuko. Two Japanese researchers, Chiba Tokuji and Ōtsu Tadao, have examined the language used in rural areas from one end of Japan to the other—language that probably relates to usage over many centuries—and discovered that it is replete with references to "returning" the unborn and to the "return" of the mizuko.[24]

These references could be dismissed as nothing other than euphemisms—the making pretty through language of that which is, if the truth were told, simply horrifying and abominable. To do so would be to miss the impact of the curious wedding here between archaic belief systems, Buddhist teachings, and the language of common folk. Language about "return," first of all, implies that what has appeared in our world—a newborn or, in this case, a nearly-born infant—has not appeared entirely *de novo*. Although many Japanese, especially in modern times, prefer to be somewhat imprecise about the "preexistence" of the fetus or newborn, there is, in keeping with Buddhism, a vague sense that a life that appears in our world or in a woman's uterus is the re-formation of a being that was before either in *this* world in other incarnations or in the world of the *kami*, or gods. We will note more about this in a later chapter.

It is important here to note that the very notion of "return" makes for a rough sketch—in fact a *conveniently rough* sketch—of a reality that no one seems to want to specify with any greater precision. There is just enough detail to keep the concept rich and open to variant interpretations. The point is to avoid so much specificity that the notion gets hardened into a rigid—or refutable—doctrine. Adumbration is of the essence.

The practical result seems clear. For the parent who wants to imagine its deceased or aborted mizuko as potentially coming back to be reborn into the same family at a time more convenient for all concerned, referring to its "return" can imply that although it is being sent back to another world for a period of waiting, it is fully expected to be reincarnated into this world—and perhaps even this family!—at some later date. In that sense the aborted fetus is not so much being "terminated" as it is being put on "hold," asked to bide its time in some other world.

In such cases the mizuko is imagined as going to a kind of limbo, a place of clear deprivation, until the time comes for its release to a better place. And traditionally, at least, the parent could do things to make sure that the mizuko would go only to a place of *temporary* repose. Lest the unseen "powers" that control such things mistake the intention of such parents, rural folk, we are told by Chiba and Ōtsu, sometimes bury their infant with fish in its mouth. This conveys a subtle meaning. Since Buddhism teaches—at least officially—that it is wrong to eat flesh, a dead child appearing in the world of the Buddhas with a fish in its mouth would, such parents surmise, surely be *rejected* for passage into final Buddha-hood. In other words, its re-entry into this world, and preferrably into their own home, could thus be guaranteed![25] Rural people often prove to be imaginative and clever manipulators—even of events in metaphysical realms.

It appears also that to some people in traditional Japan the very *simplicity* of a disposal method for such fetuses and newborns would, ironically, facilitate their rebirth into this world. By contrast, to make much to-do about a grave site and especially to provide such a child with a *kaimyō,* a posthumously applied Buddhist name for honored ancestors expected to progress far beyond this world, would be to urge the infant too far out of reach and out of mind. Until very recently, at least, simplicity was of the essence for those who wanted a mizuko to come back again.[26] Too much ritual could be as dangerous as too little.

But what if a parent were content to have the mizuko progress onward and never return—at least not into his or her own family? That is, what if the parent or parents in question happened to be, either because of advanced age or an already full complement of children, not especially eager to have the mizuko be reborn to them at some later time? For such people the very flexibility of the "return" notion provided another option. They could "return" the child to the abode of the gods and the Buddhas. Prayers could be said that would ritually facilitate the progress of the mizuko to a *place far better* than either a family that does not want it or the "limbo of infants" in which it might be temporarily housed. In that sense it was imagined that the child, after the time in limbo has passed, would make a more final return to a positively pictured location in the "beyond"—a place alternately thought of as that where ancestors and kami abide, as a heaven or Pure Land, as the realm of the Buddhas, as nirvana. The exact ways of picturing such a place could differ, but the sense that it was a fundamentally *good* place was always clear. Either way the notion of "return" was full of positive possibilities. Either way there was a real consolation for people experiencing great loss.

Ancient Indian Buddhist texts had repeatedly declared, "Component things dissolve into their constitutive parts and then again these into theirs . . . [ad infinitum]." In one sense what the peasants of Japan had done was to put metaphorical, poetic, and ritual flesh onto this notion. They had turned it into a set of images they could use and direct as desired as they faced one of the most torturous experiences of human life—namely, interpreting, and becoming reconciled to, the need to terminate a life that had been developing, although totally unwanted.

Early Buddhist doctrinal formulations had usually looked at the raw facts of life and death with impassion. In its earliest Indian forms, Buddhism comes across even to modern readers of the texts as a dry-eyed, largely detached and "philosophical" assessment and acceptance of change, death, and decay as inescapable. The three distinguishing "marks" of all existent things, according to the most basic of Buddhist teachings, is put in a pithy way: "All things are characterized by impermanence, suffering, and the absence of self." So on that level the fetus as a mizuko in the process of sliding from its relative formedness as a human into a state of progressive liquidization is doing no other than following the most basic law of existence.

Common people, however, were not ascetic monks or adept at making such a cold-eyed accounting of reality. Their approach to Buddhism was not through a point-by-point analysis of the "constituents of being." Their Buddhism, which had to make sense of life's crises in order to be of any use to them, was a Buddhism that had to mediate the old doctrines through a rich and adaptable store of images and practices connected with folklore. Their concern was not so much to have an objective analysis of "being" as to find, from within the Buddhist tradition, comfort and consolation in their often desperate and miserable lives.

And we can assume that they were seldom more miserable and desperate than when caught in the horrible dilemma of needing to terminate the life of a child in the womb. In such times the whole of the natural parental impulse was at war with their own grasp of what had become a painful necessity in their lives.

In such a bitter situation the concept and images of "return," however imprecise in some of its specifications, clearly lent them conceptual and emotional support. The pain of the situation might remain, but it would be palliated in Buddhism—as long as it was Buddhism of this sort.

・　・　・　・　・

A common phrase for the amniotic fluid which contains an embryo is the "bag of waters." Birth is connected with its breaking and with the release of this fluid. To the vivid imagination of archaic peoples it must have seemed that life emerges from a watery source.

To refer to the fetus as a "child of the waters" is to say as much. It is, however, also to note that a child so designated is one whose status is still in flux; its viability in the everyday, empirical world remains in some sense an open question. Fetuses and the newborn, especially in earlier periods of human history, had survival chances much lower than today. The rate of miscarriage, stillborn birth, and infant mortality was high.

The need for consolation is present when one child dies; it becomes even greater when children die one after another. Canonical Buddhism taught that "life was impermanent" and "all constituent things pass away." But what ordinary people really *wanted* to pass away were experiences of this type and their worry that death might mean a finality. They wanted to know that lives can be recalled—not so much from "the grave" as from the great Ocean of being. The cold primeval waters, they wanted to know, are in fact a warm matrix that is fecund with new life.

Language is the maker of scale. Consolation consists, more often than we like to admit, of concepts shaped by our imaginations and our words. It results also, apparently, from choices to look at certain things rather than at others, to use certain words rather than others. It involves choosing where to cast one's eyes: at the tender evidences of continuity—however frail they may be—rather than at the ragged, torn edges of discontinuity.

Water, we know from experience, is what slips and flows with ease through our fingers. We know it as something with an indeterminate shape. That can bring us floods, but that same fluidity makes for water's usefulness. Likewise, imprecision of image and concept can be troublesome—and also of great use. Whether we are talking about things or concepts, when we call them "fluid" we mean that they can be moved about at will and put in places wherever and whenever we might wish.

The aborted fetus in Japan is fitted into a language of this sort. Some may—and do—declare that this renders morals all too flexible: what is all so fluid and watery, they claim, can readily degenerate into a moral swamp. That may be. But before taking up that problem we need at least to understand in greater detail exactly how the human mind and religious imagination are at work here.

Chapter 3

SOCIAL DEATH, SOCIAL BIRTH

> an edge is never
> a single or a sudden thing
> (*Aleda Shirley, "The Rivers Where They Touch"*)

> The certainty of death is attended with uncertainties,
> in time, manner, and places.
> (Sir Thomas Browne, *Religio Medici*)

PASSAGE AND PROCESS

IT IS OFTEN thought, mistakenly, that complex views of dying and being born are peculiar to our own time—as if people in earlier days always and everywhere had simple, clear-cut, and uncomplicated opinions about such momentous events. It is, of course, true that modern medicine has made certain matters more complex for us, especially in terms of the kinds of ethical decisions we must make. Questions of sustaining or taking "life" get complicated when, for instance, we speak of a certain person as being "brain dead" even when by other gauges some kind of life is still present.

It is too easy, however, to project onto the past a simplicity that was probably rarely, if ever, there. Much of what we call religion and the attempt to be philosophical are born out of the human being's long-standing desire to take something *other than* the simplest and most matter-of-fact view of life and death. Throughout human history, religion and philosophy—for the most part at least—have strongly resisted the assumption that a given "life" is neatly coextensive with that complex of chemicals we call the human body. Thus the priest at the graveside intones words about the difference between the corpse that is going into the earth and the soul that has gone on to be with God. Thus too the philosopher, even if one who is skeptical about souls, wants to assert that people's deeds live after them in the memory of others and in the cumulative project of human culture. Gravestones, gifts bequeathed in memory of "x," whole universities named after departed loved ones, even Marxist heroes embalmed in public squares—these are all ways in which human beings assert that the end of life is complex but in some sense, we feel, even *ought* to be so. To reduce that complexity in a simple and thoughtless discarding of the dead not only would be, we feel, an insult to them but also would diminish our common humanity. To hold on to some type of "complexity" at these cruxes is, we instinctively feel, one of our ways of being other than, and in some sense "higher" than, animals.

Moreover, this insistence on humanizing the event of dying is something that can be implemented only through social forms. Funerals, services of memorialization, even fixing the name of the dead person to buildings, charity funds, and boulevards—all these are ways in which death is socialized and the "life" of the individual in question is perpetuated, in some sense, long after his or her breathing and heartbeats have ceased. These events are social constructions, but they are also avenues through which the human perception of the uniqueness of our humanity gets expressed. Ritual, especially the complex of events called "rites of passage" emphasized by scholars of the past like Arnold van Gennep, Mircea Eliade, and Victor Turner, is crucial in expressing this perception.[1]

The importance of ritual in Japanese life has been difficult for Western observers—and especially Western theories—to admit to. In the period immediately after its military defeat in 1945, there were many theories as to how Japan could and should alter many of its social patterns and enter the future. Some were Marxist and others offered an American-style modernization. The former placed no value on the traditional society. Its religions and its rituals were deemed harmful impediments to building a new, classless Japan and had to be swept away. The American-style program of modernization, while not hostile to the traditional culture, envisioned a secularization of society on "rational" models. In these the rites and rituals of the past were quaint and charming remnants but no more than that.

Yet, not only did Japan pull itself out of the ashes of catastrophe with stunning speed but in doing so it confounded virtually every Western theory as to what would be needed to do so. In fact, one of the striking features of Japanese life is the persistence of a whole complex of social and religious rituals—especially those that attend death. Ironically what has, in fact, been thoroughly discredited is the doctrinaire Marxist critique of such rituals as merely ideological manipulations or forms of waste foisted on a naive population. And, in contrast to those forms of modernization theory that trivialized these rites, there is evidence to show that even Japan's strong economic recovery had roots in traditional values and that these values had been enhanced by family-centered religious rituals. The cultic care for ancestors, in brief, turned out to be a benefit rather than a bane.

This is to say that both religion and social ritual seem very much alive and well in Japan in the late twentieth century. People still crowd the Shinto shrines to celebrate births, days when children pass certain age points on the way to maturity, and the "coming of age" itself at the twentieth year. They hold ever more elaborate and expensive wedding ceremonies—having, over the past couple of decades, actually evolved ways in which "Christian" weddings, complete with the traditional white dress, wedding cake, and chapel atmosphere, are provided, along with the Shinto rite, as an option for newlyweds.[2] They also, to be sure, conclude a life with an elaborate Buddhist funeral followed by an extended sequence of services to memorialize the dead.

Funerary rituals and memorials for ancestors have, it has turned out, uncommon importance for understanding the nature of the society of the living in Japan. Anthropologists were, it seems, more attuned to these realities in Japan than were the various prophets of modernization. For instance, already in 1964 David Plath, in an important essay on ancestor rites, wrote:

> In the usual Western views of ancestor worship the ancestors are seen as a kind of deadweight from the past. They are supposed to foster a past-time orientation and a solidly conservative stance among the living. This may hold for other societies, but I think it misleading in the Japanese instance, [in which] the ancestors do not demand that life continue exactly as they knew it [but rather] whatever will assure the continuity of the household line. Far from hindering change, ancestor worship in Japan at least can be a spur to it.[3]

This kind of perspective—keenly on target and prescient, in my view—should have been enough to call into question the then-prevalent view, common to both champions of "modernization" and Marxist critiques of feudalism and its remnants, that Japan would have to jettison such things as its ancestor rites in order to qualify as a truly modern society.

But this not only shows that traditions from the past can be engines for moving into the future, it also indicates that there can be great utility in the kind of social frameworks and definitions that lie over the bare facts of biology. If there is one thing powerfully suggested by Japanese ancestral rites it is that there can be a *significant gap* between physiological death and social death—and that both are important.[4]

In fact, the whole of the ancestral cult in Japan insists that dying, at least in cultural and social terms, must be a prolonged, protracted, and many-staged passing. The Buddhist memorial services are held, at least when according to tradition, on an exact schedule. The sequence of rites consists in the funeral day, seventh day, forty-ninth day, hundredth day, first year, third year, seventh year, thirteenth year, seventeenth year, twenty-third year, and thirty-third year. Thus with only one exception, it should be noted, *more and more time* is permitted to elapse between temple rites, and this fact coordinates with the perception that the deceased is *more and more rarefied*—at least as someone with whom the living need to deal. Thought to be progressively integrated into the world of the gods and Buddhas, the dead person is less and less dangerous to those who inhabit the world of living humans. Not only is he or she forgotten but the living also feel safe in forgetting.

In the long run to forget the dead, then, is not only necessary but desirable; one could not possibly keep alive forever the memory of all one's deceased ancestors. The key thing, however, is that even forgetting has a schedule and is part of a process. As Robert J. Smith observes:

> When a member of the household dies, the immediate concern is to begin the process of removing his spirit from the realm of daily life and ultimately from the entire world of men. Often the rites designed to accomplish this process are simple and direct: the spirit of the dead is elevated out of human place and time as the dead person fades from memory. At length the *shirei* [spirit of the newly dead] is said to become an ancestral spirit (*sorei*) and . . . ultimately one of the myriad deities. [On the Izu Islands] the memorial tablet for the deceased is raised shelf by shelf in the domestic altar, until on the final day it is put with the ancestral tablets on the highest level.[5]

The progressive elevation of the tablet mirrors the gradual removal of the dead from their proximity to the living. He or she is more and more of an ancestor, more and more a kami. A kind of ontological thinning takes place. And as that happens, he or she can also fade from the consciousness of the living. Attenuation is a process.

DENSIFICATION

For most Japanese that is the basic pattern of social dying. And a grasp of this is necessary because, I wish to claim, such a process has its exact *obverse*—in the processes whereby a person socially comes alive. Just as dying is not just a physiological event, so too being born into the human world is not just a matter of passing successfully out of a uterus. If in social dying there is a kind of ontological thinning that occurs, in coming bit by bit into the social world of human beings there is a thickening or densification of being.[6] The process at the beginning of a life is the structural opposite of what happens at the end. What I propose here is, I believe, crucial for an understanding of Japanese beliefs and practices with respect to infants, fetuses, and abortion.

I wish to extend and apply an argument already advanced by Kuroda Hideo in his important studies of medieval Japan.[7] Kuroda has shown, from documents of that period, that people then widely understood that the unseen world of the gods and Buddhas interfaced with the visible world of human beings in such as way that both being born into this world and exiting it through death were *processes rather than fixed points*. In that epoch, when the impress of Buddhism was heaviest on Japanese life and was congealing with folk traditions on a grass-roots level, it was assumed that a newborn gradually made the transition from "the world of the gods and Buddhas" into that of human beings and from there to adulthood. What is important to recognize is that it was assumed that only by becoming a full adult did one become, at last, a *full* human. That status was earned through passage through time and rituals, not automatically conferred by being born.

At the other end of the spectrum, of course, aging and debilitation meant a progressive return to the world of the gods and Buddhas. By common understandings and the rituals that articulated them, it was made clear to all that being born and dying were progressive events. Merely being physically born did not entail automatic entry into the community. Kuroda notes that in most instances being born had to be supplemented with a sequence of rituals—at age three, at age five, at age seven, and at age fifteen—that sequentially announced and clarified a given person's "viability" in the realm of humankind. After age sixty, when a person became known as an *okina* or "old one," and even more deeply at age seventy, when a person was regarded as a kind of living dead one, a progressive release out of the human species was assumed to be taking place—even though a physiological death had not yet occurred. Certain things were taken as "empirical" proofs of the process: the evidence of senility and memory lapses were signs of a person's progressive reincorporation into the realm of the gods and Buddhas.

Kuroda provides a very useful schematization of this whole process, with the main terms translated as shown at the top of p. 35.[8] The implication, of course, is that the stages move in a clockwise direction. As is evident from the sketch, dying socially involved becoming progessively "detached"—not only mentally but also in a deeper sense—from the world of human beings. The person at sixty years of age leaves the realm of unadulterated humanhood. He or she is drawn up progressively into the world of the gods and Buddhas and, if still physically alive at sixty or older, is regarded as an okina, an "old one" whose mind and habits are semi-divinized, less "worldly" in terms of concerns and thoughts. To be senile and scatterbrained at that age is also to be moving into the ecstasy of the other world. (Ariyoshi Sawako's superb novel about old age and senility shows this very strongly. Her Japanese title translates literally into "Persons in a Trance" or even "People in Ecstasy.")[9] Senility indicates a category change, not just a matter of brain cells and their functioning. Since medieval Japanese imagined that even after dying the okina for a while kept a human form and could occasionally visit this world, the literature of that period shows as much. A cycle of Noh drama even today

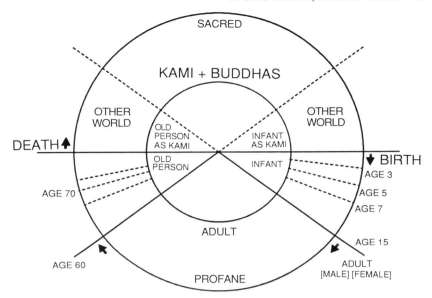

From Kuroda Hideo, *Kyōkai no chūsei shōchō no chūsei* (Tokyo: Tōkyō Daigaku Shuppankai, 1986).

is invariably opened by a "god" or else an "okina" play; in some sense there is only a negligible difference between the two.

The same is true on the other end of things. What we call "being born" is really taking progressive leave of the world of gods and Buddhas and entering that of humans. It is being induced into what is profane and bit by bit leaving a sacred dimension. In this way Kuroda explains the deep role played in medieval Japan by the "coming-of-age" rituals—understandings that are the matrix for the *shichi-go-san* [7–5–3] festival, whereby even today children at the ages of three, five, and seven are feted on an annual "children's day." Originally these festivals were times when children moved up the rank of years and demonstrated that having successfully survived the diseases and dangers of childhood, they were "making it" as humans in the human world. In the medieval period, the full completion of this was at age fifteen, at which point a child finally became *ichinin*—literally "one human." (That rite today is set at age twenty, but in Japan, significantly, it still involves public rituals on an annual "adult's day," when those who have arrived at their twentieth year officially become "adults.") Originally becoming an adult was tantamount also to becoming a full *human* and, by implication, before that the child was still betwixt and between, in the sense of not being completely separated from the world of gods and Buddhas. Emergence was gradual.

Kuroda has articulated a structure that embraced the basic view of life and death that was imbedded in a whole range of folk beliefs and practices. He has also documented this view from medieval texts. I will try to augment this basic scheme only slightly—and with a mind to showing how this material can facilitate our grasp of Japanese thinking about abortion.

It is, first of all, interesting to see how this basic view merely hinted at what happens on the empirically unseen, sacred side of the cycle and did not pinpoint anything with specificity. It held that the newborn have arrived from the world of the Buddhas and kami and that the aged return to that same world. Yet, *exactly* what happened there and to whom were matters left within a penumbra of the unspecified, providing a large and open space for interpretation of individual cases. It especially left a lot of room for uncertainty and sheer guesswork about cases of *umarekawari*, "rebirth" or "transmigration," as understood by Buddhists. That is, if it seemed right or advantageous to suggest that a certain person "x" was, in fact, a reborn version of "y" who had lived in the human world earlier, such a belief could be credible within the overall scheme. For such a person, the passage through the realm of gods and Buddhas had been a fairly rapid movement over an arc that eventuated in rebirth as an infant. The texts of the medieval and early modern periods show many instances of such speculation and, especially in the lore associated with Buddhist temples, there is a sense of certainty about particular instances. Moreover, since what really happened in the unseen world beyond death was unknown, there remained the possibility—as taught by Buddhists—that egregiously wicked or indolent persons might be reborn within species other than the human; murderers might come back as animals to be slaughtered and lazy folk as bovines forced to pull heavy loads.[10]

But in most cases the opacity of the sacred realm allowed for other possibilities, especially a sense that the dead graduated into the world of gods and Buddhas in such a way that transmigration back into this world was either unlikely or too indefinite to permit speculation. In fact, the belief in transmigration was supplemented by other Buddhist visions of what happens after death; the Buddhist texts themselves, it was realized, were not always clear about whether transmigration had to take place, and many of them stated that in most cases it was downright undesirable. There were far better options. Especially the steady growth, throughout the medieval period, of belief in Amida's Pure Land meant that one could believe that in dying people went on to become Buddhas in such places. The Pure Land was, for those who believed in it, the real name for the other-worldly repose of the dead, and it too could be fitted with ease into the overall scheme. This, in all probability, is why the word *hotoke*, designating a "Buddha," became a virtual synonym for the respected dead. It became possible to respect the dead as ancestors, to call them "Buddha"—thus using the highest appellations in the vocabulary of religion—and at the same time to feel a certain "relief" in having them move farther and deeper into the opaque and sacred realm of all gods and Buddhas.

In the case of newborn infants, however, especially those called mizuko, it was quite different. In dying they, it seems, were thought to *revert back* to the sacred realm. I take this as the conceptual and practical import of the widespread traditional terminology about "return." Whereas most people progressed in a clockwise fashion around the ambit of Kuroda's diagram, a mizuko in dying was thought to make a quick counterclockwise move to a point still near at hand. And it could do so, after all, because its entry into the human world was still so tenuous, so uncertain, so unfixed by social ritual. It was, in that sense, possible for the powers of the sacred realm to pull the mizuko back into itself.

This is of crucial import. Children, it was felt in medieval Japan, had about them an "otherworldliness," something they demonstated even by their playfulness, their inability to connect with the serious—but essentially profane—adult world of work and production.[11] In this sense the "playfulness" of children was the structural equivalent of the senility and absentmindedness of the aged; both were indices to a positive kind of unworldliness.

The period in question, it must be remembered, was one in which infant mortality was high, at least compared to what it is in more modern times. Miscarriages too, we can assume, were much more common than they are today. This is to say that the sheer number of fetuses, infants, and young children who died was relatively high. And, in lieu of today's knowledge of nutrition, hygiene, bacteria, and contagious disease, medieval people were naturally drawn to explanations of such things drawn from the worldview available to them. I think we can say with some surety that the medieval and early modern Japanese tended to interpret the frequent deaths of children as caused by their being still so close to the sacred realm that they could *with ease slip back* into it.

THE FIXED AND THE FLUID

Clearly this flattens out the overwhelming importance Westerners have long placed on what they take to be fairly precise entry points, namely, the physiological ones. While the West had its own rituals of socialization—name giving, entry into adulthood, retirement from active life, and the funeral's farewell—Westerners did not think such rituals diminished the precision of the entry point of birth and the exit door of death.

Although there is evidence that the ancient Greeks and Romans may have held views not greatly different from those of the Japanese on some of these issues, as Christianity developed its own views on such matters, notions of fluid boundaries disappeared in Europe. Christians opted for the view that human life was either present or it was not; notions of gradualism and of process were ruled to be simply wrong.

This was no doubt due to the Christian teaching that the line separating humans and God was itself a strict one and, except for the unique case of the God-man Jesus, a line that absolutely disallowed all notions of mixture, process, or gradual progress from one rubric into the other. The very uniqueness of Christ, the one and only combination of deity and humanity, prohibited envisioning any other instances. The early Christian Church poured immense energies into getting doctrinal precision on this matter and went through great ecclesiastical struggles for it. But this development, it is insufficiently noticed, had vast implications for what could be allowed—both as ideas and as social practices—within the Christian culture that subsequently developed. Christianity became a religion showing a decided preference for the hard distinction, the fixed boundary, and the precise demarcation between X and Y.

And when the matter at hand was "life," the boundaries were not fluid. The Christians rejected any kind of progressive movement between the divine and the human and in place of that held that every human being has the *imago dei* or "image of God." And that image is present just by virtue of being born a human and is present whether recognized or not.

Many historians link the social changes worked by the early Christians to this conception. Viewing other humans as bearers of the divine image meant they had to be treated well. This was, according to Elaine Pagels, "the good news that class, education, sex, and status made no difference, that every human being is essentially equal to any other 'before God,' including the emperor himself, for all humankind was created in the image of the one God."[12] And this, to be sure, implied that the newborn child had *complete possession* of the image of God, not just a first stage of something that still required time, actual maturation, and social rituals to turn into a reality. To the early Christians this meant that infanticide and the abandonment of children were heinous sins in the eyes of God.

The problem of the fetus was more difficult. In one sense it was a being in transition; the examination of a fetus in its early stage showed it still lacked some of the distinguishing physical features of humankind. Yet the impulse to extend protection to it—differentiating Christian practice as sharply as possible from that of the Greeks and Romans on this score— was strong. Augustine and Jerome, early fathers of the Chruch, were far from certain as to exactly when the soul enters the body—but they opted for a conservative, safe-side, position. As John T. Noonan, Jr. notes, "As far as Jerome and Augustine were concerned, the theoretical distinction led to no difference in moral disapprobation. They simply adopted language broad enough to condemn both contraceptive acts and acts destroying the fetus after conception."[13] The unknown was, therefore, to be treated *as if it were known.* The theological and legal history of Europe on these matters was thus set: to be part of the Christian world meant agreement with the Church's view that not only abortion but even contraception was a violation of the image of God and, as such, sins.

What I have been describing as the medieval Japanese view is, of course, very different—even though it too is derived largely from the resources of religion. In it the socialization at one side of the cycle and the desocialization at the other are also full of philosophical and ethical import. Being fully human is not determined merely by passing through a womb and is certainly not to be inferred from the mere union of a sperm and an egg. Potentiality is not actuality and there is, in this view, no compelling reason to treat it as if it were.

I stress the fact that this is a *religious* view that has gone on to find articulation in social rituals. And in this sense what happens in such cases is that a specifically *human meaning* is being placed over the bare facts of physiology. Here a great deal of the religio-philosophical weight is being shifted away from the merely physical event—expiring or being birthed— and attributed to the humanizing and social process. And it is, of course, precisely this different attribution of weight that is so difficult for modern people, especially those in the West, to understand and appreciate. Japanese today may be much less conscious of the "meaning" of all these things than were their ancestors, but there nevertheless remains even in Japanese society today a sense that the rites of passage are deeply significant, not just interesting remnants from the past. In that sense the "modern" Japanese person, much more than we tend to expect, remains in touch with these aspects of his or her own medieval world. Even when a person may not be fully conscious of such things, this religio-social framework still informs social understandings.

We should not underestimate the positive consolations that were historically derived from such a view. It has already been noted that especially in an age when infant mortality was relatively high the idea that such children were being pulled back into a basically "good" world of the gods and Buddhas to some extent palliated parental pain. Moreover, such children were often, as noted, thought to be only temporarily withdrawn from this world; with luck and well-directed prayers, the gods and Buddhas might be prompted to send the same child or children into the lives of waiting parents. This, I suspect, is the reason why until modern times it was customary not to hold funerals not only for fetuses but even for deceased children.[14] They were not part of the ancestral dead.

Clearly another "benefit" derivable from this total view of life and death was the fact that it permitted people to countenance *intervention* in the process. If becoming human depended to such a large extent on the sequence of rituals that proved viability in this world, it became more allowable for parents or others to impede that process—if there were reasons to warrant such. Since the newborn or the fetus was often referred to as *kami no ko* or a "child of the gods," it became possible to see a forced return of that child to the sacred world as something within the realm of moral possibility.

In such instances the language of *kaeru* (to go back) became that of *kaesu* (to cause to go back). The intransive verb was turned into a transitive one. These, then, were not instances of miscarriage, stillbirth, and childhood mortality but, rather, of abortion and infanticide. Human intention and agency had become involved.

It would be easy today for critics of those practices to view this merely as a language of euphemization—or for Europeans or Americans to use this kind of data to bring out the old charge that for Asians "life is cheap." To declare it so, however, would be to negate the fact that within the religious framework that gave these practices their social shape, such language was meaningful and, in the context, appropriate. To reject the use of such language is also to attack the whole religious system with which it has traditionally been closely interwoven.

PAGAN FAMILIES

It is important to remember that it was into the society just described— namely that of the medieval period—that Westerners first penetrated Japan. Long before Commodore Perry arrived in Tokyo Bay in the nineteenth century, Catholic missionaries and traders had made their way from Europe to the far eastern archipelago.

And lest it be assumed that with such a fluid view of life and death the Japanese had sunk into a moral cesspool, it is good to recall that none other than Saint Francis Xavier (1506–1552), upon his visit to Japan, wrote, "Judging by the people we have so far met, I would say that the Japanese are the best race yet discovered and I do not think you will find their match among the pagan nations."[15] This is, to say the least, rather high praise for the moral tenor of a society that, exactly at that time, countenanced both abortion and infanticide.[16]

The evidence—from observers such as those quoted in chapter 11—is that what especially impressed persons from the West was the high level of *family life* in Japan. In other words, even from sources that could ordinarily have been expected to take a somewhat critical view of what they saw, the Japanese family was something that caught attention and was singled out for praise.

What this suggests is very important. For what we seem to have here is evidence that there is no necessary correlation between the allowance of abortion and the quality—or even the overall tenor—of family life in a given society. That is, at least from what we find in this instance, there is no reason to believe that proscription of abortion is necessary to have a society in which living children are well cared for and family life is stable, strong, and beneficial to its members and to the larger society as well.

There are, of course, people in our own society who very much doubt that the quality of family life is the right measure for judging whole societies. But that is not the issue here. I wish merely to note that even if one might hypothetically grant the quality of family life as a yardstick, then— at least on the basis of the materials from Japan—there is no basis for concluding that forbidding access to abortion is important. Apparently it is possible for a society to practice abortion and still have what is generally called a "strong" conception of the family.

One can go even farther. Perhaps one of the principal benefits derivable today from a close study of Japan will be the opportunity to put to a real test some of the central assumptions that have long been held in the West concerning itself, its moral achievements, and the specific religious matrix—either Christian or Judeo-Christian—assumed to be a sine qua non for what are taken to be Western accomplishments. Ever since Francis Xavier and his contemporaries reported back from Japan that they had located a suprisingly developed and moral society—in spite of its being untouched by Christianity—such reports have filtered back to the West. What has been avoided, however, is any attempt to explore the implications of these things, specifically what they might say about some very common Western and Christian assumptions. In other words, the use of the cumulative evidence from Japan and about Japan has seldom, if ever, been faced for what it really seems to be suggesting.

I take note of this because there are many persons in the West for whom the question of legalized abortion has become a touchstone issue. The reason the public rhetoric of abortion's opponents is often so intense is because in their eyes this matter becomes the one telltale issue on which a nation or a whole civilization can demonstrate whether or not it can credibly deserve to be called "Christian." Abortion, then, can never be a matter of private choice; a whole moral universe either stands or falls dependent on the way public policy goes on this matter.

Thus public policy on abortion, for all practical purposes, is thought to distinguish a Christian society from a pagan one—and a "pagan" society is depicted both as that which Christianity opposed during its first two centuries and that which, some would say or feel, is again taking shape today. Historical matters are often brought forward, especially the fact that whereas in the pagan Roman empire abortion was permitted, the early Christians began to view it as a sin and therefore to be totally disallowed. And, since the pagan society of Rome tolerated a whole gamut of practices that the Christians came to condemn, an across-the-board moral superiority of the Christian over the pagan society is assumed to be a proven fact.

Needless to say, ever since the Renaissance there have been efforts to see the classical world of both Greece and Rome in more favorable terms, to look beyond the Christian polemic and see what it was that so many Christian writers excoriated so emphatically. What had been a Renaissance interest in individual classics eventually became a concern to describe with accuracy the Hellenistic world and its social practices.

There can be no doubt that some of those practices—slavery, for instance—the Christians rightly censured. Yet what appears to emerge from these studies is that instead of seeing things in terms of a moral and religious Christianity challenging an immoral and godless Rome, we need to recognize a more complex situation. For instance, when the relationship between religion and differing family systems is taken into account, what we see in the first two centuries of the Christian era is a struggle between, on one side, what had traditionally been the "strong" Roman family, based on kinship and reinforced by a concern for ancestors and household gods, and on the other side the new Christian churches, which were essentially voluntary and in which persons were addressed as "father," "brother," and "sister," even when they were not kin. Robert Nisbet describes it thus:

> A conflict must have existed between these novel, Christian family-like communities and the actual families in Rome. Just as the twentieth century has seen the rise of religious organizations which in effect seek to take, through conversion, children from their parents, and which on occasion are bitterly resisted by the parents of the children, so must such conflicts have existed during the early phases of Christianity. Not every *pater familias* could have taken lightly—even after his traditional authority had been diminished by the Roman state—to the loss of a son or, more often, daughter or even wife to a Christian commune.[17]

Thus one of the things about the society the Christians called "pagan" was that its concept of the kinship-based family—undoubtedly "strong" in its own way—proved an obstacle to the formation of the new voluntary associations known as Christian ecclesia.

My point in going into this is to suggest that, even when other differences are taken into account, what Westerners from Xavier to today have been encountering in Japan is a society that, at least in its concept of the strongly knit, kinship-based family, is in some ways surprisingly similar to that of ancient Rome. It too reveres ancestors and thinks of religion as deeply connected with the maintenance of the family over time and through many generations.[18]

Perhaps we need to interpret more rigorously the significance of what the Christian missionaries of the sixteenth century encountered in East Asia generally but especially in Japan. Their records document their fascination but also their confusion. By the definitions provided in the centers of Christian Europe, the societies of the far East were "pagan" and depraved. Yet the missionaries' eyes and experiences told them something very different. If this was "pagan," then pagan was not so bad!

And in the eyes of many in the West today, Japan continues to represent a perplexing civilization—no doubt in part because it is so obviously "strong" without having been part of the Judeo-Christian religious formations of the West. In that sense Japan, willy-nilly, puts a number of the West's most cherished assumptions about itself to an adequate test.

One of these, as seems increasingly clear, is the assumption that individualism—at least as we have come to know it—is an unalloyed value. I have no intention of even attempting to unpack the history and sociology of that difficult problem. Perhaps, however, a somewhat tantalizing ending for this discussion may be offered, one from a Japanese source. For if it is possible that at least *one* of the roots of modern Western individualism lies in the theology of early Christianity and in the kind of volunteerism—as opposed to the kinship-based religion of Rome—that the early Church represented and valued, then the following comment may be apropos. Yuasa Yasuo, an astute scholar of both Japanese history and Western philosophy, sees a clear connection here and has written,

> If we look at the writings of St. Paul and St. Augustine we see that their awareness of themselves as individual human beings was realized when they saw themselves standing in a state of severe and personal tension vis-à-vis a deity who is the Supreme and perfect Being. The "self" that emerges in such a context is not unlike the man who, according to Plato, has come out of a cave to find that, standing in the supreme light, he cannot avoid noticing the dark shadow cast by his own self. Our ancestors in Japan, however, saw things very differently: in most cases they did not grasp an existence of the "self," at least not in these terms. Their own conception of "self" and of being human did not arise from some awareness of confronting a God who is Absolute—but merely from the discovery of being different from the world, a world which was perceived by them rather dimly and itself quite confused.[19]

Chapter 4

JIZŌ AT THE CROSSROADS

> Great perfection seems chipped;
> Yet use will not wear it out.
> (*Tao Te Ching*)
>
> The concept of play merges quite naturally
> with that of holiness.
> (Johan Huizinga, *Homo Ludens*)

DIVINE IMPERFECTION

CENTRAL TO THE Japanese Buddhists' way of handling the human pain and moral conflicts associated with abortion is the fascinating figure known to the Japanese as Jizō. A more correct appellation is "Jizō Bosatsu," a phrase meaning "the Earth Store Bodhisattva," although many Japanese familiarly refer to him as "Jizō-Sama" or "Mr. Jizō." If we were to sketch out what is sometimes called the Buddhist "pantheon," Jizō would figure somewhere in it as a divine figure known, along with Kannon, for demonstrations of compassion and altruistic help to others.

But merely placing Jizō in a pantheon will not do. It would be tantamount to losing this figure in a crowd. And the important thing about Jizō is that, at least in Japan, he did not merely fill a niche on a shelf full of other godlike Buddhist figures. There is something special about Jizō. Western visitors are invariably struck by the seemingly widespread appearance of this figure on street corners and in cemeteries—usually with a bright red bib and sometimes with a staff topped with rings.

Although during the last two decades Japanese scholars have paid increasing attention to the history of the Jizō cult in Japan, such was not always the case. This in itself tells us something. For one of the curious paradoxes of modern Japanese Buddhist scholarship is that during most of the twentieth century—at least until fairly recently—its overwhelming concentration was on Indian and Chinese Buddhist texts. Among scholars there tended to be a corresponding neglect of those aspects of the Japanese tradition that seemed to be extratextual and to embrace the more "lowly" folk traditions. The cult of Jizō probably epitomized what such scholars of Buddhism were quite happy to ignore.

Westerners in Japan were much less ready to do so. Aspects of the more popular, "low" tradition caught their attention. Thus in 1894 Lafcadio Hearn, in his *Glimpses of Unfamiliar Japan*, picked up on Jizō and wrote, "Descending the shadowed steps, I find myself face to face with six little statues about three feet high, standing in a row upon one long pedestal. . . . The faces of the six are the same; each figure differs from the other by the attitude only and the emblematic attribute; and all are smiling a faint smile. . . . Archaic, mysterious, but inexplicably touching, all these soft childish faces. . . . [Jizō] may justly be called the most Japanese of all Japanese divinities."[1]

Even more important, however, was what was probably the first major work giving a history of Jizō. Written by Marinus Willem de Visser in 1914, it clearly shows that this Westerner, while combing the texts— without much success—for references to Jizō, was impressed with the *popular* attention paid to this figure in Japan. Although there is in de Visser's impressive study no reference to Jizō's specific significance for women who had experienced abortion or infanticide, his awareness of the extent of the common people's attention to Jizō was clearly a stimulus to his studies.[2]

Hearn and de Visser were not the only Westerners to notice Jizō. In 1928 James Bissett Pratt, an American philosopher who traveled widely in Asia and wrote appreciatively about Buddhism, noted that Jizō was a major figure in the Japanese religious sensibility—much more so than its Chinese prototype on the continent, Ti-tsang.[3]

Nowadays, of course, Japanese scholarship on Jizō has turned full circle, has become an important resource, and—bit by bit—has even begun to include references to Jizō's importance in rites for mizuko.[4] Some students of Japan now go even farther, feeling that Jizō is virtually the *paradigm* of Japanese spirituality. These scholars feel that one can understand the core of the Japanese religious sensibility if one gets a grasp of how people on many societal levels respond to the figure of Jizō.

I think there is something to be said for that. Even if one were, however, to dispute that particular point, there can no doubt of Jizō's overwhelming importance for an understanding of the religious dimension in Japanese ways of dealing with the problem of abortion. And that is simply because historically Jizō was thought to have a special relationship with children. Joseph M. Kitagawa states it succinctly: "In the course of time [in Japan] Jizō came to be regarded as the special protector of infants and children who had died—a function for which he was never held responsible in China."[5] Both exactly how Jizō came to be so regarded and why it had great implications for the relationship of religion to abortion in Japan are matters for fuller explanation later.

First, however, something needs to be said about the notion of the *bodhisattva*—at least in Japan—since Jizō fits within that category of beings. Long before Buddhism reached Japan, in the fifth or sixth century, the concept of the bodhisattva had already unfolded within Buddhism. Indian texts show that although the bodhisattva was technically still a Buddha-to-be rather than a fully-realized Buddha, it was already thought that somehow such a figure could be more in touch with the real needs of people in trouble. In the Buddhist pantheon, Buddhas, by contrast, were conceived of as beings not only perfect but also somewhat withdrawn into the splendor of their perfection. Bodhisattvas, however, were down-to-earth practioners of compassion and, especially when appearing incognito, were assumed to be ready and able to render help of various kinds. Full of altruism, they were savior figures and beings one dared to approach.

Yuasa Yasuo has drawn out the implications of this, at the same time explaining why the Japanese were so attracted to this type of figure. He writes:

> The bodhisattva completely identifies—by its own sufferings—with people who are ready to succumb to the agonies that attend the human condition. And at the same time the bodhisattva has come into our world in order to lead people to a salvation that lies elsewhere—on "the other shore" in Buddhist terms. In that sense, of course, the bodhisattva shows a striking similarity to the Christian conception of Jesus as both Son of God and Son of man—that is, someone who was incarnated as part of a mission to suffer in this world to provide atonement for sinful human beings. A different and distinctive feature of the bodhisattva, however, is that it itself is pursuing the search for truth and undergoing ascetic disciplines to that end; the bodhisattva is still exploring the complicated path towards the highest form of existence.[6]

Yuasa claims that this is crucial for understanding the religious preferences of the Japanese. He substantiates this with an argument from history. He sees great significance in the little recognized "failure" of Kūkai (Kōbō Daishi, 774–835) to enshrine in Japan a national cult devoted to the Great Sun Buddha, Dainichi Nyorai:

> Kūkai established the Great Sun Buddha as the Highest form of Absolute Being and went on to expound a mystical union as the way of religiously experiencing a unity with that Absolute. Here the thing to note, however, is that subsequent generations of the Japanese people simply did not accept his theory. In the history of Buddhism in Japan people tended to be indifferent to the Great Sun Buddha, an abstract and conceptual Buddha but extremely difficult to approach through ordinary human emotions and sentiments. The Japanese much preferred a bodhisattva type, a being that, like us, is still incomplete and imper-

fect. And if it is going to have the appelation "Buddha" it will be a Buddha which shows the characteristics associated with the bodhisattva. That is the type that the Japanese like. Typical cases of the Japanese preference are Kannon, Amida, and Jizō.[7]

Kūkai wanted his compatriots to adopt a fully transcendent and perfect being—like the kind of deity found in the West. The religious sentiments of the Japanese people, however, moved in a very different direction. As a savior figure, the Great Sun Buddha simply would not do; the problem with him was his perfection.[8]

In conjunction with some points of comparison made in the last chapter, it may help to recall that early Christian theology went in almost the opposite direction. As the perception of Jesus as Savior grew in the first century, there developed an increasingly keen sense that the only way to define his status was as equal to that of the Highest of the High. The development of orthodox teaching about Christ, as hammered out in the Church councils, insisted that only if he were fully God and morally *perfect* would he have the status and power to be the needed savior. In that cultural context, to be an adequate savior meant to have the right credentials, qualities of perfection. In Japan, by contrast, such perfection was a *disqualifier*; a being so defined and described could not meet what people expected and wanted in a figure who could save—namely, approachability and a touch of imperfection.

Jizō

The history of Jizō in Japan is basically a tale of a progressive *down scaling* of a figure that had once been a fairly lofty one in the Buddhist pantheon. When we look at the history, we see that the diminishing of Jizō—physically in icons and socially in texts—was the counterpart of a progressive growth of the public sense that Jizō is, more than any other, the bodhisattva that is close to the people. Paradoxically, Jizō's religious and social importance grows even as its stature, in a most literal sense, shrinks.

Although it is not my purpose to recount the history of this figure prior to its appearance in Japan, it is important to note that in China, where he was known as Ti-tsang, Jizō was already a figure of compassion, one thought to be especially involved in helping people caught in the underworld.[9] And in the Chinese texts of special importance to the Japanese conception of Jizō, there had been, according to Hayami Tasuku, a focus on Jizō as the savior of people suffering because caught in a forced transmigration through the six realms.[10]

This concept of the six realms (*rokudō*), absolutely crucial for an understanding of medieval Japan, was essentially a Buddhist taxonomy of the universe. It served not only for classifying the species of being but also for portraying the weals and woes that are part of transmigration or reincarnation either up or down in the scale. According to the view that became very popular in Japan, both Jizō and Kannon as bodhisattvas were always ready and willing to move *down* into these six realms to give concrete guidance and assistance to beings caught in them. The six realms as a group constituted samsara, the realm of suffering, and were in contrast to nirvana, a place above the six, where fully realized Buddhas dwelt. Even gods, importantly, were supposedly still caught in the imperfect realm of suffering. The six also housed warlike titans whose record of past killings made them compulsive bloodletters (*ashura*) and hungry ghosts (*gaki*), whose insatiable cravings made their misery only one notch better than that of the creatures in hell.[11] The point is that Jizō and Kannon, as bodhisattvas, were in places proximate to beings in dire plight and were found at the nexi where a being in transmigation might move from one rung on the cosmic ladder to another. They negotiated, by guidance and help, the right moves at such empirically unobservable junctures between one life and the next.

A sketch of the concept would look like this:

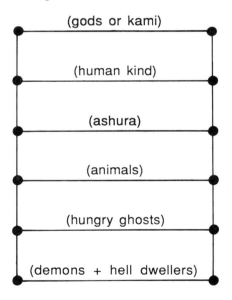

Note: ● = node locations of
Jizō and Kannon

Unlike the religious taxonomy of medieval Europe, in which all beings from God on down occupied fixed places, the Buddhist one adopted into early medieval Japan was characterized by a fundamental *fluidity*. Through reincarnating, a given being would move up or down or—just as likely—into different "lives" within the same basic rubric. Karma, the accumulation of good or bad deeds in the past, gave one either an upscale or a downscale rebirth.

But figures like Jizō and Kannon were there on the spot to help those who could not make it on their own karmic record. So compelling was this vision of the universe as six basic rubrics through which beings traveled that in medieval and early modern Japan it was customary to represent it also in the visible, physical world.

This was especially true of Jizō. Images of this bodhisattva were frequently assembled in groups of six (*roku-Jizō*) and placed either along the sides of roads or, especially, at junctures where two or more roads would meet. In this sense the metaphysical landscape or cosmology was copied back onto the physical one in a very graphic way. And, of course, this meant that Japanese people from medieval times down to the present were, in seeing clusters of six Jizō images along roadsides or at road crossings, visually reminded of the supposedly more important—though invisible—realities as taught by Buddhism. Travelers along roads were reminded of their "larger" journeys. Even today these clusters are found in many villages and hamlets in Japan—as well as scattered throughout large metropolitan areas such as Tokyo.[12] In this kind of practice the basic structure of the otherworld is thus, through what has sometimes been called the "poetry of stone," transposed onto the actual geographical landscape in which people live their mundane lives.

Equally important in the history of Jizō, however, was its iconographic downgrading. The early sculptures, for instance those of the ninth and tenth century still extant in Japan, were obviously copied largely from Chinese prototypes; like most of the icons of the period, figures of Jizō were exquisitely crafted but also austere—distant and holy rather than proximate and imperfect.[13] This, of course, is precisely what changed with time and with the movement of the Jizō into and within the lives of the common people of Japan.

Much of this movement was supplemented by a rich folklore about Jizō, which literary works incorporate. For instance, the *Konjaku-Monogatari-shū* of the eleventh or twelfth century, one of the era's most important works, includes thirty-two tales that show how socially widespread the Jizō cult had become. Most full in its attention to Jizō was the *Jizō-Bosatsu Reigenki*, a work from the late classical or medieval period, although it cannot be dated with certainty.[14]

Progressively Jizō was viewed as a bodhisattva especially close to children and itself often diminutive in size. The *Uji Shūi Monogatari* (ca. 1190–1242) includes a striking tale about an old Buddhist nun who, wanting to meet Jizō and having been tricked by a con artist into believing that he could guide her to Jizō, was brought instead to the home of a couple who happened to have a ten-year-old boy who just happened to be named Jizō. The parents introduced the nun to their child. The tale continues: "The moment she saw him, the nun was completely overcome and prostrated herself, lying there with face to the ground worshipping him. The lad had come in playing with a stick, and as he idly scratched his forehead with it, the forehead split open right down to the upper part of his face. Through the split could be seen the ineffably beautiful countenance of Jizō the Bodhisattva."[15]

Needless to say, the nun continued her adoration. The editor then draws the following lesson: "If only you pray with a heart that is truly sincere, even the Buddha will reveal himself to you." The way in which Jizō worship was developing is clearly present here. Not only does Jizō often appear incognito but it is especially likely to be present *in the form of a child at play*. The recording of a miracle such as this, then, is also meant to establish the claim that behind—or even within—every child lies a Jizō. As Hayami notes:

> In the *Konjaku Monogatari's* tales about Jizō we find that almost without exception this figure appears as a "little monk" or as a "young monk." It is often thought that this identification of Jizō with children is based on the concept that he is their special protector. Still the fact that this notion of Jizō borrowing a child's form is found neither in the Buddhist scriptures nor in Chinese stories about Ti-tsang is something that may lead us to suspect that there might be something distinctively "Japanese" implicit in it.[16]

This, of course, is a complex problem. There is the possibility, as suggested originally by Wakamori Tarō, that the child motif enters because of an archaic Japanese predilection for seeing children as frequently chosen by the kami to pass on messages to humankind—children as, in that sense, mediums.

Perhaps that is so. It is not, however, *always* necessary to predicate something intractibly "Japanese" at work in every historical departure from Chinese practice.[17] The workings of other kinds of historical factors—often social ones—can sometimes explain these things very well. I think these other historical factors are what is crucial here.

That is, inasmuch as Buddhism was making an increasingly deep impact on the lives of common people in the medieval period, they naturally forced Buddhism to make sense in terms of their concrete needs and anxieties. There is evidence to suggest that the Jizō cult was clearly developing primarily among women during this epoch, and it is, I think, not improper even in our own role-sensitive age to assume that in medieval Japan it was probably women who had the deepest concern about children, fetuses, and how Buddhism might connect with these concerns. The episodes we have from the literature suggests precisely that. For women to have been the principal creators and shapers of the Jizō cult seems not at all unreasonable.

Over the centuries of the medieval period, the images of Jizō became more and more childlike. What had once been an obviously adult and dignified figure turned into the representation of a child-monk, a figure both benign and, in the parlence common today concerning Jizō, "adorable." At the same time associations of people devoted to Jizō (*Jizō-kō*) developed. The focus of these was clearly on children. Festivals were held, for instance, that centered on both the child and the image of Jizō.[18] In fact, historians can even trace an iconographic link from the Jizō image to the "kokeshi" doll, which seems to have developed in northeastern Japan during the nineteenth century. Originally, such dolls were probably surrogates for mizuko in that impoverished part of Japan. Some scholars speculate that the name "kokeshi" even includes a nuance meaning "child removal." Later the kokeshi became an ordinary form of folk art, sold widely throughout Japan and purchased in large numbers by foreign visitors to Japan in recent decades.

There are, obviously, many ways of interpreting these changes. Japanese scholars, for the most part, have emphasized that this shows that Buddhism in Japan became more and more imbued with native folkways and modes of belief—that is, a cult of Jizō that had been formed among the elite, had once been temple-based, and had been "continental" in spirit was progressively making its way into the lives of commoners and was becoming almost indistinguishable from indigenous forms of folk religion.

Of this there is some clear evidence. In addition, however, it is important to cite at least some ways in which the child-centered cult of Jizō was important to parents—especially women—who in this period not only had expectable concerns about childbearing and childrearing but also had deep anxieties about the increasingly common practices of abortion and infanticide. As shown in chapter 6, at least by the sixteenth century some forms of child or fetus-dispensing techniques were sufficiently present in the culture to catch the attention of Europeans. It is quite likely that these were present well before that.[19]

In chapter 1 it was noted that Jizō became a figure that often elicited what we call a "double take." We have now also noted that in the *Uji Shūi Monogatari* the child in the narrative was capable of revealing the Jizō inside it. Part of this, undoubtedly, was due to a medieval taste for the "hidden meaning" and even the concealed saint. Throughout the medie-

The kokeshi dolls originated in the famine-beleaguered northeast and appear to be a folk art related to the mizuko.

val period, the icon of Jizō encouraged the observer—both by its diminution into a child-monk and by the cult around it—to see it alternately as an innocent child and a gentle savior figure. The theme of Jizō having appeared in the role of a playmate especially fit the notion of the bodhisattva as coming into our world incognito. As noted earlier, the motif of play as a mode of salvation was important in medieval Japanese Buddhism.

I stress the *doubleness* of interpretative possibilities because that seems to be what made the cult of Jizō a powerful way of emcompassing at least some of the emotional pain involved in the loss of a child, especially in cases where there had been an intentional "return" of one. If the young child, newborn, or fetus were considered to be so intimately related to the cosmic figure of Jizō—through multiple motifs of closeness—then the anxious parent could more easily imagine a safe passage of the deceased child through the difficult places in the "other" world or incarnations.

This is, I think, essentially what happens when even today the icon of Jizō often does double duty. At least this is what is intimated in the literature often given to people going to mizuko temples—literature that states, "your Jizō image will represent both your mizuko and the bodhisattva that takes care of him or her in the other world." The suggestion is that all the complex emotions and prayers of such parents can be brought together and focused on one image. Jizō represents *both savior and saved*; it receives both the prayers and the apologies of the parents who had "wronged" it—by abortion or whatever.

Jizō is the bodhisattva who wears a bib. All his great power to save suffering creatures is disguised in the appearance of an utter powerlessness presented to the world. But when this concept is turned inside out, the child or fetus who has gone on to another world has within it the potential to become there a bodhisattva or a god.

GODS WITH GRUDGES

Jizō became diminutive, thereby adding to his moral prestige, since such a change showed his compassion.

Some of the traditional gods or kami of Japan, however, were much less admirable. Tales of their doings show that some of them, although worshipped, were not above being fairly selfish. They are often the subjects of stories in which the roles they play can be mean-spirited. As gods they often appear—to borrow Nietzsche's phrase—"human, all too human." They often seem to resemble the gods of the ancient Greeks—not only because there are many of them but also because they can be vain, angry, passionate, resentful, and even retaliatory.

Part of the reason for this, it should be remembered, is that many of the

Japanese kami were thought to have once been humans. Divinized ancestors have, in a sense, the *prerogative* of being "all too human" simply because in some sense they still are. To the degree that they are thought to be still interested in what goes on in this world, they show their passions—both positive and negative. This point is an important one.

Yuasa Yasuo's historical inquiries are of value here. One of the central concerns of his major work on the religious sensibility of the Japanese is to explain what it meant for Buddhism to enter into the Japanese religious scene and to connect with more archaic forms of Japanese religion. Yuasa skillfully debunks the still-prevalent notion that the ancient Japanese were naturally "an optimistic, world-affirming people" who then went on to embrace Buddhism, "a world-weary, world-rejecting, and pessimistic" form of faith.[20] He cites important studies by Tanaka Gen that show this simplistic caricature originated with the thinker Haga Yaichi (1867–1927) and, unfortunately, gained currency in the writings of a number of important Japanese scholars. Tanaka criticized this notion as little more than a part of fervent nationalism of the Meiji period, although it had antecedents in the anti-Buddhist polemics of the preceding Edo period.[21]

What Tanaka had seen as a Meiji concoction Yuasa attacks from another direction—namely, the materials from the archaic period. His point is that historical materials will not support the notion of an archaic Japan of natural optimism subverted later by a Buddhism full of pessimism. Yuasa focuses on the early period, when many Japanese still lived in forests, and what he finds when looking carefully at such archaic materials, especially those of mythology, are references to a wide variety of frightening demons, monsters living on mountains and in rivers, swamps, and forests:

> These are demonic, having become gods that wreak revenge *[tatari]*. To human beings they bring all kinds of disasters and calamities. The natural world was thought to be alive with gods and spirits, so that people in ancient Japan lived their lives encompassed by such creatures. In these terms I think it not inappropriate to use the phrase "religion of terror" to characterize the basic structure of the beliefs of the Japanese in archaic times. The festivals they held must be seen as intended to pacify the frightening power and anger of the gods—as well as to invoke their protection.[22]

This excerpt from Yuasa's work contains a word that will be of considerable importance in our later discussions of the mizuko and abortion. "Tatari" is probably best translated as "revenge" or "retribution," although it almost exclusively refers to actions directed against living humans but originating from the world of the gods, the spirits, or the dead. It is the exacting of a penalty by powerful but empirically invisible beings; it is not the retaliation that one human being might wreak on another for a slight or a wrong. It is, moreover, played out within a religious ambit rather than an interhuman one.

Tatari, Yuasa claims, can serve much better as an entry point into the archaic Japanese religious sensibility than will unsupportable claims about a natural and native "optimism" or "world affirmation" in that period. It is, moreover, in his opinion a feature of Japanese religious life that has been remarkably constant; it shows up in every epoch of history and undoubtedly figures more than one might expect in today's Japan.

The paradigmatic case of tatari, remembered as such in Japan, is that of the early court figure Sugawara Michizane (845–903), probably the greatest scholar of Chinese learning in early Japan. Michizane was wrongfully accused of treason and was exiled. He largely vindicated himself by what he wrote during exile, in a remote province, but neverthless died there—an "unnatural" kind of death for a man who longed to be in the capital and honored for his immense cultural contribution. Death, however, was not the end of Michizane. His enemies at court very soon met multiple misfortunes and tragedies—things that were widely believed to be the revenge (tatari) of Michizane suffering in the land of the dead. In order to placate his angry soul, not only were his descendants reinstated but also Michizane himself was elevated to the status of a god. Appropriately, he became the kami of scholarship. A major Shinto shrine in Kyoto's Kitano district was dedicated to him, and even today throngs of students go there to pray for his help in passing their examinations for entrance into schools of various kinds. Michizane, once his angry ghost had been pacified, became a positive cultural force. There are people in Japan today who, half in jest and half in seriousness, would attribute Japan's current high literacy rate and educational achievements to him and his now-happy, well-placated ghost.[23]

This is the nature of tatari. It involves a revenge-seeking spirit who, bearing a grudge against those who had wronged him, takes retaliatory action from his position among the dead. But in doing so he joins the company of the gods, beings who have supernatural powers and exercise them from the "other side." A good deal of Japanese ritual life apparently has its origin in the fear that, unless rituals are performed, a maligned god will exercise baneful influence on the living.

Yuasa, however, takes an unusual approach to tatari. Trying to get some interpretative leverage on the archaic materials both through what is known about personality dynamics and from his own studies of Buddhism, he holds that it is important to recognize that any vengeful spirit (onryō) is at the same time a *being in pain*. This means that in contexts wherein it is assumed that a vengeful spirit is retaliating from the "other side" against those who wronged or neglected it, it is not only the recipient of that act who suffers. The resentment implicit in the vengeful act is not so much an expression of power as one of weakness and pain. Buddhism holds that to show resentment is also to show that one is suffering—that is, other than enlightened. This is a reason why, according to Buddhist doctrine, all gods, though powerful, are still in the realm of samsara, or suffering. Seeing gods as suffering was a conceptual tool with which Buddhism related itself to the various indigenous religions of Asia and, along the way, defined indigenous deities as powerful but less than Buddhas and bodhisattvas. Japan was no exception.

The kami's suffering leads to complexity in their relationship with living humans. They are both to be *feared and pitied*—and in that sense they are unlike the God of Jews, Christians, and Muslims, who, while a being to be feared, is never to be thought of as in need of human pity. In the Japanese case at least, this means that when there is an angry or resentful god or ancestor perceived as somehow present, the required response is not only fear but compassion. The indigenous religions of Japan, as Yuasa suggests, taught people to fear and placate the gods; Buddhism taught them that compassion for the "god in pain" is also appropriate. The kami are gods in need of help. Their "roughness" needs to be transformed into a "quietness" of spirit and, in that sense, humans can help the gods move closer to becoming Buddhas. In this Buddhist kind of interpretation, an act of simple placation can be seen as one of fundamental charity.

A RIVERBANK LIMBO

This conception of how human beings interact with gods and Buddhas reverberates throughout Japanese approaches to the abortion problem. However, it is important to try to understand the Japanese Buddhist attitudes towards abortion in terms of traditional ideas concerning the after-death destiny of children and fetuses. In order to specify the connection, we need to see it not as a set of abstract religious concepts but as a picture of how the universe works. Since a grasp of the Japanese medieval mind is fundamental to understanding how Buddhists even in the present relate to abortion, it is important to see that mind in concrete terms.

In this I take a cue from Jacques Le Goff, who has brilliantly analyzed what he calls the "spatialization of thought" in medieval Europe. In *The Birth of Purgatory*, Le Goff, a distinguished historian of the *Annales* school, has demonstrated that many things we have long taken to be characteristic teachings of classical Christianity were, in fact, inventions that arose from the rich imagination of the medieval mind. Purgatory is, he shows with rich evidence, exactly such. The concept did not exist in early Christianity; in fact, Le Goff pinpoints its "birth" as a concept in the twelfth century and as a creative response to distinct social and intellectual problems then faced by the Roman Church. Limbo, or more exactly the notion of two different limbos within Christendom, was also an invention. Many medieval Christians had difficulty accepting the idea of eternal punishment meted out to two categories of persons who, on strictly technical grounds, were "outside" the Church and otherwise quite beyond the pale. The first category embraced wise and just people who died before the coming of Christ, and the second included all infants born within Christendom but, unfortunately, unbaptized at the time of their death.

It is especially the latter group that interests me here. Many Christian thinkers apparently had difficulty with the "hard line" view that infants who died unbaptized would, simply by virtue of that fact, be forced into perdition. Le Goff summarizes: "The children's Limbo, which would continue for centuries to be an object of controversy, did not stand on the same plane as the three other regions [Heaven, Hell, and Purgatory] of the hereafter. It was the place for human beings not weighed down by any personal sin but only by original sin."[24] The distinction was crucial and the limbo of children was often conceived of as a place where souls were alienated from God's embrace but, unlike those in Hell, were not subject to ongoing physical tortures.

Le Goff reminds us how this ambivalence about the limbos entered into the great literature of the period. Dante, for instance, was torn between Christian orthodoxy on the one hand and, on the other, his affection for the great "pagan" classical writers and his own tender pity for children who had died an early death. This, notes Le Goff, obsessed Dante throughout his own long pilgrimage.[25] Therefore, in the *Divine Comedy* Virgil eventually describes a place on the outer edge of hell where both wise pagans like himself and unbaptized infants will reside forever:

> There is a place below where sorrow lies
>   in untormented gloom. Its lamentations
>   are not the shrieks of pain, but hopeless sighs.
> There do I dwell with souls of babes whom death
>   bit off in their first innocence before
>   baptism washed them of their taint of earth.[26]

This is a vivid instance of what Le Goff calls an invention of the imagination in order to "spatialize thought." It also is a way of handling a conflict between official religious teaching and human emotions, which seem unable to accept that teaching.

In the development of Buddhism in medieval Japan too *a kind of children's limbo* is imagined—and it has a central role to play in thinking about the fate of aborted fetuses. Within Buddhism, of course, the reasons for the invention of this concept were quite different from what they had been in Christianity: notions such as "original sin," "eternal damnation," and "dying outside the Church" have no near equivalent in Buddhism.

The Buddhist limbo was really a children's variant of the transitional state undergone by *all* who die. All beings, by traditional teaching, pass after death into a betwixt-and-between stage—best known in the West through *The Tibetan Book of the Dead*—and children are no exception. This stage or place is dark, confusing, and terrifying but at the same time only transitional. It is followed soon afterward by a rebirth into one of the six realms.[27]

In medieval Japan, however, it was imagined that there was a special place that constituted a limbo for children. Its name was *Sai-no-kawara* or "the Riverbank in the land of Sai." There is evidence that it was in fact based in part on a pre-Buddhist concept of a postmortem place for the dead.[28] Sai-no-kawara was envisioned concretely as a riverbank where dead children were gathered. They were thought to be miserable because, on the one hand, they could no longer be with their beloved parents in the land of the living and, on the other, they could not cross the river, which is taken to be the boundary between them and a good rebirth.

Buddhist texts had little to say about Sai-no-kawara, although the Lotus Sutra, quite likely the most important Buddhist scripture for the Japanese, in its Chinese version includes something that may have served as the textual precedent. In that sutra's chapter on "Expedient Devices" there is a section that describes many kinds of people whose piety prompts them to build characteristic Buddhist shrines called "stupas." The text says:

> Or there are those who in open fields,
>   Heaping up earth, make Buddha-shrines.
> There are even children who in play
>   Gather sand and make it into Buddha-stupas.
> Persons like these
>   Have all achieved the Buddha Path.[29]

Perhaps this was a slim basis for a full-blown notion of a limbo for dead children, but once that notion was developed, people looked back to this text for its legitimacy.

Sai's riverbank, where all dead children and fetuses gather, is, in theory at least, not a place found on our earthly maps. It lies either in some "other" world or in something of a borderline location between this world and others.[30] As a matter of fact, however, there are a number of places so designated in Japan. That is to say, the "Riverbank of Sai" label has at times been attached to places within our own empirical world. I have seen it in cemeteries, and it is well known that local people in Japan will sometimes give that name to a deserted-looking and stone-strewn riverbank in the countryside or to a desolate portion of the coast.

But these too are boundary places; they are imagined as specific locations where our world meets the other- or underworld. Modern people may tell themselves that such locations are "symbols" of intangible events in some unseen and other world, but it seems fairly clear from the kind of cultic activites that take place in such empirical Sai-no-kawara that they have popularly been taken as real nexi with other kinds of space—that is, interstices between the physical and the metaphysical.

Places having the Riverbank of Sai label, perhaps merely because they are so austere and forelorn, often are places of almost tangible power. Such power can be felt, for instance, by walking through the place so designated at the temple named Nembutsu-ji, in Western Kyoto. There is no literal river there, no running water whatsoever. The word "riverbank" is attached to approximately half an acre of identical small humanoid stones that are arranged in perfect rows—like a cemetery comprised of stone dolls, all exactly the same. In such places it is not the physical presence of running water that makes it a "riverbank" but the stones in perfect arrangement. The physical river is left to the imagination; the host of little stone Jizō icons stands as a metonym for the whole.

Such stones, however, represent not only the stones of an otherworldly/underworldly riverbank but also the children who are standing there. The conflation of meanings is crucially important. Whether the Riverbank of Sai is constituted by a natural congregation of river stones or by human hands that arranged stones in one place, the intention seems to be much the same. The underlying structure of this Japanese equivalent of the River Styx is constant: stones that are both riverbed and the children on it; the theme of a border or great divide—physical in the form of a river, metaphysical in that it runs between this world and the next.

The most impressive of the Sai-no-kawara that I visited is at the northernmost tip of the island of Sado, in the Japan Sea, historically famous because it was a place of exile for people who had become persona non grata in the capital during the medieval period. The number of notables, including Emperor Juntoku (1197–1242), exiled to Sado is large. It historically was difficult to reach, and even today few Japanese have gone there. But at the most distant point of this island is a site designated as Sai-no-kawara, which can be reached by bus and then by walking along the edge of the sea. There are no homes or businesses of any type there.

What one sees there—at least what I saw in 1990—is the abundant evidence of numbers of persons who had gone there over the years to memorialize dead children. There at that very desolate place, where the land and the open sea come together, is a collection of Jizō images and toys of every type and description. There is no temple, no priest, and no

A site of Sai-no-kawara, where the sea meets the land on the northern tip of Sado Island.

Miniature Jizō images are placed throughout the rocky terrain of the Sado Sai-no-kawara site.

Dolls on site dedicated to mizuko express the emotions of children as well as the relations of parents to their children.

The center of Sado's Sai-no-kawara is a cave with images; no priest is in attendance.

Dolls at sites such as that on Sado Island include traditional as well as modern, robot-like types.

evidence of anyone's being able to profit in a monetary way from what people do there. On the contrary, this kind of site strongly suggests it came into being as an aspect of folk Buddhist piety—most probably organized by an association of women devoted to Jizō (*Jizō-kō*).

Unlike the "happy" atmosphere in a commercially-driven temple such as Purple Cloud Temple, the Sai-no-kawara at the remote tip of Sadō is pervaded by a sense of gloom and dire loneliness. This fits exactly the mood communicated in the many Riverbank of Sai "hymns" that have come down to us from the medieval period. Such hymns are often attributed to a great Buddhist priest named Kūya (903–972), famous for his attention to the needs of commoners.[31] Some authorities hold that the attribution to Kūya is fallacious and that the work is clearly of a fourteenth- or fifteenth-century origin.[32] The words of one such hymn portray the pathos and plight of deceased children standing on the banks of the river in Sai:

This is a tale that comes not from this world,
But is the story of the Riverbank of Sai
By the road on the edge of Death Mountain.
Hear it and you will know its sorrow.
Little children of two, three, four,
Five—all under ten years of age—
Are gathered at the Riverbank of Sai
Longing for their fathers and mothers;
Their "I want you" cries are uttered
From voices in another world.
Their sorrow bites, penetrates
And the activity of these infants
Consists of gathering river stones
And of making merit stupas out of them;
The first storey is for their fathers
And the second for their mothers,
And the third makes merits for siblings
Who are at home in the land of the living;
This stupa-building is their game
During the day, but when the sun sets
A demon from hell appears, saying
"Hey! your parents back in the world
Aren't busy doing memorial rites for you.
Their day-in, day-out grieving has in it
Much that's cruel, sad, and wretched.
The source of your suffering down here is
That sorrow of your parents up there.
So don't hold any grudge against me!"
With that the demon wields his black
Iron pole and smashes the children's
Little stupas to smithereens.
Just then the much-revered Jizō
Makes an awe-inspiring entrance, telling
The children, "Your lives were short;
Now you've come into the realm of darkness
Very far away from the world you left.
Take me, trust me always—as your father

And as your mother in this realm."
With that he wraps the little ones
Inside the folds of his priest robes,
Showing a wondrous compassion.
Those who can't yet walk are helped
By him to grasp his stick with bells on top.
He draws them close to his own comforting,
Merciful skin, hugging and stroking them,
Showing a wondrous compassion.
Praise be to Life-sustaining
Bodhisattva Jizō![33]

Here, of course, we encounter a good deal of bathos and melodrama. The whole is probably best understood as a piece of religious drama. As a matter of fact, Manabe Kōsai has shown that during the Edo period this simple plot served as the germinal idea for a dramatic game very popular with children; in it one boy represented the demon and tried to capture as many other children as possible, while another represented Jizō and tried to rescue them.[34]

Whether as hymn that takes form as drama and game or as one replete with its own dramatic elements, the structure is the same. The setting is on the bank of the River of Sai—that is, in the interstitial place between the world of the living and that of the dead. The basic libretto of the riverbank hymn is based on an interchange between four types of characters:

1. The children, newly deceased, as a group
2. A demon
3. Parents of the children, offstage and back in the land of the living but brought forward by recollection
4. Bodhisattva Jizō

The plot is minimal: in essence nothing more than the picturing of the children's sorry plight; the entry of the demon with his pronouncement that their suffering is due to the fact that their parents back in the world are neglecting to perform "memorial rites" for them; the demon's willful destruction of the small stone stupas made by the children; the glorious entry of the Buddhist figure with the name of Jizō; and finally the act whereby Jizō takes up the children as their rescuer and surrogate parent in the place where they now are.

The fundamental difference between the figure representing the demonic and that representing the good is basic; the displacement of the demon by Jizō is so swift and complete that there is nothing even resembling a real "struggle" between them. Jizō sweeps into control of the situation just by coming on stage. Actual physical conflict between the forces of good and evil, so characteristic of melodrama in the West, never gets off the ground here.

There is also no slaying of the representative of the "evil" side, something that may be fairly significant. What constitutes real "drama" in the Buddhist view of things often seems to have less to do with a quasi-military *victory* of good over evil as it does with an unequivocal demonstration that goodness is strong, reliable, and ready to save those in need.

The dead children's basic plight, as vividly portrayed in the riverbank hymn at least, is that of getting access to the resources that can save. It is a problem of a perceived *distance* or barrier—geographical, emotional, ontological—between the desperate one and the source of help. In this case that source of salvation is desperately needed by recently deceased infants and children existing in the limbo between the world where their parents still live and another that seems to be a place of death that is final and irrevocable.

But two more aspects of the drama deserve special notice: the element of parental guilt and the figure of Jizō. Because the whole question of parental guilt will return for extended comment in chapter 9, here it may be enough simply to call attention to the deep ambivalence, even *resentment*, in the hymn's attitude toward the deceased children's own parents. The words of the demon are put forward, importantly, as something other than a mere fabric of lies. Nowhere do the text's words contradict the demon's claim that the children on Sai's riverbank suffer, at least in part, because of these parents.

The effect of this kind of drama on parents can be imagined. Some of the parents expected to be moved by this finger-pointing would, we can assume, have been feeling guilt merely because their ritual remembrance of their dead child was lacking. Others, however, would probably have had a deeper sense of guilt, especially if they worried that their child might be on the Riverbank of Sai due to their own decision to put them there, through abortion or infanticide.

The drama on the Riverbank of Sai shows all the basic elements in their most raw form: innocent children suffering in limbo due to no fault of their own, the darkest elements of the cosmos represented by a demon, parents so preoccupied with their own lives back in the world that they forget their suffering dead progeny, and a compassionate Jizō who not only remembers but saves.

The story and the cosmology it articulates are quintessentially medieval. Nevertheless, in a surprising way all the basics of these, even when now interpreted largely as "psychological" truths, have carried down through the centuries and shape the way many in Japan think about—and behave toward—the mizuko of today.

PART TWO
HISTORICAL PROCESSES

Chapter 5

EDO: AN ERA IN VIEW

> Both read the Bible day and night;
> But you read black where I read white.
>
> *(William Blake)*

> One must hide depth.
> Where?
> On the surface.
>
> *(Hugo von Hofmannsthal)*

SQUEEZE-PLAY

MANY EXPERTS maintain that in order to understand even contemporary Japanese society it may be the Edo (or Tokugawa) period (1600–1867)—more than any other—that needs to be understood. One rationale for that view, at least in the past, was based on the supposition that during those centuries when the shogunate in Edo was in power, Japan was completely isolated from the outside world. Thus, it was assumed, this was precisely the time when Japanese society was in a kind of cultural "hothouse," able to develop according to simply indigenous patterns and proclivities that were not likely to be mixed with outside influences either from continental Asia or, as had happened in the antecedent sixteenth century, from a Christian, expansive Europe. Those who stress the total isolation of Japan during the Edo centuries also often romaticize it as having had real benefits—inasmuch as Japanese culture was in a sense "free" to be itself.

Others have seriously doubted that a good face should ever have been put on such a degree of isolation and self-enclosure; the modern philosopher Watsuji Tetsurō (1889–1960) claimed that in its adoption of an isolationist posture the Edo was, in fact, the *least* typical of the Japanese epochs.[1] Still other scholars more recently have raised serious doubts about the evidence for the supposed total seclusion; Ronald Toby, for instance, has shown that during the Edo years there was a much more active diplomatic and cultural exchange going on with Japan's Asian neighbors than was previously suspected.[2] In addition, of course, knowledge of the West and from the West was, however blocked and filtered, penetrating into Japan—especially in matters of science and technology.

For the purposes of this study—namely to grasp how contemporary Japanese tend to relate abortion to religious ideas—the Edo period clearly seems to be of crucial importance. This was the period when conflicting ideas about sexuality and reproductivity became sharpened. In addition, precisely because data about population trends in this period are so much fuller than for earlier periods, we can more easily view how notions of the ideal family may have influenced practices of birth control. Moreover, many of the Buddhist folk practices that underlie contemporary mizuko ritual practices took on a definite shape during the Edo. Japan from the early seventeenth to the mid-nineteenth centuries, then, is of great importance for our investigations.

There is something also intrinsically interesting about intellectual life in this epoch. Construed for too long as one in which governmental thought control stifled the life of the mind, the Edo was in fact a period of intense, committed, and polemic argument and writing. As Olof G. Lidin has noted, "At no time was there a static situation. The whole of the Tokugawa era vibrated with intellectual activity, and the relatively simple picture of around 1600, when Ieyasu began his rule, became successively more complicated as the decades passed."[3]

One of the things I wish to show in this study is that in Japan's Edo period abortion was a subject of contestation. It shows itself, however, within wider ideational struggles over reproductivity and productivity. Confucians, neo-Shintoists, and Buddhists did not agree on these matters. The intent of this chapter is to contextualize such issues within the wider spectrum of ideas in the Edo era.[4]

Immediately we face an ironic situation. Although we can claim that it is impossible to grasp modern Japanese attitudes toward abortion without seeing how they were shaped by Buddhism in the Edo period, the West's knowledge of Buddhism in that era is grossly inadequate and strangely contorted. The reasons for that deserve a brief note.

One is that the scholarship of Japanese Buddhist specialists themselves, at least until the last two decades, largely deprecated and ignored the Buddhism of the Edo period. To a certain extent specialists accepted the Meiji denunciation of Edo Buddhism as "corrupt" and focused their studies on the Buddhism of earlier periods—especially that of the Kamakura (1192–1333), a Buddhism believed to have been much purer, more intellectually vigorous, and closer to continental origins. Buddhist scholars themselves largely ignored the Edo period—except for attention to a few exceptional figures.

Even more harmful to such studies has been the unproven assumption that Buddhism simply fell completely or virtually out of the picture, at least out of Japan's intellectual life, during the centuries of the Edo.

Although Western scholars have poured vast energies into studies of non-Buddhist intellectual life in the Edo period, Buddhism has been an egregious blindspot within those studies. This is in part because such studies have tended to be controlled by a fairly narrow conception of "intellectual" life—taken primarily as a study of polemical treatises rather than more comprehensively to include the history of mentalities and symbols. Prejudgments as to what is "rational" have also gotten in the way—as if the whole story of the mind in Edo Japan were merely one of an ever more refined movement toward real "rationality." Needless to say, within such a set of presuppositions Buddhism has been easily dismissed as irrational, folkish, superstitious, and irrelevant. The general assumption in much of Western writing about this period has been that, for all practical purposes, Buddhism was simply "dead."

The peculiarity of this assumption can quickly be shown. Publishing itself provides a refutation. Uesato Shunsei has examined the records of publishing in certain key years of the Edo era, and the data he has collected show that between one third and one half of all books published were on Buddhist topics. Moreover Buddhist books outnumbered those of Confucianism by a margin of five to one.[5] Even if many of these were of a popular rather than polished nature, it becomes, to say the least, rather difficult to declare a system of thought "dead" or even moribund when it informs the *largest* single category of publications in a given epoch. Moreover, a number of learned, sophisticated arguments for the Buddhist position were published during the Edo period—treatises that have tended simply to be overlooked by most scholars of that era.[6]

This is not to say that Buddhism did not lose significant ground in intellectual circles. But, as Herman Ooms has shown, that did not happen as quickly and as thoroughly as either its contemporaneous critics desired or most modern Western intellectual historians have assumed.[7] Although I think it accurate to say that what had for many centuries been Buddhism's "hegemony" in Japanese intellectual life was broken in the Edo period, its influence was far from gone and its vitality was still present. For nearly a thousand years before Edo, Japanese Buddhists had argued mostly *among themselves*, but that was now no longer true. The difference was that from this time on there were serious and powerful rivals, and certain portions of intellectual territory had to be ceded to them.

There can be no doubt that Buddhism at the outset of the Edo period was caught in a squeeze play. Many Japanese in leadership positions, fully aware that the Chinese had decidedly relegated Buddhism to the sidelines and elevated neo-Confucianism as the philosophy of state, were in favor of doing exactly the same. Korea too had undergone a neo-Confucian revival and had literally removed all monasteries from the capital, thereby "returning" Buddhism to the mountains, its place of original strength in China and Korea. There were these continental precedents. On the other hand, Buddhists in Japan had enough sympathizers among those who made policy to find places where it could hang on—even in urban contexts. Therefore, in contrast to both Chinese and Korean Buddhism, Japanese Buddhism remained at least a contender in the larger intellectual arena. Its crisis, as James Ketelaar clearly shows, came in the late nineteenth century, but within the twentieth century key intellectuals such as Nishida Kitarō, Watsuji Tetsurō, Miki Kiyoshi, and others were able to see in Buddhism substantive bases for their own intellectual projects.[8] Such a reemergence of Buddhism at the very center of Japanese intellectual life in our century would have been highly unlikely if it had, in fact, gone into anything like the kind of total eclipse in Edo that some historians have claimed.

Buddhism survived in the Edo both by emulating the government's rigid, hierarchical bureaucratic structure and by becoming part of it. The pyramidal organization of temples, already begun in the Muromachi period, was continued in Edo—with main temples at the top, above three lower levels. The vertical structure was matched by a horizontal expanse. Of great use to the authorities was the division of all of Japan into Buddhist parishes (*danka-seido*). To ferret out Christians still in hiding after the ban on Christianity in 1614, Japanese families were required to be officially affiliated with a Buddhist temple. Since every village and town had to have a temple, there was a tremendous increase in their number— from 13,037 in the Kamakura period to 469,934 in the Edo.[9]

Of course, since every Japanese was thereby registered at a Buddhist temple, the government's collection of population statistics as well as many other kinds of data had become a relatively simple matter. The Buddhist temples had not only saved themselves from extinction but now also had been given a public rationale for a good deal of institutional growth. Priests, at least to the extent that they kept the records and took the census, had also taken on an additional role as a type of civil servant.

Debate can—and still does—swirl around the question of whether Buddhism in the Edo period saved its institutional skin at the cost of being eviscerated of most of its spiritual life. Certainly it often had to be at the beck and call of the shogunate. Certainly too many monks found their positions sufficiently secure, so that they learned how to live "the good life"; the fiction of Ihara Saikaku (1642–1693) is replete with stories of priests living in luxury and spending a good deal of their time in brothels.

To be sure, the perception of the Edo Buddhist clergy as venal and pleasure-bound has some basis in fact. And, of course, since it has often been commonly assumed that the life of pleasure and the life of the mind cannot possible conflate, a ready conclusion has—especially in the

West—been that this is enough to show that Buddhism was intellectually "bankrupt" or "dead" by this point in Japan's history.

That, however, begs some large questions. And those are the questions that are germane to what we most need to explore.

PLEASURE—QUARTERED AND ENLIGHTENED

It may well be that the perception of Edo Buddhists as having a clergy largely addicted to indolence, privilege, and pleasure is the result of exaggeration and defamation by persons who had had a generalized distaste for Buddhism. Martin Collcutt suggests that such charges in the nineteenth century were made largely by those "Japanese who often were ideologically hostile to Buddhism themselves or by Western observers inclined to view Buddhism as an obstacle to Christian missionary success in Japan."[10] Thus what we are dealing with is not only the—notoriously difficult—problem of trying to take the "spiritual" pulse of a past era but also of trying to do so through the works of polemicists who were predisposed to disparage what they described.

We need to note a few things that can advance our discussion of how Edo Buddhism articulated views and attitudes toward sexuality, children, and abortion. First it is necessary to grasp the significance of the fact that many Edo Buddhist monks and priests habituated the pleasure quarters of the larger cities and had ongoing sexual relationships with geishas and prostitutes. There was something very much open and aboveboard about much of this. In the seventeenth century, Saikaku wrote novels about not only rich merchants but also Buddhist priests taking up long-term liaisons with women of the pleasure quarter. Because such novels are generally assumed to have had a basis in fact, they have usually been interpreted merely as indices to the corruption of the Buddhists or to a kind of Japanese "this-worldliness" working to subvert and domesticate an otherwise "otherworldly" Buddhism found on the continent.

Because, however, celibacy was the official Buddhist ideal, it elicited a totally opposite complaint from the critics of Buddhism—namely, that it was an "otherworldly" norm that requires a virtually asexual people. Indeed, one of the ironies of the period is that Buddhism was simultaneously charged with being too otherworldly *and* with being too worldly. And, because the scope of Buddhism was large and monks were numerous, there were enough of both types to fit what the creators of each stereotype—although they were opposite—needed. Celibates and profligates were both within view.

As for the latter, those who indulged in sex and the life of the pleasure quarters, it is noteworthy that they tended to do so quite openly and often claimed it was *part of their religious practice*. We need to take careful notice of this—in part because it has been so misunderstood in the past. For instance, precisely because much of the Buddhist tradition, both on the continent and in Japan, had held out abstinence as an ideal, it has often been thought that whenever Buddhists seemed to "affirm" sexuality, it was because their Buddhism had become only an empty shell covering a kernal of the indigenous and folk traditions, traditions that from early times valued sexuality positively.

Since we are here thinking of "tradition" as more often the product of bricolage than a narrow, straight channel out of the past, it would seem important to recognize that within the Buddhist tradition there was both a rationale for strict celibacy and one for an affirmation of sexual life, even though the former had by far the heavier textual and institutional weight on its side. For us to try to see *both* as having places within the "tradition" does not mean that historically the proponents of the one position did not disagree with—and even condemn—the other.

It is important to see that metaphors of sexual union had been part of the stock of imagery used by Esoteric Buddhists in Japan from the eighth century on. The rituals wherein practitioners were encouraged to envision the unification of the Great Womb Mandala with the Great Vajra Mandala were, to our knowledge, kept on the level of visualizations—but the language of sexual union was clearly present as an analogue to the desired spiritual unification of the practitioner and the cosmos. James H. Sanford, whose thorough research has contextualized this matter, summarizes the above type of Buddhism as follows: "[The] tendency to emphasize the biological differentiation of male and female and then move on to the resolution into oneness of this duality in the act of physical intercourse is to be explained not as references to literal sexual congress but as symbolic allusion to the ineffable 'coincidentia oppositorum' non-duality of higher spiritual states."[11]

In the medieval period what had been implied became more explicit—during the development of what is known as the Tachikawa School and its rituals. The practitioners of this group for some centuries led a quasi-underground existence, marginalized socially and clearly "heretical" in the eyes of most Buddhists.[12] Because the rituals of the Tachikawa group involved sexual intercourse and the use of sexual fluids as well as skulls, there has been a great reluctance among Buddhist scholars to see connections between it and the larger, orthodox part of the tradition.[13]

Although the evidence seems clear that the marginalization of the Tachikawa was successful—including activities "in the 1470s when orthodox Shingon monks simultaneously incinerated a large batch of Tachikawa books in Kyoto and buried a second set on Mt. Kōya"[14]—the suppression of the rituals themselves did not mean an expunging of the notion that sexual intercourse could be valued as religiously meaningful.

Sanford suggests that some of this valuing of sexuality also probably underlies the poetic language of the important medieval Zen monk Ikkyū (1394–1481). While Ikkyū sometimes felt that his own visiting of brothels was inconsistent with his Buddhist vows, at other times he quite boldly insisted that sexual union was a medium through which he found the basic truth of Buddhism. His poems in celebration of his union with his blind lover, Mori, are classics and are openly erotic. In analyzing the imagery of one dense poem, Sanford finds an allusion to Ganesa, the erotic elephant of Indian religious lore, and comments, "In medieval Japan (and later) there was a rather worldly popular cult to this buddhicized divinity that centered around the mildly erotic bifurcated image of a male and female 'Ganesa' standing in embrace. Both the image and attendant ritual were sexually toned in almost all aspects."[15] It is important to note that by Ikkyū's time there was a latitude within Japanese Buddhism such that his wisdom and spiritual attainment were widely hailed even though his sexual behavior bordered on the scandalous.

The difference between Ikkyū and the Edo Buddhist monks is that in Ikkyū we still see rather self-scrutinizing attempts to find ways of seeing brothel visits as, by some stretch of the religious imagination, compatible with Buddhist practice. The whore-mongering monks of the Edo era, by comparison, seem to have had fewer compunctions.

"Enlightened play" became one of their favorite themes. It was a theme found at times within earlier phases of Japanese Buddhism,[16] but in Edo the arenas of play and pleasure became—for some monks at least—what they liked to regard as the true practice halls of their religion. More traditional monks, such as the great poet Ryōkan (1757–1831), expressed their ludic satori in innocent games with children, but the more "worldly" Buddhist clergy habituated the brothels of the pleasure quarters.

It is certainly not difficult to see complicity between such monks and those who profited from the era's prostitution. Social historians have not been able to document the actual extent of this, but it seems clear that monks, many of whom were unmarried, contributed substantively to the cash flow of the pleasure quarters.

Again it should be noted that we are discussing only a portion of the Buddhist clergy and, at that, a percentage we cannot determine. Many clergy of the Edo period continued to command public respect for the quality of their lives and vocations. Nevertheless, the literature of Edo contains enough satire directed against playboy monks to let us see an element of public resentment concerning their behavior.

It is, of course, difficult to know how much of this monkish consorting with women was due to a desire to find enlightenment even in such ways and how much of it arose from sheer hedonism. We can be fairly sure, however, that the contemporaries of these monks saw much more of the latter than the former in their behavior.

What can we draw from this? Although we are short of the materials to make anything even approximating a satisfactory evaluation of the actual state of clerical morals in this period, we can make a few comparisons. For instance, the difference between Japanese Buddhist monks of the period and their Christian counterparts in Europe is considerable. Although, for instance, many parish priests in thirteenth-century Europe lived openly with concubines, such behavior was interpreted as concessions to "the flesh," not activities that could by any stretch of the imagination be interpreted as "good" or spiritually useful.[17] In the Christian context such actions were sins and not capable of being transformed into virtues through complex interpretive moves.

Whereas sexual activity on the part of Catholic clergy occurred in spite of the whole Christian tradition and at the risk of personal perdition, that of Japanese monks was, at least in their own minds, sometimes sanctioned by a certain intellectual development within the Buddhist tradition—one that interpreted play and dalliance, even when sexual in nature, as one of the modes in which the enlightened mind could exhibit itself.

Undoubtedly this provided ready pretexts for abuse. However, I am not interested in judging whether this was "good" or "bad" Buddhism. It will suffice to note that, at least in some ways, this development was the following out of one trajectory of practices and ideas launched in a much earlier period. Moreover, since there was a different but parallel development in the late Tantric Buddhism that developed in India and which was also evident in Tibetan Buddhism, it will not do to attribute this, as some have done, merely to a pattern whereby Buddhism was being subverted by a powerful, indigenous *Japanese* worldview.

Roughly parallel developments, in Tibet, for instance, it should be noted, overturn a common assumption, especially in much Japanese scholarship, that something often called the "indigenous Japanese worldview" was, especially in this irruption of hedonism, eating away at Buddhist "negativities" from below. On the contrary, we are suggesting here that if the notion of "tradition" can be defined with sufficient breadth, then what was going on in this affirmation of sexual activity had at least something "Buddhist" about it.

This makes for a considerable change. Up until recently, for instance, it was common to view what happened to the word *ukiyo* as a classic instance of the subversion of Buddhism by "Japaneseness." Such claimants pointed out that in the literature of the early medieval period this phrase is written with Chinese characters meaning "world of grief" caused by the transitoriness of all things. In contrast to that, by the Edo period the phrase *ukiyo* had begun to be written with totally different characters, ones that mean "floating world"—that is, it unambiguously referred to life in the pleasure quarters and to the bohemian community of artist habitués found there. When the old Buddhist *ukiyo* is written with different characters so that the world of sorrows is transformed into the world of sexual pleasures, it was argued, the linguistic alteration constitutes a trick being played on Buddhism by something that is itself deeply "Japanese." In this, the native, affirmative genius is coming to the fore.

Some recent studies, however, suggest that even this alteration was a kind of deconstruction *from within* Buddhism. In other words, the bases of this deformation of meaning are themselves Buddhist. What propels it, then, is the Mahayana logic whereby since things cannot remain independent entities, they necessarily include their opposites and turn into them. The underside of the world of sorrows is really that of erotic pleasure and, conversely, such pleasure eventually embraces sorrow.[18]

Thus, although Saikaku lampooned Buddhist monks—in addition to many other segments of society—in his posthumously published *Saikaku Oridome,* he was encapsulating a sequence of thought that some monks would have taken as normal and doctrinally sound. In a chapter entitled "Second Thoughts about Passions," he writes, "Life is like a day of fun. We are born at dawn and in the evening we die. In fact, life is really not much more than a naptime dream. But of all the things that can capture a man's fancy, one thing that has never failed to arouse a man's interest, both in old times and new, at home and abroad, is frolicking with courtesans."[19]

This, however rapid a logical leap, epitomizes what at least some Buddhists in the Edo period embraced. Thus, the kind of wordplay that transformed *ukiyo* as "sad world" into *ukiyo* as "pleasure world" was itself a form of "play" that some Buddhists interpreted as the heart of their tradition. What looks on the surface to be a rejection of Buddhism by wordplay turns out, in fact, to be "good" Buddhism after all.

．　．　．　．　．

However, we need to draw these discussions into a place where they can possibly tell us something about the trajectory of Japanese thinking about abortion. It is assumed that we cannot easily grasp the formation of religious attitudes about abortion without seeing how sexuality itself was understood. And having seen that within medieval and early modern Buddhism in Japan there was an attempt—however controversial—to interpret sexuality as religiously positive, we need also note that such interpretation focused on sexual relations between men and women *without having progeny* as the goal of such relations. In fact, from what we can determine, the avoidance of having children result from the sexual union of monks and women was a clear desideratum.[20] It must also be conjectured that monks who unintentionally impregnated their partners were not loath to have such women seek abortions—or even to assist in finding or financing them.

We cannot deny the likelihood that such monks were involved in what surely were occasions of great suffering on the part of the women with whom they consorted. Pusillanimity and social irresponsibility were almost certainly part of this picture. This, however, does not negate the importance of again noting a striking difference from the religious and moral ethos of Europe at roughly the same time.

Some experts may wish to place qualifications on what James Brundage has called "the Christian horror of sex" in medieval Europe.[21] Nevertheless, there does not seem to be anything comparable in Europe to the Japanese Buddhist use of sexual union as either a religious symbol or, as increasingly became the case, as itself a context for religious realization. Although Protestant developments led to notions of sexuality as a positive dimension of a married couple's companionship, the idea of sexuality as conducive to reproductivity always remained in the picture. In Europe the notion of sexuality as *intrinsically good*—that is, without having progeny as part of the goal—arose primarily within the secularizing dynamic of the Renaissance. In fact, particularly within the Catholic Church, there has remained a set of strong objections to such a view.

Kanaoka Shūyū, a Japanese scholar of Buddhism, gives us an unusual but perceptive view of this. Since for many Europeans religion and Christianity are virtually the same, the Renaissance view of sexuality as intrinsically good—even without progeny—easily came to be viewed as an antireligious and anti-Christian perspective. Kanaoka finds in Western writers—Baudelaire and de Sade for instance—a keen sense that in rejecting the Church's view of sexuality they are rejecting Christianity *as a whole*, especially teachings about original sin. In Asian history Kanaoka finds no comparable kind of dilemma.[22]

I think Kanaoka is essentially correct and that he has uncovered an important difference between Christianity and Buddhism. It is one that has resurfaced with new force in the debates over abortion. From within both the Catholic Church and the ranks of fundamentalist or evangelical Christians, there appears to be a very strong tendency to castigate abortion-rights advocates as having a view of sexuality whose roots lie in anti-Christian and antireligious "humanism." To that degree attitudes about abortion are taken as indices to views of sexuality and those, in turn, are interpreted as litmus tests of whether one is part of Christianity or part of an anti-Christian movement. Especially in the rhetoric of certain fundamentalists, the question of abortion becomes an issue of resisting a whole intellectual world of *anti*-Christian values that have been gathering force since the Renaissance.

In some sense, then, what in Europe developed within the Renaissance, and often as a conscious rejection of Catholic teaching, was in Japan a development largely within Buddhism itself. Although this very development left many Buddhists open to sharp criticism from their peers, it provided at least the makings—and fairly early—of a way of picturing sexuality as valuable apart from its role in reproduction. In fact, especially when Buddhist monks themselves were involved, separating sex from the making of progeny was a matter of considerably importance.

FAMILY ACCOMMODATIONS

This is, however, not to suggest that Edo Buddhists were—or, more precisely, could afford to be—indifferent to the family and what are often called "family values."

It has already been noted that during this period many people—most especially those possessing or wanting political power—were keenly aware that ideas have consequences. No idea was regarded with indifference. Concepts, philosophies, religious tenets, and even the homespun notions of folklore—all were subject to scrutiny to see what within them posed potential dangers to the political powers that be.

The Edo was a period during which not only people but also ideas were closely monitored—no doubt the chief reason that the era's detractors sometimes portray it as the time when the world's first "totalitarian state" came into existence. That emphasis on broad and tight control was, of course, part of a program of national pacification, possible only in Edo because the long political fragmentation of Japan had been brought to an end by a succession of strong warlords, each of whom moved the country closer to unity. The Edo period was not only designed to be an era of peace but also proved to be one. Government, however, intended to lean heavily on people. Pacification meant an engineering of society; persons and institutions that wished to survive were expected to show they were functional and useful to the overall national program.

Buddhists were, as suggested, caught by that need. They had to learn to *live within* a somewhat restricted operational and discursive range. But it also meant they had to devise ways to live as deeply and intensively as possible within that range and, in fact, to find ways of circumventing the imposed limitations. They had been moved out of their early hegemonic place in intellectual matters and no longer had anything approaching easy access to the ruler. Part of the "survival technique" of Buddhists during the Edo period, then, consisted of forging ever deeper connections with commoners—especially rural people—and assimilating Buddhism to the practices of folk religion.[23]

The developing cult of Jizō was, then, only one of many during this period. Many local deities, long believed in by common people, were taken up into the practices of Buddhists—with the ready explanation that folk gods were really only the old manifestations of an original Buddhist essence. This process had begun earlier but now proceeded apace. It would, of course, make it difficult for later students of the period to distinguish what was Buddhist from what was "folk," but that was a price to be paid.

The second way in which Buddhism was maintained by its adherents as important in Edo society was by becoming established as the institutional support of the family. And it did so by becoming the de facto formal context within which the cult of ancestors—and thereby the Japanese family itself—was maintained. This too was the development of a trend that had begun in the earlier Muromachi period; as Tamamuro Taijō showed some years ago, what is often called in Japan "funeral Buddhism" was not just a creation of the Edo government authorities but part of the way in which Buddhist temples two centuries earlier had extended their influence into the lives of the masses. Tamamuro analyzed the content of the various "oral records" (goroku) that in Zen show what the great teachers have said. Those of the early thirteenth century were almost 100 percent devoted to topics related to meditation and its practice. By the fourteenth century, however, 50 percent of the goroku were connected to rites for ancestors and, especially in the Sōtō school of Zen, this rose to almost 100 percent by the fifteenth century.[24] This happened as Buddhist monks increasingly found themselves addressing groups of common people rather than cloistered fellow monks. It also shows the radical shift of emphasis undergone by Buddhism as it accommodated itself to the needs of the masses.

This turned out to be a skin-saving move for the Buddhists. During the Edo period they came to be attacked, often very severely, both by neo-Confucianists and later by neo-Shintoist partisans, who often had much easier access to the rulers. In such a situation the Buddhists did their best to show that even if they no longer held intellectual hegemony in Japan, they remained institutionally useful. As noted, they did that primarily by letting their extensive parish system be used by the government as part of its bureaucracy. The widely spread system of Buddhist temples and priests easily became useful to the central authorities because by requiring that each Japanese person be registered at a temple the whereabouts of the entire population could be known. Ostensibly the demand that all the citizenry be registered at Buddhist temples was in order to disclose and root out any remnants of Christianity, but the effect of the new connection between the government and the parish system was that the authorities now had a means for keeping fairly close tabs on the entire population. There was a symbiosis: the Buddhists received a kind of rationale for their very existence by performing such a socially useful role and, on the other side, the government received from the Buddhists a ready-made mechanism for tighter social control.

Some have felt that in the Buddhists' allowing themselves to be so used they saved their skin but lost their soul. Twentieth-century views of Edo Buddhism as decadent came not only from the detractors mentioned above but also from the fact that anyone could easily imagine an expectable and negative impact resulting from the government's policy of harnessing the Buddhist clergy to do its work.

During the Muromachi period (1334–1573) the large general population had been recruited into Buddhism—for the most part by having people get used to needing to carry out rites for dead ancestors either in temples or with Buddhist monks as officiants. In the Edo period it became a requirement to be a Buddhist. Perhaps most common believers did not expect more from Buddhism than that the priest would say mass for dead relatives—and for that believer when he or she died. Priests, on the other hand, often did not expect much more from their parishioners than attendance at such rites. This led to what later critics have called "funerary Buddhism"—with monks often little more than the directors of funerals, the chanters of requiems, and the collectors of donations.

This led, however, to retention of the Buddhist institution as having at least some role in the lives of *virtually all* Japanese. Since in Japan the rule of celibacy was less and less observed in strictness, priests of various schools felt relatively free to marry. Some took wives and had children of their own. Earlier Rennyo (1414–1499) had been something of a pacesetter. The priest who made Kyoto's Hongan-ji into one of Japan's largest temples, Rennyo married five times and had twenty-seven children.[25] In most Buddhist sects, it gradually became the custom for temple priests to hand the custodianship of their temples down to their sons. In other words, what had once been a celibate clergy without progeny eventually tended to become a hereditary one, an ironic but historically important development in Japan.

Whatever this may have meant in terms of a possible "departure" from the ideas and methods of earlier Buddhism, the link-up with the ancestral cult and the transformation of many temples—especially those in urban areas and small towns—into family temples meant that Buddhism in Japan was increasingly identified with family values. The Muromachi trend continued and, if anything, intensified in Edo. Texts and sermons of the period increasingly laid emphasis on Buddhism as a way of binding families together and ensuring their perpetuity through time. This is not to say that the ideal of celibacy did not remain or that there were no temples and monasteries that kept alive the traditional modes of meditative life. It is merely to note that especially during the Edo period Buddhism in Japan was identified strongly with the family and family values.

In these ways Buddhism as an institution became increasingly "conservative." Individual monks might create scandals and bring down a fair amount of criticism by habituating brothels and pursuing luxury within the confines of their temples. But the Buddhist institution itself was viewed publically as one of the main cogs—perhaps even the *chief* cog— in what is sometimes called Japanese "familyism." Buddhists commandeered the rites for ancestors. Monks passed their temples and traditions down to their own progeny for generation after generation. Temple grounds in Japan—in contrast to China and Korea—were for most people where cemeteries were to be found. It was to the temples, therefore, that people went to remember ancestors and be reminded of the import of family continuity over time.

This was happening, we need to note, during a time when Confucian and neo-Confucian scholars were often berating Buddhists as having no social utility and—on the basis of logic rather than the actual facts of the age—as *inimical* to familyism. But this was more rhetoric than reality. And it was due to the fact that, although such polemicists often had access to those in political power, Confucians and neo-Confucians in Edo Japan did not have anything comparable to the Buddhists' vast network of temples.

There is, in fact, something extremely odd in the anti-Buddhist rhetoric of the period. Conceptually borrowed as it was from anti-Buddhist charges leveled much earlier in China, it repeats the claim that Buddhism, useless and otherworldly, needs to be rejected and peripheralized. Yet, such rhetoric seems, in fact, to inadvertently testify to conditions exactly *the opposite* of what is claimed. That is, a hard look at these claims would suggest that Buddhism's critics were disturbed by the continued worldly tenacity of an institution they judged should already have been relegated to history's slag heaps.

Confucianists and neo-Confucianists had, by far, the stronger family ideology. Yet Buddhist institutions—especially by undergoing the changes they had—had effectively transformed themselves into the de facto protectors of both ancestors and the family. All this was strikingly different than what had happened in both China and Korea. Japanese Buddhists had either found or been given an important social role. They had turned their religion into "funerary Buddhism," but funeral Buddhism was also family Buddhism. The stridency, therefore, of their detractors tells a story—but perhaps more concerning their frustration than their strength.

The price the Buddhists paid for this weathering of attacks was to be recognized only much later. In the late nineteenth century, especially after coming to see what European scholars had discovered and came to call the "moral integrity" of the earliest Indian Buddhists, many Japanese came to have much self-doubt about the authenticity of their own Japanese version. Likewise, after Japan's defeat in 1945 there was another period of soul-searching among Japanese Buddhists and a deep critique of the historical sacrifice, by being so easily used by the state in Edo, of "true" Buddhism for the sake of getting social security—a sacrifice seen now as having been repeated in the 1930s and 1940s.[26]

This, some would claim, is a price that simply had to be paid. Japanese Buddhism may be less "pure" than that of some other lands, but it is an important part *of society* rather than that which provides an ideal and viable alternative only *off the edge* of ordinary society. Without trying here to decide on this matter in any definitive way, we can at least note that historically Japanese Buddhism came to have a function of reinforcing the strong family values of that culture and of a conservative state that has "familyism" as one of its principal ideological supports. It is, of course, much more difficult to see how Japanese Buddhist institutions can easily gain the leverage to more of a questioning or even adversarial position vis-à-vis things that may be going wrong within the society or its government. A trade-off of a role as critic for a socially secure role seems, at least to many observers, to be right there.

RITUALS, RESOURCES, AND WASTE

One further criticism of the Buddhists deserves a closer look. Perhaps the aspect of Buddhist life that most stuck in the craw of many Confucians was what they saw as its easy tolerance, if not encouragement, of all kinds of "wasteful" behavior. Many Confucians seem to have been temperamentally and ideologically concerned with being economical. "Waste" was something they abhorred and were on the lookout to expose in any of its forms. Actually the Confucian thinker who spearheaded the anti-Buddhist movement in China, Han-Yü (768–824), did so in part because of what he detected as extravagant waste by pious Buddhists in their festivals.[27] The charge against Buddhists as being extravagant was an old one.

In Japan Miyoshi Kiyoyuki (847–918), one of the earliest figures to be self-consciously a Confucian, long before the Edo period scored the Buddhists for their "extravagance" in funeral rites.[28] In the eyes of many Confucians, how Buddhist monks spent their time and how much Buddhist believers spent on pilgrimage and religious festival were downright wasteful.

In Edo these charges became sharper. A choice example comes up in the writings of Ogyū Sorai (1666–1728), often taken to be the leading Confucian of the epoch. Concerned as he was to promote an economic policy making maximal use of coinage, Sorai wrote, "[Recently] the quantity of copper coin has decreased. Matsudaira Izu no Kami, with true insight into the meaning of the boundless benevolence and mercy of Buddha, melted down a great Buddhist image and made it into copper coin. . . . All temple bells and other useless copper objects should be melted down and this would provide as much copper coin as could be desired."[29]

The language is arch. Sorai suggests that those who subvert—even in fairly drastic ways—what Buddhists themselves were defining as "piety" are often more in keeping with the Buddha's own intention. In fact, of course, Sorai, in a way that would have left most Buddhists incredulous and stunned, asserts that economy matters and piety does not. His advocacy of such a melting down of ritual equipment was complemented by his censure of the ancestral practice of burying coins with the dead. To his way of thinking, China led the way in these matters, especially because paper money took the place of metal coinage in many of the activities of piety.[30] Here was where the Chinese were "rational" and the Japanese were not.

The thing to note here is that he not only argued that paper money could easily be used to substitute for coins jettisoned as charms, but called for taking Buddhist temple bells and even treasured icons and reducing them to metal for recycling as currency. This fit his view of Buddhist priests as "useless" in society.[31]

It is important to see that for Sorai the criterion of political and social *utility* tended to subordinate and even to cancel out most other kinds of values. Although at times championed in the twentieth century as a thinker in whom a kind of modern "rationality" shows itself, Sorai's criterion of utility, if implemented as he proposed, would wipe out not only most of religion but also most of what we think of as art. He saw magnificent Buddhist sculptures as so much raw metal that should be turned out more profitably as common currency and Buddhist priests as males who should be driven out of their relatively contemplative lives and put into the harness of the world of "real" work.

To the Buddhists this epitomized a rather frightful constriction of the human spirit. Of course it also threatened them institutionally inasmuch as an ambience in which people would be willing to make donations was itself a sine qua non for the Buddhist clerical order (sangha). Temples, temple monasteries, temple schools, and the very sustenance of monks and nuns—all these were totally dependent on the existence of a laity ready and able to make donations. Thus a "rationality" such as that found in the writings of Sorai was bound to set off shock waves within the Buddhist community.

But Buddhists also saw a parsimony of spirit in this kind of proposal. Beyond the fact that it was a blow to the institutional vitals of Buddhism, Sorai's criterion of calculated utility also completely missed the Buddhists' point, namely that generosity benefited the donor as much as the recipient. *Fuse* or "charitable giving" was, in the Buddhist context, traditionally understood as a virtue that at the same time constituted the initial step on the road to enlightenment. What the ancient Buddhists had called the virtue of *dāna* or "giving" was understood to be a kind of matrix out of which a whole new, enlightened personality could be built. A passionate act of giving away precisely what the conservative, calculating mentality would want to hoard—this itself was taken as "opening" the donor to a whole realm of new possibilities. Liberal giving liberated the donor—from self-constriction. What Georges Bataille noted of the Buddhist lamaism of Tibet would apply to Japan's Buddhists almost as well: "[L]amaic enlightenment realizes the essence of consumption, which is to open, to give, to lose, and which brushes calculations aside."[32]

The distinction here was not, as those who sympathize with Sorai sometimes imply, between a "rational" way of thinking and an "irrational" one. Economically driven cutbacks directed against the religious impulse are sometimes—although not always—like the animus against art as a "waste" of materials and labor. Not in any way reducible to a simple matter of whether or not "rationality" is present, the gap between Buddhist and Confucian views of these things is considerable and important.[33]

This point of difference continues, as will be noted later, even today within Japanese thinking concerning rites dedicated to the memory of aborted fetuses. A good deal of the public criticism of such rites in Japan arises from a sense that such rites are a "waste." Those who defend the rites, on the other hand, will sometimes claim that one cannot afford—for other reasons—to refrain from such donations of time and monies. The matter remains unsettled.

SCHOLARS AND THE BEDROOM

Critics from another quarter also saw Buddhists as wasteful—of human semen and fertilizable ova. In a move that would eventually have a profound effect on modern Japanese attitudes concerning reproductivity and abortion, the Edo movement known as Kokugaku developed what must be seen as its own *religious view of* sexuality, one which differed sharply from that of the Buddhists.

It is important to see that criticism of Buddhists in the Edo period came not only from Confucian quarters but also from thinkers who self-consciously defined themselves as *Kokugaku* or "National Learning" scholars. Although they are sometimes referred to in the West as "nativists," I will use the term *neo-Shinto* to describe their position. It is important to see that during the Edo period what had long been an ambience of fairly mutual tolerance—even mutual support at times—between Buddhists and the practitioners of Shinto slipped seriously. By the end of Edo it had fallen apart completely and physical violence had erupted.

This is not the place to survey the development of Kokugaku; others have done that very well.[34] The rationale of the genesis of this movement is fairly clear. Partially in imitation of earlier Confucian criticisms of Buddhism but partially too because they had their own objections to it, many of the thinkers involved in the National Learning movement not only attempted to revitalize Shinto as Japan's original and autochthonous faith but increasingly looked in a hostile way at Buddhism for being of foreign origin and against what they themselves took to be the native grain.

Of great importance to us here is to single out one great change in the Kokugaku view of things, because it had such a deep impact on Japanese thinking about religion and abortion. The greatest scholar in this movement, Motoori Norinaga (1730–1801), had studied neglected Japanese classics and found in them certain affirmative feelings—including feelings about sexuality—that he thought had been denied and repressed by both Buddhism and Confucianism. Matsumoto Sannosuke has shown that later Kokugaku scholars, by contrast, were much less concerned about affirming sexuality per se than about the importance of sexuality as linked to *quantitative production and reproduction*.[35]

It is valuable to recall how this focus on sexuality started. Kokugaku began as a research topic adopted by a group of exceptionally qualified scholars, who in the sixteenth and seventeenth centuries became newly interested in uncovering what the indigenous Japanese mentality had been like before it underwent its long period of tutelege to the Buddhism and Confucianism adopted from continental sources. They turned back to the oldest myths and collections of Japanese poetry in order to separate what they took to be the Japanese "original" from external influences. Because they were interested in what was *Japanese* as distinct from what was Chinese or Indian, their scholarly inquiries were focused on things deemed native to Japan.

At the outset, it should be noted, there was no overt hostility to either Buddhism or Confucianism; one of the original scholars, Keichū (1640–1701), was himself a Buddhist priest. Ryōkan (1758–1831), a Buddhist monk and one of the great poets of the era, was a student of Kokugaku who obviously wanted to bridge what others were increasingly declaring to be the incompatibility between what was really Japanese and what was of Indian or Chinese origin.[36]

As the neo-Shinto movement gathered strength, its increasing jingoism objected to Buddhism not only because of the foreign origin of the faith but also for what was taken to be the Buddhists' "outlandish" position regarding human sexuality. Jingoism was here mixed into what amounted to a passionate concern to show that reproductivity was incumbent on all Japanese as individuals. Buddhist monks, even if not themselves practicing celibates in this era, had within their own historic tradition sufficient emphasis on celibacy to make them easy targets for charges leveled by the neo-Shinto party.

Although the late Kokugaku texts that make these charges will be looked at in detail in chapter 7, it is of value here to note that within this movement a religious mystique was gathered around the fact of human sexuality, especially the capacity to produce children and to do so in appreciable numbers. In their possession of sexuality, human beings—and the Japanese most especially—were intended to be present-day emulators of the primal couple, Izanagi and Izanami. The myth in the *Kojiki* (taken, incidentally, more and more literally within Kokugaku) had, after all, stated it in unambiguous terms: Izanagi and Izanami had recognized the difference in their bodies as male and female and had forthwith had sexual union to produce children. They were progenitors and fecund. To many of the neo-Shinto thinkers this implied that any sexual union of male and female was itself a recapitulation of the archaic couple's joining: the man and woman coupling were like *musubi no kami*, "the gods that are joined." Sexual coupling and reproducing were "godlike" acts.

As the fervor of the neo-Shinto movement grew, it was easy to show that Buddhist scriptures, by contrast, often looked on celibacy as a desired state. In brief, it seemed clear to these critics of Buddhism that their opponents not only lacked a religious ideology that could embrace procreation as a value but had institutions and norms that often went in exactly the opposite direction. And in many ways they were, of course, right.

Exceptions surely existed. As noted, a priest such as Rennyo might father twenty-seven children. Moreover, by taking over funerary rites Buddhists had become part of familyism. But still Buddhists were hard-pressed to show in their own tradition a *religious basis for fecundity*. There was, as noted, a part of the tradition that gave religious meaning to sexual union. But that still was not what the later Kokugaku scholars had in mind, and they were, therefore, correct in assuming that Buddhists would have trouble imagining reproductivity as itself a religious value.

The union of man and woman was something that the sexually "free" monk of Edo could envision in positive terms. But that was far from visualizing this activity as of necessity eventuating in a child. Such monks no doubt could find a good deal of compatibility between their own views on sexuality and those, for instance, of Motoori Norinaga. But the *later* Kokugaku drive was geared to maximal reproduction. And it was precisely in this, as we shall see, that the conflict between neo-Shinto and Buddhism became most acute.

.　.　.　.　.

Although it is distasteful to produce neologisms gratuitously, we perhaps need one here. I find no available word for what the Buddhists were unable to accept. It was something even stronger than natalism, something we may do best to call *fecundism*. By this I mean the attribution of religious value and significance to reproductivity, especially if large numbers of progeny were a major part of the intentionality of sex. Quantity is important in fecundism.

Buddhists in the Edo period had relatively little trouble endorsing the family as social unit that was at its best when strong—and often strongest when the living treated honored ancestors as somehow still involved in family matters. That the continued rites for ancestors required new generations of children to carry on the rituals was a given. That conjugal life in the family would likely produce children was also an accepted fact—a natural one. Yet fecundism was not part of what Buddhist belief took real religion to be. And because it was, by contrast, a litmus test for neo-Shintoists, this was bound to be an arena in which real conflict would eventually develop.

Chapter 6

EDO: POPULATION

> Human life cannot in any way be limited to the closed systems
> assigned to it by reasonable conceptions.
> (Georges Bataille, *Visions of Excess*)

> Neither the word, *civilization*, nor its adjective, *civilized*,
> comprehends all that can be valuable in a people. But the
> Japanese are civilized. Japan is a civilization; it is full of
> human achievement as contrasted with natural wealth.
> (Henry Zylstra, "A Letter from Japan" [1945],
> *Testament of Vision*)

A Road and a Plateau

THE PRESSURE of ideas is one thing; the pressure of bodies—especially in large numbers—is quite another. The Edo was an era during which whole philosophies were pitted against one another in interesting ways. It was also one in which certain facts about Japan's population constituted a hard factor which, however unnoticed at times, had its own impact on the development of ideas and the struggle over them within society. The connection between these salient features of the demographic landscape and the trajectory taken by intellectual and religious developments in the Edo period has to date gone unstudied. But we leave this connection untouched at the risk of a skewed view of Edo intellectual life. In order to redress this even partially I will make a partial and preliminary attempt to see how these features were related.

One of the most vivid portraits of Japan's density comes from Engelbert Kaempfer (1651–1716), a German physician attached for a while to the Dutch settlement on the island of Dejima in Nagasaki harbor. In 1691 Kaempfer managed to gain permission—virtually unheard of for a European during Japan's "closed" Edo period—to travel in Japan's interior. He accompanied the head of the Dutch merchant community in Dejima on his tribute mission to Edo and wrote about what he saw. Among his reports is the following:

> It is scarce credible, what numbers of people daily travel on the roads in the country, and I can assure the reader from my own experience, having pass'd it four times, that Tokaido, which is one of the chief, and indeed the most

frequented of the seven great roads in Japan, is upon some days more crowded, than the publick streets in any of the most populous town in Europe. This is owing partly to the Country's being extreamly populous, partly to the frequent journies, which the natives undertake.[1]

Kaempfer noted that the Japanese were doing an inordinate amount of traveling, a good deal of which was due to the Tokugawa shōguns' requirement that all local daimyōs spend alternate years in residence in Edo; this unusual tool for nationwide surveillance was meant to prevent rebellion by local lords, whose wives and children were permanently in residence in Edo as the equivalent of hostages to the central government. This system was in place for over two hundred years, until 1862.

Even without that reason for crowded highways, as Kaempfer noted, Japan was *very densely populated* place in 1691—as it remains today. Kaempfer, we now know, had every reason to be amazed at what he saw. What he was personally witnessing as the press of people along Japan's principal highway is something that demographic historians have subsequently confirmed with their own analyses. Experts on Japan's population see the Edo period as one in which some extraordinary developments took place.

Hayami Akira estimates that during the first hundred years of the Edo period Japan's population doubled; at the beginning of the seventeenth century it had been somewhere between ten and eighteen million, but by 1725 it had reached thirty million.[2] At this time Edo, with around a million inhabitants, was the largest city in the world.[3] Moreover, it is quite possible that at that time Japan alone had three of the world's ten largest cities: Edo, Osaka, and Kyoto.

The facts seem clear. At the outset of the Edo period, Japan was already one of the most densely, if not *the* most densely, populated nation in the world. Moreover, during the first hundred or so years of Edo, that population grew enormously and did so in a way that led to extreme crowding in the urban centers. Nevertheless, after 1725 it somehow leveled off. Remarkably there was a period in mid-Edo when the Japanese population ceased its trajectory of rapid growth. Nothing can show this more clearly than the graph on p. 91, constructed by two American scholars.[4] The striking feature of the graph, of course, is that precisely during the period from the early eighteenth century to the middle of the nineteenth there is a significant leveling out of the otherwise steadily upward curve. It is, even more interestingly, the only such detectable one in the whole of Japanese history—at least where such things are able to be charted.

The reasons for it have fascinated demographers and historians—in part because the Japanese data is extraordinarily rich, derived as it is both

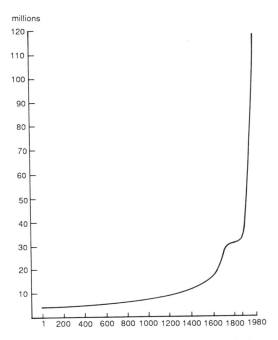

millions

From *Kodansha Encyclopedia of Japan*, ed. Gen
Itasaka et al., s.v. "population."

from national surveys required by the shōgun as well as from the temple
records that exist, as noted above, due to the government's requirement
that all people be registered as members of temple parishes. Here is where
the co-optation of Buddhists into the goverment's system of national surveillance gave a rich dividend to modern researchers in terms of unusually
detailed records of the era.

Japan's population plateau during the latter half of the Edo period deserves attention, however, for other reasons as well. It is important to
recognize how different it is from the trajectory in Japan's near neighbor,
China. Although between 1721 and 1846 Japan's population remained
more or less stable, China's population between 1749 and 1819—that is
during a contemporaneous but even shorter period of time—*doubled!*[5] It
is likely that no statistic is more important than this one in telling a tale
about differences during the time when East Asia's two giants were about
to start out on their strikingly different trajectories into the modern era.

What *does* this tell us? Not that Japan was underpopulated but that
having reached a certain level after a century of very rapid growth, its
population *stabilized* for a century and a quarter. The latter half of the

Edo period was in this respect totally different than the first half. The tale told by the demographers' statistical tables is one of Japan, at least in comparison to China, bringing its population under control and reining in what otherwise had threatened to be a runaway situation. The operative word here, of course, is *control*.

Such control, whatever its source, should be noticed. But to speak of control is necessarily to speak also of human volition, namely human beings' willing into existence the conditions that would, in effect, put a stop to what had till then been Japan's rapid upward population curve. And since we have nothing to indicate that this was a policy of the Japanese government, it means that decisions about having fewer children than had once been the custom were being made within the "bedrooms" of the Japanese citizenry.[6]

As a matter of fact, we find that government officials were, if anything, very hostile to anything that would put any kind of clamp on population growth. Daimyō officials particularly were very eager to prevent anything that might result in demographic stagnation.[7] Thus the inescapable conclusion must be that decisions to limit family size were made on a very private and personal level, and these decisions, moreover, were made *in spite of* government prohibitions.

But was it necessarily a matter of choice? Could it not have been due to circumstances beyond human control that the striking population plateau came into existence? This, after all, was the point classically advanced by Thomas Robert Malthus (1766–1834), who held that three things very much outside the domain of private reproductive decisions are bound to bring population down or keep it leveled off: war, famine, and epidemic.

How does the theory of Malthus play out in Japan? In a word, very badly. During the period of documented population stability, 1721–1846, Japan was experiencing an unprecedented spate of peace; the "national seclusion" policy of the Tokugawa regime meant that Japan was engaged in no external military exploits. Moreover, its stringent domestic controls meant that even though there were peasant uprisings, internal bloodshed was not enough to influence population in any significant way. Thus the impact of warfare as a control on the Japanese population would seem to have been negligible.

Likewise famine, although certainly a factor during certain short periods of scarcity, was not so pervasive that it would have played a significant role in reducing or stabilizing the overall population. In their studies of Edo population, Susan B. Hanley and Kozo Yamamura hold that in past studies the number of deaths attributed to famine has been greatly exaggerated.[8] It appears, then, that the second of Malthus's "positive checks" was also not enough to have impacted significantly on the Japanese population.

And more recently Ann Bowman Jannetta has exploded the relevance of the third part of the Malthusian triad—epidemic. In her study of contagious diseases in Japan during the period in question, she shows that diseases were "much less important as a cause of death and a stabilizer of population in preindustrial Japan than they were in preindustrial Europe."[9] Japan's relative geographical isolation as well as what seems to have been very effective policies to keep bubonic plague and typhus, the big killers elsewhere, from entering through Japan's ports, provided what Jannetta calls a *cordon sanitaire* around Japan.[10]

The conclusions to be drawn from this are intriguing. With Malthus's theories not being applicable in this instance, we are left with the problem of finding other means to explain Japan's remarkable, 125-year population stability. Moreover, since Malthus seems to have defined quite adequately the "irrational" factors that ordinarily operate to decimate or limit populations, it seems appropriate to look in the Japanese case for an explanation that depends more on "rational" and willed control.

MICRO AND MACRO

An odd and—especially because of the way we must word it—seemingly absurd question then arises: What are human beings to do when there is a conspicuous "lack" in a given nation's allotment of humankind's wars, famines, and pestilences?

The question was never explicitly raised in those terms within Edo Japan and is, of course, our way of retrospectively viewing the situation. If we can agree that the Malthusian and other "positive" checks have often been operative for much of our modern history, we are forced to recognize that Japan during its plateau period stands as a peculiar exception. For all practical purposes, Japan's relative geographic isolation, especially when reinforced by the Tokugawa "seclusion" policy, cut that archipelago off from the "benefit" of population control brought about by battles and by certain bacteria. Internally, food production was—with some egregious but largely local exceptions—sufficient to prevent the decimation of any large portions of the population.

What then, in lieu of the emptied granary, the slaughter of battle, and the devastating pest, could the Japanese use to keep their population within control? What would be sufficient to create the remarkable plateau of 1721–1846? For that would have ordinarily been *precisely the period* during which the population of Japan would have grown by leaps and bounds. So too it ordinarily could be expected that an already densely populated nation, one having three of the world's largest cities, would have become even more crowded than it in fact was. Hypothetically speaking, if things had gone in Japan the way they were then going in China and—now surely hypothetically—a long-lived Englebert Kaempfer had traveled the Tōkaidō again in 1750, he would have had to make his way through twice as many people as he had seen there in 1691.

In such a context, the food shortages would have become not local but nationwide and chronic, and the struggle for survival would have become intense. The internal strife and bloodshed that were part of the peasant revolts beginning around 1750 would, in fact, have been much more widespread and devastating than they were.

What then kept the population so controlled? The answer that has become increasingly clear to scholars is that what prevented a demographic upsurge in Japan was a combination of infanticide and abortion. This is the important conclusion to which researchers have come over the past half-century—with American scholars coming forward with some of the most interesting data over the past two decades.[11]

Therefore, although government officials repeatedly tried to prevent any such inroads on population growth, it seems clear that the practice of infanticide and abortion in the Edo period was adopted by the general population in spite of the proscriptions. If Japan's population curve was leveled between 1721 and 1846, it was because common people took recourse to these methods.

It seems now fairly clear that the growing dependence on abortion and infanticide during this period was, in fact, the wider extension of a practice that had begun well before the Edo period. The problem of documenting that claim arises because prior to the Edo period and its rich records—especially those of temples—we have less reliable ways of tracing these practices with exactitude. Some scholars, especially in Japan, have held that infanticide and abortion were almost exclusively Edo period phenomena but, although there was probably a dramatic increase then, it is clear that by the end of the Muromachi period (1334–1573) such practices were common enough in Japan for some of the Europeans present there to take notice and comment on them.[12]

There are at least a couple of examples of this. Although, as we have seen, St. Francis Xavier (1506–1552) declared the Japanese "the best race yet discovered," a Jesuit named Gaspar Vilela (1525–1572), employing biblical symbols of famine in Egypt, wrote from Japan, "We fear the lean cows of Pharao and pray that the Lord will not let them come here, because it is heart-breaking to see how many children are killed in such times."[13]

Likewise, an Englishman, Richard Cooks (d. 1624), whose stay extended well into the Edo and who may be the first to have branded the regime tyrannical, wrote copious criticisms of Japan and, as the final touch, included the following: "The most horrible thing of all is, that parents may kille their own children so sowne as they are borne if they have not wherewithall to nourish them, or the master his slave at pleasure, without incurring any danger of the law, the which I have known comitted by parents to two younge children, since I came to Hirado."[14] Vilela and Cooks found these practices, it should be noted, "heart-breaking," "horrible," and, in their view, caused by famine.

But what is this about famine? Did we not claim above that famine was far from being the reason for the stabilization of Japan's population? Much of the seeming contradiction here may be due to the difference between micro and macro measurements. Vilela and Cooks were, either by personal witness or by hearsay, aware that in Japan conditions of famine could and sometimes did influence parents to kill their children. In that sense they knew—or at least could envision—the close-up situation. When faced by a person emaciated with hunger or when walking through a town or portion of the countryside where numbers of famished and dying people could be seen with one's own eyes, it is certain to be the close-up or "micro" view that is taken. We have no reason to dispute the facts of wide starvation in earlier periods of Japanese history nor of local areas of famine in the Edo as well.[15] A witness in such situations registers the acute pain of starving people, may think of it as "unprecedented," and will tend to attribute many things—including what he or she has heard about infanticide—as the result of such famine.

The historical demographer looks, however, at a larger overall picture and makes a comparative judgment. His or her "macro" perspective takes in data not noticed by the on-site observer; from there things look different. For instance, it becomes clear that, at least in contrast to earlier periods, the practices of infanticide and abortion were not limited to the starving and desperate peasants in the country. On the contrary, they were often the practices of people living in the large and overcrowded urban centers. And, if we follow out the conclusions of the research of the American scholars who have worked on this topic, famine or even the prospect of hunger were in all likelihood *not* the cause of much of the practice of infanticide and abortion in that period and in those places. Thomas Smith states the striking conclusions concisely:

[In the village of Nakahara] there can be little doubt that one of the reasons for low registered fertility was the practice of infanticide. This comes as no great surprise, given the literary and legal evidence for infanticide in Tokugawa Japan. What is surprising is that the practice does not appear to have been primarily a response to poverty: large landholders practiced it as well as small, and registered births were as numerous in bad as in good growing years. Also, infanticide seems to have been used to control the sex sequence and the spacing of births and the sexual composition and final size of families. In short, it gives the impression of a kind of family planning.[16]

What Smith calls a "kind of family planning," discernible in all of this data, has made for a small revolution in thinking about this aspect of early modern Japan.

The implications of this deserve to be drawn out a bit. If the practices involved were just as common in urban centers as in rural areas and just as often found among well-off persons as among the impoverished, it becomes clear that many people in Edo Japan were limiting their children in order to enhance the quality of their lives. Eng and Smith even claim, at least in their data, to have seen the evidence of attempts to bring about a near balance of the sexes—something astounding in view of the usual assumption that, since infanticide permits maximal choice in the sex selection of offspring, a traditional society would have chosen to kill females and let males live by a large margin. Eng and Smith found the facts to be different: while families wanted to be sure that they had males, once that was established they moved toward a near parity of the sexes.[17]

RATIONALES AND RATIONALITY

We need to recognize what a revolution in thinking is involved in this. On the scene, Vilela and Cooks had said it happened because there were too many mouths to feed. They were not wrong in many instances but merely ignorant of the fact that far more cases of abortion and infanticide in Japan were part of privatized family-planning strategies.

Marxist-oriented scholars too have tended to favor the notion that infanticide was caused by famine. During those postwar decades when Marxist ideas had a wide hearing in Japan, it was common to assume that infanticide was caused by the peasants' starvation, which, in turn, was really the result of the greed of the ruling class. The ideological compulsion to prove the negative consequences of political oppression made it impossible for such scholars to recognize that, in fact, many urbanites in Edo Japan probably limited their families merely to increase their own wealth.

Then, of course, there was also the "embarrassment" factor. Given that, at least until recently, Western scholars generally assumed that infanticide would only be found in primitive or unenlightened societies— and, therefore, by definition not in Europe or America—there was something inherently embarrassing in acknowledging that infanticide was practiced quite widely in Edo Japan. Infanticide would also, of course, tend to reinforce the old Western notions of an Asia in which "life is cheap."

While it seems clear that infanticide was more widely practiced in Asia than in Europe, the difference now appears to have been one more of relative frequency rather than of a deep *civilizational* difference. Although not all historians are willing to go as far as Lloyd de Mause in seeing infanticide as widespread in Western contexts,[18] there is sufficient evidence of its existence in medieval and early modern times to suggest that a hard and fast line between the West on one hand and primitive or Asian societies on the other can no longer be assumed. Moreover recent studies on the practice, in Christian Europe, of abandoning children indicates that, although by far the preferred method of disposing of children there, the actual mortality rate was so high that any case made for the moral superiority of this practice must also be questioned.

The population of Europe would have grown much more than it did if in the early modern period there had not been the "release" mechanisms of disease, war, and emigration. Serious famine, which was only at Europe's "wretched extremities, Russia at one end, Ireland and Spain at the other,"[19] would have been much worse if, like Japan, the other Malthusian "checks" and emigration had *not* been available. In truth, the wealth of Europeans—through colonialism especially—grew tremendously during the time frame under consideration. The fact that the Japanese, without either the Malthusian checks or emigration available to them, resorted to abortion and infanticide cannot be taken as any index at all to a moral superiority on the part of Europe.

Correspondingly, there is no need for Japanese students of this problem to sense that the data is something shameful. Thus too there should be no need to depend any longer on a Marxian or quasi-Marxian rationalization for Japanese infanticide in terms of brutal conditions imposed by rulers on peasants in a feudal society.

The facts of the matter seem too clear: there were two primary reasons for practicing infanticide and abortion during the Edo period, and they differed for different portions of the population. To many rural people—most especially in the northern areas where the crop yield was often miserably meager and real famines were commonplace—the prospect of yet another hungry infant in a farmhouse already lacking enough food would, most certainly, have given people sufficient reason to consider "returning" it to the world of gods and Buddhas.

At the same time, however, there were no doubt many other people in Japan—perhaps the majority—for whom the "return" of a child made sense in terms of gaining or keeping the things that made for a richer, better life. For them it would seem to have been exactly as Hanley and Yamamura stated it: "We find evidence that the people in these villages followed customs that resulted in maximizing per capita income and thereby in maintaining and improving their standard of living."[20]

For such people, the experience of a better life as a result of such measures was a positive reinforcement. It was part of a pattern whereby people had the growing sense of *gaining control* over their own lives and happiness. For those in desperate straits, that was perhaps only a modicum of control. But for those better off, townsfolk primarily, it was quite a bit more. Concerning them Eng and Smith remark, "These goals required foresight and the ability to carry out long-range plans; qualities not usually associated with a demoralized or desperate people."[21] A trajectory for the future was set.

A key to understanding the implications is to recall how greatly this contrasts with what was happening in China. During what was surely a critical span of time, the population of Japan's continental neighbor doubled while Japan's leveled off. This meant, of course, that in China the sheer number of mouths to feed was much larger—and, while Japan was beginning to industrialize, required a much larger proportion of the national labor force to sustain.

But it also meant a different kind of *experience*. The people of Japan, quite contrary to what their Edo rulers wanted, discovered both as individuals and as families the positive benefits that accrued from taking steps to limit their children. They found out that life—not just the quantity of goods but also qualitative things—could be greatly improved. This, moreover, was self-reinforcing. Family planning had positive results and these, in turn, made such planning itself clearly desirable.

That did not happen in China. One result has been that down to the present day China's battle against its own population pressures goes on. And then it comes as dicta from the top down, as government "policy" rather than the ingrained and self-reinforcing practice of the people themselves. Not only are the sheer numbers vastly different but the *historical experience* in the modern period has been virtually the opposite of Japan's. It is, I suspect, quite likely that nothing more fundamental than this lies at the basis of the great difference between the two East Asian giants in modern times—a difference in historical experience that stretched right down to the present. China goes on fighting what in many ways is still a nineteenth-century battle against an explosive population—and issues edicts to do it; Japan, basically stabilized, plans the technological and cultural developments of the twenty-first century.

We can gain an insight here into how "rationality" often gets itself constituted. What is striking about the pattern of population control in Japan is that it looks "rational" only in retrospect, namely, as *we* see the long-term impact. It was, of course, rational to the people who practiced it, because they realized benefits from it. But it was not rational at all to the authorities, whose concern to have an adequately productive and tax-contributing populace made any kind of birth control abhorrent and highly "irrational." They, interestingly, would have viewed rationality in the terms of the Reverend Thomas Malthus, who wrote, in his *Essay on the Principle of Population*, 1798, "[T]here is not a truer criterion of the happiness and innocence of a people than the rapidity of [population] increase."[22]

The eighteenth and nineteenth centuries were, in Europe but also in Japan to a somewhat lesser extent, periods when concepts of rationality were in the air. Governments and the advisors to governments often thought they knew fairly well what rationality was and how it might be applied to the planning of whole societies. Malthus was interested in that; his entire work was an attempt to show that threats to population (that is, war, famine, and epidemic) are "good" in that they encourage human "exertions" to meet them. Malthus was interested in thus justifying the essential "rationality" of the God who had made the world to include the sufferings of the starving. The daimyō of Japan were also interested in what might be "rational" in terms of mustering maximal resources for the benefit of their domains and themselves. They were getting their notions of "rationality" from Confucian and neo-Confucian advisors.

The general population, however, was going about things differently. They were uninterested in rationality per se. They in practice rejected what the "rationality" embraced by their rulers demanded of them. What they found as rational for themselves was far more pragmatic, part of life-situation decisions rather than an overarching notion of mind and rationality.

CULLING—BY MAN AND BY GOD

Finding what was beneficial for themselves meant finding language that would help. And that, in turn, meant not so much the language of logic as that of metaphor. What is especially impressive about the family planning of the common people of Edo Japan is that they devised metaphors to grasp and embrace their goals.

One of these metaphors has already been examined—"return." Infants and fetuses not permitted viability were sent back to the realm of the gods and Buddhas. An alternative linguistic tool for this purpose was drawn, however, from the agricultural world. Since the term became the chief one to encompass the birth-control techniques of the period, it is important to understand it clearly.

The term is *mabiki*, which literally means "the culling of seedlings," especially in rice fields. The agricultural analogy and its intention are pat-

ent: just as the growing of rice may yield a better crop if along the way
certain weaker seedlings are removed, so too in human affairs the culling
of some infants and fetuses may be desirable. Families, so the rationale
undoubtedly went, needed thinning out as much as did rice fields glutted
with more seedlings than could possibly survive. What was good for the
crop quality of the harvest was assumed to be a "good" as well for the
field of seedlings that was the result of human beings having sex. The
human hand applied to the cultivation of rice had to be guided by wise
choices, taking certain plants as worthy of continued life and others as
not. Man's hand—or in this case, certainly *woman*'s hand in the form of
the midwife's—applied to the "field" called family had to be equally wise,
discriminating, and guided by something of an informal plan.

This is a nuance of the word that seems to have gained wide currency
during the Edo period. At least that might be inferred from the fact that
although the word *mabiki* shows up in the *Nippo Jisho*, the Jesuit Japa-
nese-Portuguese dictionary published in 1603 in Nagasaki, the reference
is only to having things grow well and makes no mention of this term as
used for culling humans.[23]

The direct application of this term to the realm of human reproduction
had several important implications. The first of these, as suggested above,
is the recognition of human volition in the act. Choice and deliberation
are involved. In addition, however, precisely because agriculture is a domain in which human action cooperates with natural processes, there is
implicit here also the idea that the culling of humans, like that of rice
seedlings, is so much in keeping with natural processes that it is all but
necessitated. To refrain from mabiki in human affairs would be to go
against one of the rules of nature.

While this was undoubtedly a semantic usage that could palliate some
of the natural feelings of guilt associated with culling one's potential
progeny, we should not ignore the fact that the analogue would not have
been totally forced. The Japanese of the time no doubt had seen certain
unfortunate results from *not* practicing mabiki—in the form of mothers
whose repeated childbearing left them weak and illness-prone, in the
form of inadequately spaced newborns who were either sick or quickly
dead, and, certainly, in the form of a drain on household resources caused
by the birth of too many children. Mabiki had its own inner logic—both
in the rice field and in the household.

Besides, mabiki suggested not the reduction of resources but the intelligent use of them. The farmer who culled his seedlings did so to ensure an
overall better crop. The husband and wife who "selected" their own offspring—so the analogy went—did so to gain an *overall better family*. To
cull was to make strong what remained. It was also to give added strength
to the totality. The people of Edo did not have to know of Darwin in

order to see a certain sense in this. They knew quite instinctively that governmental condemnations of mabiki were not—at least for them as individuals and families—really rational.

It was, of course, impossible to say as much to the authorities. Their concern for maximal population and taxes was single-focused, being apparently unable to entertain the view that sometimes less might mean more. But that is precisely why mabiki, a term seemingly coined by the age, was so powerful. In it was an implicit critique of the unilinearity of governmental ideas; with a single powerful metaphor it provided a refutation of the necessity of the view held by govenmental officials.

It is, I wish to suggest, an exact illustration of the kind of moral bricolage discussed in chapter 1—one fitting, I think, Stout's concept of such bricolage. The "rationality" here was that of a specific people within a specific historical situation—people, moreover, trying to explain largely to themselves how they might mentally and morally adjust to a perceived need to "return" some of their own potential offspring to the otherworld. The rationality here was largely put together out of various things—in this case perhaps primarily through concepts like *return* and a new linguistic usage given to the mabiki practiced by rice farmers.

Malthus, it is good to recall, was in some sense not so very different. He would have been horrified at the prospect of people practicing mabiki as deliberate acts. Yet in his view God himself was doing something not dissimilar. Malthus, it is often forgotten, was, in his theories of population, primarily interested in justifying the ways of God to man: he wanted to explain why the human suffering caused by disease, wars, and famine were—at least in some larger view—rational. His conclusion, one by which he thought God was exonerated, was that population pressures, however much they cause suffering, also generate human talents. Near the—often unread—end of his celebrated essay, he writes, "The exertions that men find it necessary to make, in order to support themselves or families, frequently awaken faculties that might otherwise have lain for ever dormant."[24]

A man of his age, he saw this as the propellant whereby ingenuity and even "Reason" are produced. So all the suffering, starving, and dying makes sense in larger terms. Malthus was, it should be noted, prone to think of the high percentage of suffering and death in societies peripheral to Europe as due to their being the lesser parts of a "system," one in which Europe would show the best results in terms of "exertions," awakened faculties, and rationality. God had, it seems, designed the whole system for Europe's sake! The nontemperate parts of the world, where famine was rife, were the parts he—intelligently it seems—needed to sacrifice so that ingenuity and reason could flourish in Europe. God, it would seem, practiced mabiki on a global scale.

Malthus, wanting to show God's ways were rational, himself in the end used a botanic metaphor to make his point. In order to explain why the suffering, less noble portions of the human population—that is those not in temperate zones (as Europe and America are)—still were part of the larger system and its fundamental rationality, Malthus saw the world not as a rice field but as an oak tree. He wrote, "The most valuable parts of an oak, to a timber merchant, are not either the roots or the branches, but these are absolutely necessary to the existence of the middle part, or stem, which is the object in request."[25] That is, God, who is eminently reasonable, made the world well. Early on he made things so that the wars, disease, and famines of the world—especially costly to peoples who are like the undeground roots or the useless end twigs of an oak—would stimulate the middle portion, the trunk of the tree, which is comparable to temperate-zone peoples—to their destined strength, utility, and value.

God the Father was, in some sense, *the expert* at mabiki. The system he devised made it necessary for whole peoples to be his mizuko. Here too—in the domain where philosophers and economists try to "justify the ways of God to man"—metaphors were used to do most of the work. Perhaps all of it.

Chapter 7

EDO: POLEMICS

> Impiety—Your irreverence toward my deity.
> (Ambrose Bierce, *The Devil's Dictionary*)

HEAT AND LIGHT

ONE OF THE THINGS this study is intended to show is that although in contemporary Japan there is—at least in comparison with the West—relatively little public debate about abortion and religion, this *was* an issue of considerable public importance a century of so ago. Japan, in a word, had its own "abortion debate" much earlier than the West. Although some issues were different, others were the same.

In this chapter an effort will be made to show the principal sources at our disposal in any attempt to reconstruct what that "debate" was all about. Excerpts from certain texts of the 1830s and 1840s will be given in translation and analyzed in terms of what they tell us about the trajectory of Japanese thinking on these matters.

First, however, there is value in noting something else that may be surprising. We are so accustomed to being told that in Japan many of Asia's major religious philosophies were accommodated to one another and led a harmonious coexistence that it may surprise many in the West, at least initially, to learn that during much of the Edo period there were intense and often passionate disagreements among Buddhists, Confucians, and the partisans of the newly self-conscious thinkers who identified with the nativist Shinto tradition. When it came to their respective visions as to where Japan as a society ought to be moving and what constituted the wise course to be taken by rulers, Confucians, Buddhists, and the neo-Shinto partisans of Kokugaku often looked at things very differently. It was natural, then, that this generated verbal attacks. In earlier epochs intersectarian debates among various Buddhist sects could themselves become quite fierce. But the Edo was in many ways that era in Japanese history when polemic among quite different philosophies became sharp. In that sense it was, more than earlier eras, one of polemic and "debate"—most often in print rather than in actual verbal discourse.

Because a good portion of this polemic was intended to be heard, evaluated, and even judged by rulers—both shōguns and local daimyōs—it was argumentation on which scholarly and advisory careers often hung. Although for a thousand years or so of Japanese recorded history prior to the Edo epoch it had been the Buddhists who held a kind of intellectual hegemony over the land, this situation changed in the seventeenth century. Although there was not quite the sudden and total switch to official neo-Confucianism that was long thought to be the case, it was in the Edo period that Buddhism first gave up its long-standing hegemonic position and then, especially as the era advanced, largely receded from the front line of contenders for attention from rulers and officials.

It was earlier suggested that there is something odd in assuming that Buddhism was dead. The fact that a majority of books published in the period were Buddhist is alone a reason to question such assumptions. The content of some of the best of these has in recent years been under study in Japan—and is shown to be much more intellectually vigorous than earlier supposed.[1]

Then, too, there is the peculiarity of assuming Buddhist weakness when its detractors deemed it far too strong. For instance, one of the period's major anti-Buddhists, Nakai Chikuzan (1730–1804), argued that the Buddhists must be forced out of teaching positions in the school system of the day. The stated rationale was the old charge that Buddhists teach disengagement from society.[2] But Nakai's problem seems to have been the opposite, namely, that Buddhists were far *more* engaged—at least in the educational system—than he wanted them to be.

Buddhists were, in a word, not nearly as "otherworldly" as others desired them to be. Imai Jun puts the matter succinctly: "We do well to understand the Buddhists of the Edo period in the following terms. It was not a matter of them taking flight from the world by moves that involved leaving the householding life; rather, what they did was forge together an ethic of Buddhist world involvement and develop an emphasis upon Buddhism as useful in the world of practical affairs."[3] This view not only fits what Buddhists themselves were saying at the time but also suggests the real story behind the Confucian rhetoric against them. This is to say that we must read the age not only from assumed light in the arguments but also from the intensity of their *heat*.

The attacks of the neo-Shintoists, coming both later and with more power, proved far more difficult for the Buddhists to meet. Since Confucianists themselves had teachings derived from China, they could hardly make charges against the Buddhists for adopting "foreign" doctrines. But the neo-Shintoists could. Their claims was based on the assumption of a pure Japaneseness, and they were able to turn the screws on Buddhists on this point at least.

Another school of thought, known as "Mito Learning" because it originated in the Mito district, became virulently antiforeign and used Buddhism especially as an object of attack.[4] Especially in Mito itself anti-Buddhist sallies were mixed with more general and pervasive xenophobia. By the second half of the nineteenth century, this eventuated in a "movement"—sometimes with official approval—to rid Japan completely of Buddhism; it went under the banner of *haibutsu kishaku*, literally "Destroy the Buddhas and kick out Shakyamuni." This led to a good deal of physical destruction of Buddhist temples and icons as well as some deaths.[5]

Merely as a matter of survival, Buddhists most of the time had everything to gain from adopting practices that stressed compatibility and language that would cool down the rhetoric of the charges against them. They made the most of their difficult situation—in part simply by becoming "all things to all men." In addition, it is very clear that *silences* were strategically maintained on points where open clash could have invited harsh measures. For the most part, however, throughout the Edo period Buddhists pretty well retained their place in Japanese life through their deep involvement in the major public education system, their participation in rituals and folk festivals, and especially the ample opportunity the widespread temple system provided for monks to mingle deeply with the masses and give counsel on practical affairs.

MABIKI'S CONFUCIAN CRITICS

My concern here, however, is not with the whole extent of this period's polemics but only with how they were refracted through the age's thinking about abortion. To claim, however, that there was a "debate" about abortion in Japan during the first half of the nineteenth century also necessitates saying that what remains in existing records is all on one side—namely, that which opposed the practice of mabiki and also indirectly the Buddhists who, we are led to believe, were understood to have what would now be called a "soft" position on mabiki.

To the extent that Buddhists had such a position in the Edo period, they appear to have avoided saying so in print. Given the fact that the opponents of mabiki invariably had the support of governments on this issue, the "wisdom" of never making a *public* justification of mabiki is clear. To do so would have been to risk too much. Yet we can assume that there was, at least in certain quarters, a Buddhist willingness to "wink" at mabiki practices. That is, although monks would have given vocal support to the government's fecundist policies in public statements, their words *in private* likely were quite different. They probably were much more "understanding" of their parishioners' needs or desires to control family size through mabiki.

Moreover, "Buddhism" in this context was not limited to what was under the control of the clergy. There was also the growing phenomenon of the voluntary associations of devotees of Jizō (*Jizō-kō*) and these, we can assume, were laypeople and perhaps largely composed of women. And their Buddhism was certainly one that saw Jizō's compassion as extending to themselves as women who at times had no option but to practice mabiki.

This suggests that Buddhism did not, at least in many instances, problematize the matter of mabiki. Writing concerning the Edo period, George A. De Vos notes that for Buddhists at this time abortion was removed from the area of religious sanctions.[6] Although there was, in fact, no common consensus among Buddhists about the details of fetal life, and there were condemnations of abortion in the Buddhist classics,[7] we can assume that the actual "position" of Buddhism on this issue in the Edo period was much as De Vos suggests—namely, in the direction of wanting to keep this as a viable option in people's lives. Besides, of course, the notion that even a fetus or infant is "recycled" by making a temporary "return" to the world of the gods and Buddhas removed a good deal of the sense of this as a form of killing. Language surely softened these deeds.

In any case, the Buddhists appear to have had a much "softer" position on this matter than their opponents. Many of the era's most severe attacks on mabiki came from Confucians and neo-Confucians. Because they often had access to the government, they also could easily claim that, at least by the most simple kind of calculations, mabiki deprived rulers of potential subjects and therefore of revenues as well.

Economics may have been at the heart of matters. Words about "humankind" and its particularity, however, filled the rhetoric. Nakai Chikuzan, already mentioned as one of the age's principal polemicists, traveled to distant Kyushu and wrote,

> Among distant relatives in remote areas there are many impoverished people who do not have progeny. In terms of the [Confucian] concept of true humanity these are instances in which such humans show themselves inferior even to the beasts. The abominable thing is that people get inured to such things and do not think them unusual. In Hinata and its environs [today's Miyazaki] it is especially egregious and a practice that even the upper ranks of the samurai are adopting. I hear much more of this than I can tolerate.[8]

The idea here is that what is a "natural" virtue exhibited by beasts—who reproduce readily—should a fortiori be characteristic of human beings. Confucians and neo-Confucians, often fond of contrasts between humans and lower forms of life, would be doubly enraged to find more "virtue" on this point in animals than in human beings.

Satō Nobuhiro (1769–1850), during his trips to the northeast and southwest of Japan's main island, found mabiki practices widespread and wrote,

> I have heard that long ago in the Western world there was a great nation whose king killed 3,300 children every year to use their livers to make medicine for the kidney which would give him power over women. Everyone who hears this story is shocked and condemns this inhuman practice . . . but at present in the two provinces of Mutsu and Dewa [northern Japan] alone, no less than 60,000 to 70,000 infants are killed annually. And yet I have not heard of anyone who is shocked at this and condemns the practice.[9]

Satō does not go into the tremendous difference in reasons—an unnamed European king's sexual whims versus poverty in Japan's northern hinterlands—but assumes his argument is rational and will be self-evident.

In many ways it is clear that Confucian attacks on mabiki practice were based primarily on the notion of it as a *waste* of people. In that sense, it was structurally similar to what we saw in an earlier chapter as the tendency of some Confucians to score religious practices as a waste of resources and energies. Sorai's desire to melt down Buddhist icons to make coins was not terribly different from arguments that mabiki was a waste of persons who, if allowed to live, would have produced tax revenues for the coffers of rulers.

These are only two examples of what in Edo Japan was a constant Confucian objection to mabiki.[10] It is clear, however, that they neither had the moral authority to enforce this nor the wherewithal even to monitor it. In fact, precisely because Buddhists had more pervasive contact with the masses and could be expected to feel the need to respond to governmental directives, Confucian moralists in the Edo period repeatedly tried to solicit the help of Buddhist priests in getting their anti-mabiki message across to common people.[11] The fact that all these efforts had very limited success is shown by the need for ever more heated rhetoric and by the evidence of the population plateau described in chapter 6.

SHINTO GODS AND HUMAN BABIES

While it is important to remember that Confucians found the practices of mabiki abhorrent, many of the most important and interesting arguments against it were leveled not by them but by the apologists for Kokugaku. These came in the early and mid nineteenth century, a time when, in the view of Matsumoto Sannosuke, the rhetoric of the Kokugaku movement had gotten increasingly ideological as well as overtly political. The movement was gathering force as a revival of Shinto—but at the same time was increasingly nationalistic and political. Here I wish to present and look closely at what was said about mabiki in three texts by three major neo-Shintoists of what is called the *bakumatsu* or "close of the shogunate" period in Japanese history.

Matsumoto, in fact, succinctly puts the contents of the following texts into their larger context. In late Edo-period texts neo-Shinto's comprehensive ethical and social program was trying to inculcate the following: "The need for industriousness in home industries, the prohibition of abortion, respect for social distinctions, the proscription of luxurious living, the right way of spousal relations, the rearing of children, the education of fetuses in the womb, the mutual understanding of five-person family units, respect for village elders, and the prohibition of meat-eating."[12] The concern about abortion, then, was one part of something much more comprehensive.

Although actually the last written of the three texts considered here, the *Yotsugigusa* of Suzuki Shigetani (1812–1863), written in 1849, is a good aperture through which to begin to see the neo-Shinto mentality. Suzuki writes,

> For a couple to have children and heirs is part of its supreme duty with respect to the realm; it is not a matter of private inclination. We must keep in mind the fact that the wealth of the nation and the adequacy of its military preparedness depend completely on the quantity of her people. You may have very good soil but if you do not have the available bodies to farm it, it will again become just barren waste. A castle too, even though well-built, requires soldiers to defend it. Exactly in this way the thing that is most needed in our own time is a large population.
>
> This notwithstanding, some people, pressed by poverty, kill and bury their own children. It is really only in China that this evil practice has existed with any great frequency, but the word is now out that this heinous practice at some time or other crossed the sea to come into our own land too. I hear of it taking place from time to time out in rural areas and among the poor. Sometimes women who are pregnant take potions in order to induce abortions and rid themselves of their children.
>
> At other times they make arrangements with midwives, wait full term, and then suffocate the newborn—either by throwing it into rushing waters or by burying it. This kind of thing goes by the name of "mabiki" or "thinning out"—on the analogy of what is done to rice seedlings in the fields. Even though the people who do these things are shameless, desperately poor, and ignorant, we must note that it is beyond the pale of humanity for a parent to kill its own child, or let it become the food of dogs and wolves, or else consign it to

waters with the result that it eventually becomes food for the bellies of fish. This is such an evil practice that nothing else can be compared to it.[13]

Suzuki is explicit about technical aspects of mabiki and about his reasons for holding it to be immoral.

The fact that these practices deprive the nation of potential soldiers and farm workers is paramount in his considerations. Children are, he goes out of his way to say, not the private possession of their parents but of the state, and it is the state's needs that come first. It is not so much a matter of a fetus's intrinsic value as its being a potential producer and soldier. Although Suzuki recognizes that it is their poverty that induces the peasantry into such practices, he is not moved to pity them. Instead their acts are seen as selfish and against true morality—here defined as what is needed by the nation. The nation and what is good for it are of paramount concern in any estimate of behavior.

Another Kokugaku critic of these practices was Miyauchi Yoshinaga (1798–1843), who in his *Toyamabiko*, of 1834, wrote,

People are born into this world due to the grace of the gods and emperors. There are some who forget that these are the source; they then entertain the wicked idea that by their own acts they bring their children into existence. The next thing they do in their selfishness is to abort the fetuses that they have come to think of as their own. That shows how debased they really are. As mentioned, although it is solely due to divine favor that something grows in a womb, such people let the fetus develop for five or six months—just to the point where it has begun to take on either male or female sexual characteristics—and then, absolutely devoid of mercy, take such a time to be good for aborting the child. In other cases they let it go full term for ten months—that is, to the time when the facial features are developed and the gods are beckoning such a child to be born, like a beautiful jewel, into this world—and then let it be born only to crush it to death by sitting on top of it. This is most surely a sin in the sight of the gods and those who practice such things are sure to receive retribution during their own lifetimes. Perhaps their punishment will come later in the form of a complicated childbirth in which the mother loses her own life. Or else such parents will later find it impossible to conceive again—so that they will go childless into old age and with no one to take care of them. In this way they will receive the punishment of the gods and their family name will die out.[14]

Here again is the idea that children are possessions of the state rather than of their parents; the corollary is that it is privatized selfishness alone that would impell parents to refuse to let a fetus mature into a live birth. Miyauchi, however, makes the Shinto basis of his viewpoint clear: children are due to the grace of the myriad gods and Japanese emperors, who are in his view gods themselves.

Miyauchi, it is important to note, also makes much of the notion of *tatari*, or retribution, and sees it as very much part of the Shinto he espouses. Women who practice mabiki, he proclaims, may experience divine retribution in terms of subsequent complicated deliveries, even death while giving birth. Couples may also be infertile. Those who sin against the state, in effect, sin against the gods and as such are likely to find their own sexual and reproductive lives impaired. The concept of tatari comes into sharp articulation here.

Finally, the views of Miyahiro Sadao (1798–1858), as given in his *Kokueki Honron*, of 1831, deserve quotation in full. He explains his position on mabiki as follows:

> The reason for my objection to these things is that if the population is meager, it will be difficult to accumulate wealth and thereby develop our country. Because the august gods have in their hearts the intention of making all things abundant, they provide the world with human beings who have seeds in their own bodies. The gods intend humans to be prolific—just as they intend vegetation to grow abundantly on the earth. Ordinary folk, however, may not have an adequate grasp of these things; they assume that children are something merely made at home by a man and his wife and are uncertain whether the gods are involved or not. Being selfish and greedy they mistakenly think that having a lot of children will simply deplete the family's wealth. Thus after they have had one or two children they set about destroying all subsequent ones by abortion. These acts are despicable. Why do people assume that heaven would give us children that have no value? What we need to realize is that all such children, for better or for worse, are given us by the gods and that through these children our nation can be developed as a well-populated place, one that bustles with people. Surely it is clear that if people, due to their own selfishness, simply abort their children, we will end up as a nation without a sufficient number of people. . . . It is, of course, true that if you have a lot of people you will need sufficient food to feed them all. But the thing to remember is that a large population also produces excrement in abundance. With nightsoil in good supply we can have fields that will give us rich harvests . . . whereas the practice of abortion leads to a decrease in the supply of nightsoil. To say we need more people, however, is a far cry from saying we need more Buddhist priests, as if they were in any way beneficial for our land. . . . To transform unenlightened young lads into Buddhist priests is itself a sin before our gods. Males are born equipped with male sexual organs and these, when developed so that there can be passion between a man and a woman, are organs that can be used for what they are intended—that is, procreation, for increasing the number of people in our land. Such organs are the visible signs of a mandate received from the gods. There-

fore, it clearly will not do for males to become [celibate] Buddhist priests. Is one to assume that the great gods of creation made us with a part of our bodies that is to go unused? On the contrary, it is the will of the gods that this thing, the sexual organ, follow its natural course, one that leads to conception and the birth of children. In the human being there is no organ more important than the sexual one. This is the reason why it would surely be a transgression of the will of the gods if we were to fail to make full use of the precious tools we have been given to procreate and have offspring. . . . [15] Wickedness consists in not following the will of the gods. The examples I have noted here have been abortion and infanticide; the profession of belief in Buddhism; and the polluting of [sacred] fires [by cooking meat in them].[16]

RELIGION AND (RE)PRODUCTIVITY

Of the these three, Miyahiro's is in all probability the most interesting set of arguments. Because they are also most clear about how a neo-Shinto objection to abortion would be formed, they deserve our closest attention. Miyahiro holds not only that children are the gift of the gods in some generalized sense but that each one is specifically intended by the gods of Japan to enter into this world. To have an abortion, then, is not only an act of greed and selfishness on the part of parents but also a deliberate act that runs contrary to a process that the gods have intentionally begun. It is an impious defiance.

Miyahiro is also convinced that the gods wish and will a *quantity* of life on earth—vegetable as well as human. Since he assumes that the gods have a special interest in the well-being of Japan and the Japanese, it is perfectly reasonable for Miyahiro to conclude that they want Japan to be "a well-populated place, one bustling with people." A vision of Japan as both highly productive in an economic sense and highly reproductive in a biological one is the essence of this religio-political view of things. Quantity is terribly important to him, and carries over even into his argument—perhaps "charming" to us but deadly serious to him—that many people can produce a good quantity of excrement. Night soil increases agricultural production. Abortion, by contrast, reduces the night-soil supply by cutting down on the number of the humans who are, in effect, the machines that manufacture such human manure.

Here *homo faber* is not so much the human who makes tools as the one who has become a tool. As Harry D. Harootunian astutely notes, "Between the sowing of species and the sowing of rice, Miyahiro recognized no barriers."[17] The gods and the state are taken to have a total program for the development of Japan, and all Japanese individuals and family groups are, willy-nilly, meant to follow in lock-step and be part of the means to realize these ends.

It is for that reason that Miyahiro, like many of his fellow neo-Shinto ideologues, could find absolutely no utility in the institution of the Buddhist clergy. He zeroes in on what is wrong with such priests. In essence, his objection to Buddhists is their practice of *celibacy*, which, although honored "in the breach" by many priests then, was still their "tradition." Miyahiro takes that tradition as itself a sustained and literally *embodied insult to the gods.*

This is because, at least for Miyahiro, reproductivity—or his own Shinto version of the biblical "be fruitful and multiply" mandate—is the essence of piety. As Harootunian has noted, in Miyahiro we clearly see "the powerful pull of Shinto as it was reformulated into a popular and agriculturally oriented religion in the late-Tokugawa period."[18]

In such a context, the Buddhist priest—at least if he is "traditional" and celibate—is by virtue of that celibacy in open contradiction to the most sacred order. Here sexuality is an expression of divine purposes, because it is the engine of fertility. Buddhist priests who have sexual organs that are not being used to produce progeny are a travesty of what the gods intend the (Japanese) human being to be. "Is one to assume that the great gods of creation made us with a part of our bodies that is to go unused?" Miyahiro asks.

It is not at all difficult to see why these Kokugaku writers pleased rulers of all kinds to such an extraordinary degree. Daimyō were, especially in "lean" years when bad weather gave meager crops, intensely eager that there be more productivity. The miserable plight of farmers was something of little import to them. To their minds, strictly quantitative and calculating in a most simplistic fashion, having more human bodies working in the fields was the best guarantee against diminished crops and lost revenue. Abortion was hurting their own incomes, and such a practice had to be stamped out at all costs. Conversely, it was important to see both reproductivity and productivity as important to the gods as well as the state. It is, then, not accidental that they cast production in the language and ideology of a religion. Fecundism was the order of the day.

They carried this very far. As Jennifer Robertson has shown, the later Kokugaku thinking led also to the production of *nōsho,* farm manuals that not only gave much practical advice for increasing crop yield but also, in a pseudoscientific fashion, fantasized—sometimes with graphic illustrations—about what was taken to be the humanlike sexuality of rice seedlings. The sexuality of ordinary plants was exaggerated and overdrawn in order to instill in the populace the makings of a kind of "gender-bound theology."[19]

All this must be viewed, of course, within an actual context, in which Japanese farmers frequently faced personal shortages of dire proportions. Numbers of them and sometimes whole villages knew death by starvation. Their attempts to organize protests and small revolts have been extraordinarily well documented in recent years.[20] Yet the bottom line for Japan's rulers during these years was always the same: their own concern about income loss and their near-total lack of concern for the plight of the peasantry.

In such a context, peasants often had no real option other than abortion and infanticide. Neo-Shintoist ideologues called such practices "selfish" and the height of impiety. Politically minded Confucianists saw in them only the "waste" of various kinds of potential.

The technology of abortion in Edo was largely in the hands of doctors of the Chūjō school. They made and used suppositories for "extracting old blood" or "spoiling fetuses." Mercury was the principal active agent in them.[21] This notwithstanding, it can easily be assumed that the services of such doctors were too expensive for poorer people and they necessarily had recourse only to ruder, more dangerous means to extract fetuses. The brutality of method was also probably more likely where there was more fear of detection. In this period, when the senryū form of verse commented on social situations, one of them—surely referring to a pregnancy—went as follows:

What's developed here
Will, by Chūjō's methods,
Soon be turned to water.

BUDDHIST BRICOLEURS

There was condemnation of abortion from the Confucians on secular, economic grounds and from neo-Shinto apologists on religious ones. We must recognize that the plight of the peasants was not, at least to the advocates of either of these positions, reason for countenancing any practice that would lead to a drop in, or even a leveling off of, population. An infamous response, common in the era, to those who claimed the peasants' lot was miserable was "peasants are like rape-seed; just as such seeds release oil only if squeezed, peasants produce only if treated the same way."

From what we can derive from the data of the time, the only source from which there seemed to be at least an "understanding" of what drove people to mabiki—even if not an outright condoning of it—were certain members of the Buddhist clergy. Such priests, certainly far closer both physically and emotionally to both the peasants and the townsfolk, were likely to feel compassion—one the principal Buddhist virtues—for their plight. This sense of compassion can be expected to have been present, even when—as was the case—the Buddhist clergy were themselves at times recruited to carry the anti-mabiki message to the masses.

Still, to be so used was not the same as being committed to the program. We can, I believe, see a fair amount of attitudinal fence sitting, perhaps even mental resistance, on the part of Buddhists to the notion that the people must be pressed into having as many children as possible. As noted above, Miyahiro's diabtribe against Buddhists comes in the context of his condemnation of mabiki. This deserves a closer look.

Although he does not overtly say that Buddhists were giving any articulated opposition to his own cause, it is not too difficult to see a hint of that. When he writes "When we say we need more people in our land that is a far cry from suggesting we need more Buddhist priests," this is not merely to say that Buddhists are useless in some neutral sense. He goes on to say that Buddhists themselves have practices that clearly show that their fundamental ideology differs from those of the neo-Shintoists. They turn young boys into monastics and, thereby, away from the "divine" mandate to be reproductive. They have a philosophy that tolerates the non-use, and therefore the "waste," of sexual organs, organs that the gods want to see maximally used for making children. In that sense Buddhists are not sufficiently "religious"—at least in terms of what Miyahiro thinks to be the essence of religion.

And, of course, he was right in that. However much some of the era's monks may have been happy to be sexually active in brothels, they—as noted earlier—did not do so with the aim of producing offspring. Of course there were priests who had taken wives and had children. But Miyahiro knew that, although rationales for this had been in the works for centuries, the Buddhists themselves were on some levels hamstrung by the part of their tradition that had the greatest textual weight, namely, the part that clearly made the celibate monk the ideal.

Miyahiro knew that and knew it well. He faulted the Buddhists for having a tradition that not only did not prize reproductivity as such but included the monastic practice as a way of implementing nonreproductivity. The Buddhists were in a terrible bind. In actual argument they could not win either way. To go public and say they believed in Miyahiro's version of maximal sexual reproductivity would have made them open repudiators of both Shakyamuni and the bulk of their own central tradition. On the other hand, to say openly that the peasants' need to practice mabiki should even be "understood" would be—especially in the context of the age's inflamed rhetoric—to defend a position that was tantamount to blasphemy vis-à-vis the kami and lèse-majesté with respect to the emperor. Miyahiro and others were turning the screws on the Buddhist clergy, trying to expose something deemed implicit in their position and their religious code—celibacy itself for instance—that in their own ideology constituted insults to the nation, the gods, and the emperor. Buddhists, in their view, were not only unpatriotic but even antipatriotic. And their refusal to embrace fecundism was a part of this. And on this point the Buddhists maintained silence.

Silence may have been wise policy, but that does not mean it is impenetrable. That is, we are not prevented from trying to untangle and lay out the differences here. Although his rhetoric was strident, Miyahiro was not too far off the mark. Even his charges help us to clarify a certain trajectory in Buddhist thinking. In other words, we can be helped even by detractors such as Miyahiro to see something of the structure of Japanese Buddhist thinking about sexuality and reproductivity.

In fact, Miyahiro correctly grasped that within the Buddhist practice there was an implicit position, which, in brief, maintained that *religion and fecundity are not connected.* Miyahiro rightly read it as the opposite of his own position, namely, that reproductivity is the essence of piety. Although Buddhists were traditionally committed to the protection of existing life, they did not grant any religious value to the generating of new life. For monks, having children was an encumbrance to strictly religious aspirations; Shakyamuni referred to his own newborn son as "Rahula" or "hindrance." A refrain running throughout the scriptures is that birth, like death, is pain—not merely to refer to the pain experienced by a woman in labor but to characterize the whole of life. Birth was, according to the early Buddhists, a necessity; but that did not make it "good."

The practical implementation of this view of having children is that, for the most part, Buddhists in Asia have been opposed to abortion—at least officially—but not at all to contraception. That is, they see opposition to abortion as one of the implications of the need to refrain from homicide; at the same time, there is absolutely nothing wrong with preventing conception.

One of the four reasons for expelling a monk from the community had long been the intentional taking of life and this, it was made clear, referred also to embryonic life.[22] One text tells of a woman who, while her husband was away from home, became pregnant by another man. From a monk who received alms from her, she received a preparation that aborted her fetus. The Buddhist community concluded that the monk, although full of remorse, could not be retained within the clerical ranks.[23]

Contraception was very different. A carefully weighed statement on the topic of "birth control" in the *Encyclopaedia of Buddhism* differentiates clearly between contraception used merely to facilitate a promiscu-

ous life-style and that which is used "as an aid to judicious family planning [when] the intention is the avoidance of causing unnecessary misery
in economic and social life."[24] The latter use is viewed as consonant with
Buddhism's emphasis on health as inclusive of positive measures for body
and mind.

Social well-being is also a valid reason for contraception—and even for
such measures to be adopted as government policy. Although this should
never mean enforced sterility to deprive the people of their legitimate
power, an enlightened government, we are told, may adopt birth control
as an instrument of its public policy, with a view to solving a related
number of political, economic, and social problems that have risen
among the people it governs consequent to an excessive birth rate.[25] Buddhism, it is claimed, can have absolutely no objection to that.

Thailand, a largely Buddhist culture, has provided a frequently noted
instance of success in birth control. A study of it during the 1980s concluded,

> We believe that the pace of decline [in fertility] has been facilitated by certain
> aspects of the Thai cultural complex, in particular the Buddhist outlook on life
> and the position of women in Thai society. Buddhism as practised in Thailand
> emphasizes that each individual is responsible for his or her own salvation
> and this undoubtedly contributes to the general tolerance often associated
> with Thai culture. Buddhism contains no scriptural prohibitions against con-
> traception, nor is Buddhist doctrine particularly pro-natalist. . . . Moreover,
> women in Thailand have traditionally experienced relative social and economic
> freedom.[26]

Even casual observers have noted, for instance, that the population pressures in a Buddhist nation such as Thailand are much less severe than in
non-Buddhist India or in the Philippines, which has a largely Catholic
population.

T. O. Ling notes that in Thailand, at least, things are more complex
when it comes to abortion. The public Buddhist stance is very much opposed except when necessary to save a mother's life (91.8 percent in
favor) and for unmarried women (12.7 percent). Ling believes the latter
number is due to "the strong emphasis in Thai Buddhism on the importance of the family context in the rearing of children."[27] Most significantly, however, although in one study almost all women disapproved
of abortion, as many as 25 percent admitted to having taken "action"—
that is, herbal preparations with an abortive effect—to "restart menstrua-
tion" after having missed a period.

Ling sees things as quite different in Sri Lanka, where at times even
contraception has been condemned. The reason for that seems, however,
to be a matter of demographic politics. In the words of one monk, widely

used birth control "would annihilate the Sinhalese people in the course of 20 years." In other words, precisely because the Buddhist Sinhalese population is pitted against a much larger non-Sinhalese one—including support from the Hindu population of the Indian subcontinent—what is perceived as the need to maintain adequate numbers becomes important. Among his conclusions, Ling notes, "In Buddhist countries the acceptance or non-acceptance of population control policies will therefore depend to a large extent on the communal situation, i.e., the relation of Buddhist to non-Buddhist groups within the population."[28] The point of importance, however, is that in the absence of such a concern about a "population war" against other kinds of peoples, even the traditionally "stricter" Buddhists of South Asia tend to have little objection to contraception.

Moral rules, however, are always contexts for negotiation. And what we see in the case of Japan—surely at the geographic far end of Asia and certainly also a place where the population density was very high even some centuries ago—has been the taking of these things one step farther. My claim is that more or less clandestinely in the Edo period and much more openly in the second half of the twentieth century, Japan's Buddhists have shown a tendency to condone not only contraception but abortion as well.

The variation all the way from Sri Lanka to Japan is interesting. It reflects not only a difference in the way the tradition is interpreted but also the impact of other pressures—such as population density—on the reading of a religious tradition. This is a classic case of what can be called moral bricolage and the differences that result from it. The Buddhists of Sri Lanka are probably one extreme and the Japanese the other. The Sinhalese are intensely aware of threats from a competing, non-Buddhist population and are, consequently, most emphatic in wanting to ensure the birth of potential Sinhalese babies. The Japanese lay stress on other matters. The interpretation of tradition, although not merely a reflector of social conditions, is certainly moved in certain directions by them.

One further thing needs noting: although Buddhists were traditionally to refrain from "taking life," their position was not that of the Jains of India, whose concern for life was deontological. The difference is important. Citing the Jains as an instance of absolute scrupulosity in measures taken to avoid life taking, John A. Miles has argued that much of the "pro-life" rhetoric in current abortion debates often disregards the fact that "respect for human life is not an absolute rule within the Judeo-Christian tradition."[29] It seems, in fact, that only the Jains have that—so much so that occasionally the consistent Jain has died by starvation rather than eat animal flesh.

Buddhism is not Jainism. Monks even in South and Southeast Asia are permitted to eat meat if the animals are not killed expressly for them. They are not fanatical about avoiding the accidental killing of insects or even small animals. Of course, in medieval Japan things went farther—considerably. As more and more of the warrior class was introduced to Buddhist teachings, there were doctrinal, even ethical, accommodations to the warrior livelihood. How to be both a warrior and a Buddhist became one of the key discussion nodes wherein doctrine was forced into a marriage with the realities of lay practice in medieval Japan.[30] It is not too difficult to see how it became possible to move from accommodations such as these to allowances for mabiki as well.

Chapter 8

SEX, WAR, AND PEACE

> Demographic "promotion" is just one more step towards
> symbolic extermination.
> (Jean Baudrillard, *Simulations*)

> Oh, brother, I am weeping for you.
> Never let them kill you, brother. . . .
> What does it matter whether Lüshun castle fall or not?
> That kind of thing has nothing to do with us shopkeepers,
>   has it?
> Never let them kill your brother!
> The emperor does not come out to fight.
> How can his noble thoughts allow
> That his subjects should fight bloody battles
> And die like beasts, mistakenly believing
> It is honorable to die?
> (Yosano Akiko,
> *"Never Let Them Kill You, Brother!" [1904]*)

THE MEIJI PUSH

THE NEO-SHINTO program in the world of ideas was undoubtedly going somewhere. It had national visions and goals: a strong Japan able not only to hold its own in the nineteenth century world of the Western colonial powers but in some real sense also itself "imperial." The story of Japan in the later half of the nineteenth century is too well known to need detailed description here. Before that, even within "secluded" Japan there was, of course, a growing sense of how aggressive and demanding the Europeans could be. (In the sixteenth century, Japan had had one taste of an intrusion by the West.) When Suzuki Shigetani wrote, in 1850, of "military preparedness" as part of the reason why Japan needed all the children it could produce, it was not that he had no specific future emergencies in mind. India and other parts of Asia were then already colonized by European powers.

The newly articulate nationalist movements in nineteenth-century Japan were, to a certain extent, saying "It won't happen here!" And when an American, Commodore Matthew Perry (1794–1858) arrived with his "Black Ships" in Edo bay on July 8, 1853, there could no longer be any doubt that the danger was real. From that point on many of the politics and policies actually implemented in Japan were a following out of what the neo-Shinto scholar-polemicists had a decade or two earlier stated as desiderata. In 1868 a new emperor, Meiji, was in place and in this "restoration" a much more activist role was given to the imperial person. Industrialization on a large scale and under national direction was taken up with alacrity.

And, as if to implement Miyahiro Sadao's 1831 vision of a Japan that would be "well populated" and "bustling with people," the crackdown on mabiki was complemented by an active promotion of the concept of the large family. Whenever historians overstress the "newness" of the Meiji period, they tend to overlook the fact that the Meiji government did not differ much from that of the Edo in its willingness to subordinate, if not sacrifice, people's well-being to the goals of production.

With a nation newly coordinated towards centrally defined goals, Meiji Japan was also much more effective than its Edo predecessor in natal promotion and, its logical counterpart, the proscription of abortion. Laws outlawing both infanticide and abortion were promulgated and enforced soon after the beginning of the Meiji era in 1868.

And for the most part they seem to have worked. What had been a stagnant population and a flatness on the demographer's graphs took an upswing—so that by 1920, for instance, the population of Japan had burgeoned to nearly fifty-seven million. Faced with what was seen as a clear challenge from the West, the government of Japan made a decision to play demographic "catch up"; the ensuing all-out Japanese effort to make up for the population "stagnancy" of the Edo period was so successful that by the 1920s and 1930s journalists and politicians in the West had begun to perceive Japan as the opening wedge of a "yellow peril" or "oriental horde" poised to engulf the world. These were decades when nations in the East and West eyed each other with suspicion. In such a situation, population policies and demographic growth were seen as indications of imperialist goals adopted on the opposite side.

Meiji men were encouraged to produce. And Meiji women were enjoined to reproduce. This is not to say that women were not drawn into the labor pool used in the intensified effort to industrialize the country but merely to note that increasingly it became a woman's patriotic duty to produce children. This lashing of women's reproductive capacities to national goals was to remain in force until the end of the Second World War. That is, the practical implementation of the fertility-and-fecundity position of the Edo rhetoricians was carried out in a program that went through the Meiji (1868–1912), the Taishō (1912–1926), and the first twenty years of the long Shōwa (1926–1989) periods.

Notions of the strong family became bound up with those of the strong nation. Kano Masanao depicts in great detail exactly how a relatively private domain, the family, got "sucked up into the nation-state" so that in 1870 even the "modernizing" step of granting commoners the privilege of bearing surnames also made it easier for the central government to keep tabs on individuals.[1] On one level it was an egalitarian step in that it extended the surname right, till then a restricted privilege, to all persons in the realm; on another level, however, it meant that from that point on all individuals were organized into families and all families were to be part of an organized "national family." Family life was encouraged as part of a mechanism of national productivity, and such a program included both carrots and sticks.

This, as Carol Gluck points out, does not mean the family was not under stress and undergoing change. It does suggest, however, that official rhetoric from the central organs of the state had its own program. She writes, "In the face of gesellschaft, gemeinschaft was invoked; confronted with increasing individuation and even anomie, ideologues enshrined the family—the hyphenated metaphor of the family-state in effect sanctifying the family at least as much as it domesticated the state."[2] Words were crucial in marshaling the people.

It is not that Japan was unique in this. In his provocative 1977 study, *La police des familles,* Jacques Donzelot demonstrated, from eighteenth-, nineteenth-, and twentieth-century French materials, how a modern or modernizing government, while addressing social conditions deemed bad, actually extended its *control* over individuals and their family life. Care and even charity, when in the hands of government with laws, courts and police, also becomes regulation, intrusion, and even invasion into the family, a realm some would have preferred to keep as the fortress of privacy.[3]

Of course in the Edo period the population had been under surveillance. During that time various systems were employed whereby groups of households, most often in five- or ten-household units, were consolidated for mutual protection but also for reciprocal watchdogging.[4]

In Meiji Japan, however, such "policing" of the populace became much more sophisticated. The evolution of a concept of national family was not unconnected to the establishment throughout the land of the *kōban* or police-box system.[5] In the 1930s and 1940s, a network of "neighborhood groups" was organized by the government to assist in its effort to keep tabs on the entire population. The people of Japan were having to become accustomed to a modern government with increasingly more modern methods of surveillance and increasingly more intrusive policies.

Jizō—Weeping and Phallic

Needless to say, in this increasingly militarized and imperialized context, demographic promotion became even more important than it had been. Japan's 1905 victory in the Russo-Japanese War came at a cost of 60,083 killed in battle and 21,879 lost through disease.[6] Wars such as that brought territorial gains but lost lives. And to lose lives was to lose population. In such a context there was, at home, a priority placed on mothers' producing sons to fight and die in such wars.

It comes as no surprise, then, that the campaign for even more intense procreation heightened and, conversely, anything that threatened to impede high-quantity childbirth was viewed with government hostility. When Margaret Sanger (1883–1966), the American leader of a birth-control movement, visited Japan in 1921, her activities were closely watched by the police, her pamphlets were confiscated, and a good part of her lecture tour was canceled.

The crackdown on abortion became ever more severe. It had earlier been illegal, but in 1907 penalties for its practice were made much more stringent. The journal *Seitō* (Bluestockings), in the forefront of modern writing by Japanese women and of the expression of women's concerns, was closely watched by government censors. Those censors banned a June 1915 issue that included an essay by Yasuda Satsuki counseling women to have abortions if they thought it necessary, and quite expectably they easily sanctioned an issue of the same journal two months later when an article by Yamada Waka declared both abortion and birth control to be sinful.[7]

The police themselves were directly involved in efforts to frighten people who might be tempted to practice abortion. It seems clear that, even as late as the 1920s and 1930s, the police distributed what were called *mabiki ema*. Ema were small votive pictures, and mabiki ema were a type that graphically portrayed the physical and spiritual hazards of abortion and infanticide.

Historians' keen recent interest in these pictures was kindled initially in Japan because Yanagida Kunio (1875–1962), the lionized founder of folklore studies in Japan, had written in his own autobiography concerning his vivid memories of having seen such mabiki ema in the 1880s. They were, he wrote, hung for public view in the town, in Ibaragi prefecture, where he, from about age thirteen, lived with his older brother. Yanagida wrote further:

What I most vividly recall from the approximately two year period when I lived by the Tone River were the painted ema, donated by someone, that hung in a Buddhist temple by the riverside. It was in a hall that enshrined an image of Jizō and was located on the right when one entered the hall. The scene painted on the votive plaque showed a woman strangling a newborn infant with a twisted towel of the kind that is often worn around the head. A reflection of the same woman seemed mirrored in the paper-screen door behind her—except that in the reflection there were horns that had begun to sprout from her head. Off to one side there was the figure of Jizō, who stood there in tears. Even though still a child, I grasped the import of all this and even now in recalling it I shiver in my inner being.[8]

Recent researchers believe they have located the very temple—named Tokuman-ji—that Yanagida frequented a hundred years ago. They are also quite certain the same votive tablet has been found.[9] It is assumed that a considerable number of such mabiki ema had been distributed throughout that area. The fact that the police had been involved in their distribution became, at least after the war, something of a political problem, and it appears that most such ema were subsequently destroyed.[10]

Having analyzed a considerable number of such mabiki ema that they themselves discovered, Chiba and Ōtsu come to a quite surprising conclusion regarding the dates on the ema. Even taking into account that losses from the earlier period have been greater, they conclude: "Looking at the dates when these votive tablets were made and dedicated, we find many more from the Meiji period, when mabiki practices had supposedly declined, than from the Edo period, when they are thought to have been very common."[11] What we can surmise is that even though the Meiji government had a wider arsenal of tools both to promote population and to curb abortion and infanticide, these may have been much less effective than had earlier been thought. Although the population climbed dramatically, this does not mean that abortion, now necessarily much more clandestine than it had been in Edo, came to a halt. Although even much more "back alley" than before, abortion clearly continued even when the police were on patrol and the government celebrated family life and maximal reproductivity. The very intensity of the campaign with ema testifies to that.

And what has happened to the figure of Jizō in all this? From the evidence of the votive tablet of the Tone River temple and others, Jizō is, at least in part, a bodhisattva that weeps over the death of newborns and fetuses. In this context Jizō too becomes part of the panoply of means used to discourage such practices.

We know from other sources, however, that Jizō was capable of quite another rendering, namely as a phallic form. In that sense this seemingly saintly and innocent Buddhist bodhisattva can, under the aegis of a carver's tools and an onlooker's imagination, quite readily take on the aspect of a potent fertility symbol.

In the view of some, however, the actual history is exactly the reverse: Jizō the Buddhist bodhisattva, at least in Japan, is really an ancient phallic symbol reconstituted and made respectable. Yanagida in his own studies leaned in that direction and indirectly hinted as much. Although he was circumspect about any direct references to sexuality, Yanagida placed Jizō within the ambit of folk religion and Shinto rather than Buddhism.[12] He felt that Jizō, at least in modern times, retained virtually no Buddhist meaning.

Yanagida was a man of the Meiji and, in some sense, even a perpetuator of the Kokugaku stress on Shinto and indigenous forms—at the expense of those, such as Buddhism, that came to Japan from elsewhere.[13] Thus when he notes that Jizō, like the indigenous Dōsōjin deity, was a figure found frequently at crossroads, Yanagida not only assimilates the two but tends automatically to grant a priority to the Dōsōjin form and meaning. And since the Dōsōjin figures typically are a male and female together—and at times even together in an erotic embrace—any association between them and Jizō tends to transfer some of the erotic and reproductive symbolism of the former to the latter.[14]

Although it seems Yanagida went too far in dismissing the Buddhist elements in Jizō, there may have been, especially at the local level, connections between Jizō and the Dōsōjin cult. That helps us account for why in some of the representations of Jizō the erotic and fertility themes become quite explicit.

Whether or not icons of Jizō are phallic may in most instances be "in the eye of the beholder." Surely many stone icons of Jizō, especially if they are worn by the weather to the point where the facial features of the bodhisattva are scarcely detectable, dot the countryside of Japan like simple upright pillars of stone. For such to be viewed as ithyphallic would not, it seems, require much stretch of the imagination.

And sometimes too the artist has pushed the matter. A sculpture in Ueno, in Tokyo, is very explicit. Referred to as the "bearded Jizō," it is, when viewed from the front, a man holding a staff and carrying a body-length cape. When this same Jizō is viewed from the rear—as everyone, of course, is invited to do—the cape has become a glans and the whole figure has an unmistakably phallic design.[15]

What are we to make of these? A common interpretation is that such figures express the Japanese "national personality," which is by nature affirmative of sexuality—so much so that the sexual element shows up even overtly in symbols that are supposed to be religious. In this way religious phallicism is interpreted as evidence of "Japaneseness," a trait of the national personality that is always and everywhere present. Similarly

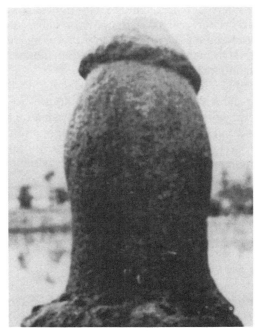

The Jizō at Ueno in Tokyo is a caped man when seen from the front and a phallus when seen from behind.

the open sexuality becomes the native or Shinto element, something surfacing even in Buddhist icons that have their origin abroad and are "negative" about sex.

This interpretation, however, is very problematic. It seems to have its origins in Kokugaku's jingoist effort to differentiate a "positive" Japaneseness from "negative" elements that came in from outside. But it also reads the icons as representing an ongoing, a-historical thing called the Japanese national character. Finally, such an interpretation tries to dissolve the ambiguity: Jizō's *real* meaning is only as a symbol of sex and fertility and everything else is dispensable "cover," a Buddhist overlay that has no real role in what this figure really means.

This interpretation will not suffice. In forming an adequate alternative to it we need, I think, to relate the ambiguity of this image to the *social history* of the period under discussion. That is, we must ask whether that very ambiguity may have been socially useful. Perhaps the clearest thing about the Jizō imagery is that whether dedicated to aborted fetuses or meant to enhance future fertility it is associated with people's deep *anxieties about reproduction*. And such anxiety was, we must recall, greatly deepened when a woman or a couple had already disposed of a fetus in the past. The opponents of mabiki, as we noted, aggravated guilt by emphatically declaring that mabiki was a sin, one that would likely make its practitioners infertile or incapable of giving birth successfully in the future. The tatari, or revenge, of an aggrieved child would, it was often said, find an outlet in the future reproductive or family life of its parents. They were explicitly taught to worry that an abortion could bring harm or death to living offspring.

Thus rather than an indication of some kind of happy, natural attitude about sexuality, the widely distributed Jizō sculptures in Japan tell us a tale about fear and worry. And this was a worry that an act of mabiki had offended the gods and that the gods would punish in return. The fact that the majority of the extant ithyphallic Jizō come from historical epochs when reproduction was a politically sensitive matter in Japan is itself worthy of notice. That is, in times when abortion was criminalized and women were, in fact, marshaled by state purposes to do their duty as maximal childbearers, it makes sense to see the prevalence of these figures as connected with social facts such as these. But more can be said.

AMBIGUITY AS A RUSE

Japanese scholars suggest that at least since the Edo period much of the Jizō cult had the bulk of its support from local groups, comprised mostly of women, organized into confraternities to take care of the Jizō icons.

This continued down through the Meiji, Taishō, and early Shōwa periods. I would insist, however, that we need to see this as more than an expression of spontaneous piety. That is, I think it important to see that such women were also propelled into devotion to Jizō by a good deal of anxiety over what was happening to them as women and mothers.

To Jizō are attached a variety of functions and attributions. The two of greatest importance for us are: *mizuko Jizō* for deceased children and fetuses and *koyasu Jizō* for assistance in conception and birth. Many Jizō icons easily embrace both of these functions.

The fact of this double aspect may initially seem like a puzzle. Prayers for increased fertility and successful childbirth may—to us at least—seem strange if addressed to the same deity to whom are directed prayers on behalf of children intentionally "returned" to the unseen world. We may wonder whether such people were not mentally confused, simultaneously wanting to bring more children into the world and getting rid of others already on the way. Yet there is nothing illogical in this; the social context can explain it well.

In fact, the linkage between the Jizō who ensures good births and the one who takes care of children intentionally jettisoned from the womb and from this world is not difficult to see. A woman or a couple that decides not to give birth to the fetus currently in the womb may have every reason to want a child conceived at some later time. If this is true for persons today, it would certainly have been true in Japan during the time under consideration. The immediate reasons for not wanting a child could have been many: unintended conception while unmarried, physical depletion because of recent illness or childbearing, current famine, or unusual "hard times" for the family—these and other reasons would have been enough to convince Edo, Meiji, Taishō, or Shōwa women or couples to resort to the mizuko alternative. At the same time, however, such persons would want to do all in their power to retain their potentiality for childbearing. "Not now," for many such people, obviously would not have meant "never."

In one sense there was probably what we might call an "irrational" element in this—namely, a deep fear that the very act of making a mizuko was a "sin" of the type that might bring retribution in the form of later infertility or miscarriages when wellborn babies would be desired. This is precisely a common structure of fear in Japanese couples who today get abortions; it makes sense to think that Japanese in earlier ages would have had even more fear of such tatari or retribution. A later chapter will explore how this structure of belief concerning revenge from the other world has carried down to the present day.

This anxiety about retaliation from wronged mizuko compounded what must have been a fear of the authorities as well. It is important to keep in mind that no matter how much women within their own societies might understand one another's need for recourse to mabiki, since the third quarter of the nineteenth century these had become criminal acts that were severely prosecuted. The whole ideology of the period was bent on producing a sense of motherhood that would make women feel a kind of sacred, patriotic obligation to bear all the children they possibly could. Not only was there an informal, local surveillance of this aspect of private life but the police, as we have seen, were also actively providing communities with little votive tablets that graphically portrayed practitioners of mabiki as horrible creatures, demonic child-killers whose unseen but real visage included bestial horns that had sprouted on their heads.

Such women had reason to fear harm from both supernatural and governmental sources. In *all* such contexts of anxiety about reproduction, the prudent course would have been for a woman not to avoid Jizō but to pay close—even lavish—attention to him and what he symbolized. Jizō was, in Buddhist terms, a bodhisattva who could reverse the karmic effect of bad past behavior. Here was a figure that, if properly treated, would care for a parent's past mizuko in the other world and at the same time keep alive the possibility of conception if needed or desired later. A parent who, by attention to Jizō, could palliate the negative effects emanating from a wronged fetus also could, with much less fear, expect success in marital relations, in giving birth, and in raising the siblings of the mizuko. Jizō made all the critical difference in this. Parents may even have thought that Jizō might be able to keep the intrusive Meiji police and government at bay.

However irrational such anxieties may seem—at least to a more modern and "emancipated" consciousness—it should be noted that the persons concerned were living within their own time and the possibilities it allowed. And in that sense there were elements of surprising *rationality*. That is, obviously people's fear did not so cripple them that they refrained from infanticide or abortion when they deemed such to be necessary or desirable. In fact, we can assume that the structure of religious belief gave such women the capacity to circumvent the government's strict prohibition of abortion. We can assume that they, knowing their own bodies and knowing also their personal or family finances, were in fact making totally rational choices when they decided to terminate a particular pregnancy. Yet they also knew that the termination of a particular pregnancy was not meant to be the end of reproductive capacities. They clearly knew the difference between "not now" and "never." They also knew that the government was not, by its policies, allowing them to make such a choice.

Jizō did. Jizō for them was not just a Buddhist bodhisattva but a whole fabric of possibilities—within other worlds but also clearly within this one too. And that would seem to have been the meaning of seeing the Jizō of fertility and easy births as essentially one with the Jizō of dispatched fetuses. There was, I suggest, uncommon reasonableness in the thinking and symbolic world of the women who gave their own shape to the Jizō cult and organized their confraternities to that end.

Of course, especially before 1945, *to be seen* paying at lot of personal attention to a Jizō specifically identified with mizuko would have been less than prudent. After all, the government was fiercely opposed not only to infanticide but also to abortion.

This raises an interesting possibility. In contrast to contemporary Japan, wherein abortion is legal and people feel unafraid to make open visits to temples or cemeteries exclusively devoted to mizuko rites—and advertised and labeled as such!—during the period when abortion was illegal in Japan the designation of Jizō that would in any way hint at abortion seems to have been next to nonexistent. What we find during the Meiji, Taishō, and early Shōwa eras is a more "generic" Jizō, or a Jizō with a variety of other specifications. These allowed, I suggest, for a *necessary* and much-valued ambiguity. In the era of close surveillance, it was largely in the "heart" of the devotee that the *real reason* for attending to such a Jizō could lie hidden; although in fact it could have been to pray for an aborted fetus, to all outer appearances it could also be to pray for another conception. Who except the worshiper could possibly know? It is quite likely that many of the omnipresent "easy birth" Jizō of that period served in this double, ambiguous way as well. For even in prayers the subtext can differ dramatically from the main text or from the public purposes for which the "house" of prayer was supposedly established.

The subtext can even at times be a *subversion* of the main text. The fact that Japanese women were not always praying for fertility at such shrines and temples in Japan is shown in a recent study. During the Meiji period, among a rather wide set of quasi-superstitious practices to avoid conception, Japanese women also went to shrines and temples, but they carried rather unusual gifts, and close attention to these is illuminating. For instance, in some Buddhist temples there can be found sideshrines devoted to Kishimojin, an Indian demoness (Harītī) who, according to legends, devoured children by the thousands until she was converted by the Buddha. In her converted, Buddhist form, however, she is usually invoked by women seeking to be fertile or to have an easy childbirth. This is the usual understanding and use of such shrines—very common especially in temples associated with the Nichiren school of Buddhism. New studies, however, show that in the city of Kanazawa, women turned the practice to virtually opposite goals. The usual custom was to bring some kind of household pot or container—as a symbol of a uterus needing to be filled—to Kishimojin. Some women, however, brought containers with an opposite message. For offerings they brought cloth bags whose bottom had not been sewn closed or bamboo water ladles whose bottom had been torn away. The implicit request, then, was not for fertility but for its opposite.

Likewise, although at shrines known for assisting fertility it was customary to present stones as a tangible expression of one's prayers for a child, some women took an opposite approach and presented their stones to the Shinto god of the toilet, the place where one disposes of things that have passed *through* the body.[16]

These were not so much rejections of religion per se as they were a turning of religion to personal purposes different, and even at odds with, the normal institutional intention. Out of their own private needs, these women were creating their own variants within the larger religious system of symbols—and doing so in inventive ways.

Not all powerful supernatural figures could be expected equally to grasp a woman's real situation. Tactics had to be adjusted. Jizō, it was assumed, was ruled by the virtue of compassion and could, therefore, usually be expected to show mercy not only to aborted children but also to their desperate parents. A bit more obdurate were the Shinto kami, primarily because from antiquity many of them were related to fertility and fecundity; since compassion was not classically their main characteristic, they had, in fact, to be "turned"—that is, implored and perhaps even tricked into becoming allies. The women who took their stones to the god of the toilet rather than the god of fertility were doing precisely that.

Most difficult and intransigent among all authorities, of course, were the mundane ones, the government and the police. There was no recourse but to deal with them by ruse. Jizō's very ambiguity, then, provided such women with a way of circumventing the authorities, a mode of what should be recognized as the astute and self-protective cleverness often shown by common folk. For these persons, perhaps compelled, by a sense of sorrow or guilt, to mourn and do rites for their mizuko and at the same time afraid of detection by the authorities, there were generic and "easy birth" Jizōs in abundance. Moreover, who could fault a woman for noncompliance with the goverment's fecundity program if she were to be *seen* publically paying obeisance to a bodhisattva dedicated to "easy births" and one that many saw as having a phallic shape?

An ambiguity in the meaning of icons is often attributed to a conceptual fuzziness in religion itself. But that is the interpretation of the theorist in quest of a pure, unmetaphorical "rationality." It also happens to be a peculiarly modern kind of quest. Common people, by contrast, often take a more pragmatic approach. The multivalence of religious symbols fits their real need. To some extent, their religious-symbol system is their own creation—not just, as Marxist theory would have it, a system imposed on them by authorities wanting to profit from it. To the extent that the symbols are their own and are for their own ends, believers can treat them as *malleable*. This also means for them that icons can provide ways of covering up an "inner intention" with an "outer form."

Actually, Japanese history includes some fascinating examples of the strategic and creative use of ambiguity in religious icons. Most notable are those used by Japan's "hidden Christians" during the centuries when Christianity was prohibited there. Great cleverless was exercised. Multiple Buddhist images, especially those of Kannon, clandestinely served as icons of the Virgin Mary. Teacups had hidden crosses in their designs.

If the clever piety of Japan's hidden Christians had been creative enough to find ways to worship Mary under the guise of images to Kannon, what would have prevented oppressed Japanese women from praying for the well-being of their own aborted fetuses in rituals devoted to a figure, Jizō, who could always at least *publicly* be referred to as the divine figure who ensures many and safe births? Such women may have had no intention whatsoever of bearing more children. In their own minds they could be hidden "naysayers" in an era when they were being pushed by the government to have more children. In public, however, they could be widely seen going to pay homage to Jizō, a sometimes ithyphallic figure and well-known giver of children.

Jizō, I am suggesting, provided precisely this kind of ambiguity. For women who wanted no more pregnancies it was a ruse. Perhaps here was a classic case of what some social scientists refer to in Japanese society as the capacity to maintain both *honne*, "one's natural, real, or inner wishes and proclivities," and *tatemae*, "the standard, principle, or rule by which one is bound at least outwardly."[17] Here was a way of acting so as to show total, even "religious," compliance with the government's pressure on women to give maximal uterine yield, but having in fact been involved in mabiki. It is, then, no reason for surprise that figures of Jizō could be found all over the land and were worshiped by women in vast numbers. Jizō in these times and for women with such needs was clearly the god of choice.

WAR AND FECUNDITY

One of the great ironies of modern Japan is that whereas the resource needs of a burgeoning home population were often cited as reasons for the necessity of military conquest in other parts of Asia, the Japanese government soon found itself calling on its people to produce even more people to be able to bear arms. But males sent into the military, especially if dispatched abroad, were not at home to father children. More seriously, an increasing rate of death in battle meant that the real population of Japan began to suffer precisely when its need for soldiers was at its greatest.

To the rulers of Japan these were disturbing facts. As Japan's war in Asia progressed, it became clear to them that the birth rate had to be advanced. Between 1920 and 1940, the population had grown from nearly fifty-seven million to seventy-three million, but that was, in their eyes, not sufficient. Already in 1934 there had been as many as 965 arrests for abortion crimes. And, as Ella Wiswell's fascinating and candid account of mid-1930s village life in a rural area of Kyushu indicates, village people were aware that abortions were prohibited by law, although they strongly felt that farming families were having more children than could reasonably be cared for. In discussing measures for birth control, Wiswell found her women informants eager to hear what she had to say about contraception in America. She writes, "I explained how [contraception] works. They asked: And your government does not fine you? I said it does not. Here, they said, the government punished you for doing such things, so you must have five, ten, twelve—any number of children. That is why people must emigrate to America; there are too many children here, they said."[18] This was in 1936. Although it is possible that the women knew a fair amount about "contraception" through mabiki methods, they seem not to have mentioned that to Wiswell. Dominant in their consciousness and in their words to her was the fact of the government's stringent policies.

During precisely these years, the Japanese government became worried about a laggard population growth, which was not up to what it had been before 1937. By the early 1940s, further incentives were introduced. A tax on single persons was introduced. The employment of women over twenty, who were expected to be married, involved in reproduction, and at home for such purposes, was restricted. Loans were given to those planning marriage. Families with more than ten children were promised free higher education for them.

A deep ambivalence about women moving into the workplace, as Thomas R. H. Havens has shown, characterizes this period. With their own workforce needs in wartime, England and America brought larger numbers of women into the factories; by contrast, many in the Japanese govenment, who were facing a labor shortage that was, if anything, even more severe than that of their enemies, retained the concept of women being needed at home.[19]

In 1940 a National Eugenics Law reiterated the illegality of abortion and made the penalties more severe than ever. In 1941 marriage-counseling centers were set up in order "to cause women to move from an individualist view of marriage to a national one and to make young women recognize motherhood as the national destiny."[20] The wife of General Tōjō Hideki, prime minister from 1941 to 1944, was personally pressed into setting an example. She "cheerfully announced that 'having babies is fun,' and told her fellow country-women to shirk all luxuries so that they could afford to raise large families."[21]

Natalism was the order of the day—in a most literal sense. It was as if history were playing out a scenario that neo-Shinto thinkers such as Suzuki Shigetani, Miyauchi Yoshinaga, and Miyahiro Sadao had written down a hundred years earlier. Now, however, there existed the enforcement powers of a centralized government such as these neo-Shintoist writers had not had in their own time. During war, a hundred years later, their themes were being articulated into edicts and policies: the relinquishing of private selfishness in reproductive matters, the absolute priority of national goals, and the coupling of the ideal of a large population to the staffing needs of the military. Such policies echoed the texts of a century earlier: "For a couple to have children and heirs is part of its supreme duty with respect to the realm." "A castle, even when well-built, requires soldiers to defend it."

What the militarist rulers of the early 1940s did not have to make explicit was that having children was a *religious* obligation. This was so thoroughly worked into the national polity that it was already perfectly clear to all. It was not necessary to say explicitly, "the gods intend humans to be prolific," or to fantasize in public about deities made happy by sexual organs doing what the gods had fashioned them to do.

The religious importance of devotion to national goals was perfectly well known to the wartime Japanese. In ways that would have immensely pleased the nativist Kokugaku scholars of the late Edo period, Shinto by the 1930s and early 1940s had been given a hegemonic place in the national panoply of religions. Official verbiage about the equality of all religions in Japan disguised the fact that by virtue of there now being something called "State Shinto" this form of religion, identified by a nationalist state as indigenous rather than imported from abroad, had in imperial Japan become not just a type of civil religion but one very tightly and ritually intermeshed with the Japanese goverment and its designs. Joseph M. Kitagawa traced this development from the Edo period: in the offical suppression of Buddhism in the 1870s; in the establishment of a Tokyo shrine, later named *Yasukuni* (pacifying the nation), to honor those who had died in the royalist cause; and in the progressive cultification of the emperor as a Shinto deity.[22]

If the neo-Shinto thinkers of the 1840s worried about Buddhists and the fact that the Buddhist principle of "house departure" and celibacy might have a baneful effect on fecundity and nation building, there was no comparable concern in the 1940s. Buddhists by that point had, with only minor exceptions, been completely co-opted and drawn into the nationalist religious program for all. The government had become total. Such totalitarianism sucked up all religions into its goals.

LEGALIZATION

During the early phase of World War II, when Japan was fighting an aggressive war in China, almost 200,000 Japanese troops were killed. This number was later greatly superseded. By tallying in civilian deaths and even the many Japanese who died by starvation and disease in the months after war's end in 1945, it is reasonable to state that 2,500,000 Japanese lost their lives.[23] While considerably less than the numbers of Soviets, Chinese, and Jews killed in that war, the Japanese losses were heavy. The rate of Japanese deaths, both military and civilian, rose incrementally as the war years passed. In the final days alone, approximately 250,000 died in the nuclear blast over Hiroshima and another 120,000 in that of Nagasaki.

During that war, Osamu Dazai, perhaps one of the premier Japanese writers of our century, traveled back to his ancestral home in northern Japan. His fascinating memoir of these travels is superficially in line with government policies of the day. But subtle notes of discord can be detected. I find an especially interesting one in the following passage:

> "That's the memorial shrine for the war dead over there. They've just finished it," Keiko told me, pointing upstream. "The shrine Daddy's so proud of," she added softly, with a smile.
>
> It seemed to be a splendid building. Mr. Nakabata is on the board of the veterans' organization. No doubt he demonstrated that gallant spirit of his when it came to work on the shrine.
>
> We had crossed over and stopped at the foot of the bridge to talk a while.
>
> "I hear there are so many apple trees now, they cut them down in places—they call it 'thinning,' don't they?—and then plant things like potatoes instead.
>
> "Maybe it depends on where you are. I've never heard of them doing anything like that around here."[24]

After so much patriotic chatter about the war dead and heroism, Dazai rather abruptly moves the conversation to rumors of "thinning" in the apple orchards. That, however, is emphatically denied by the locals.

The juxtaposition in the text hardly seems accidental. Perhaps in this subtle way Dazai is putting his own gloss on the pious talk about death in war. Although it is the government's doing, is it so different from the horticulturist's thinning of orchards? Or the rice farmer's culling of rice seedlings?[25] Perhaps Dazai was suggesting that the war was involved in population control—much like Malthus's God, who uses wars, famine, and disease to sharpen the wits of the Europeans.[26]

In any case, World War II took its toll of Japanese and by the end of that war these facts were both undeniable and unpalatable to most people. The death of so many Japanese was quickly followed, in 1945, by the death of the ideology that had propelled the war. In the days, months, and years of the postwar period, the Japanese became deeply aware, through their own bitter experience, of how ironic and tragic the *actual* results of a program of demographic promotion can be. Natalism, especially when pushed by a totalitarian state, can itself lead to death on a mass scale—even the depletion of a population. In Japan the horrible experience of the war discredited the nineteenth-century claim that above all the Shinto gods wanted to see Japan as "a well-populated place, bustling with people."

In the immediate postwar years during the American occupation of Japan, there was a population growth—not dictated by policy but a natural result of the repatriation of many Japanese men and their return to a more normal family life. As the ironies multiplied, it was *then* that a "baby boom" occurred. What the wartime natalists had dreamed of in terms of population was happening after the war was over and they had been stripped of power.

Such a birth rate, however, was not really a boon in a nation still suffering a severe scarcity of resources. Many babies were unwanted and could not be cared for; the rate of infanticide and abandonment rose dramatically. These conditions for mothers and children led to the politics necessary to bring about, at long last, the decriminalization of abortion.

In July 1948, in a move supported by members from the ranks of all five major political parties, the Eugenic Protection Law was passed.[27] Among its provisions was one that, among various reasons for permitting abortion, stipulated the "health of the mother." It was not difficult to interpret that as including mental well-being. In 1952 a further amendment to the law left matters up to the discretion of a physician, who did not otherwise have to justify his or her decision to any governmental authority.

Although occasioned by the dire conditions of the postwar context, the steady move in the direction of a liberal abortion law in Japan must also be seen as a conscious attempt to put aside once and for all the politics of natalism. It is interesting to note that this liberal sequence of laws was passed during a time when Japan was officially under American occupation. Opinions of observers differ considerably as to whether this legislation passed in spite of resistance from General Douglas MacArthur and his staff or with their tacit approval.

During the following decades, abortion in Japan became, for all practical purposes, *the* chief means of birth control. This has been partially because of a persistant unwillingness on the part of Japanese males to be co-responsible for birth control.[28] Condoms are easily available and, in fact, in most urban centers are sold in coin-operated dispensers. Yet the medical establishment in Japan has resisted efforts to have "the pill" readily available. Coleman comments, "At its heart the doctors' stance reflects a lack of interest in providing contraception. Although there are specialists with genuine apprehensions about the widespread effects of pill use, such concerns are not sufficient to explain the medical community's support of a categorical governmental ban on one of the world's most widely used contraceptives."[29] The claim by many in Japan's women's movement—often shared by observers from outside Japan—is that it may well be because abortion is so lucrative to doctors that they have resisted making the Pill available.[30]

In any case, as Coleman and others have documented beyond doubt, the abortion rate in Japan is so high largely because for so many couples it turns out to be the main contraceptive method. He writes, "The Japanese pattern stands out among affluent industrialized countries because married couples rely heavily on induced abortion. . . . [Many couples] rely upon condoms and the calculation of the female reproductive cycles. A country that is ultramodern in so many other respects has a family planning technology that was created in the 1930s."[31] If there are to be changes, they will, it appears, come about primarily through the efforts of the women themselves, including their lobbying for such change.[32]

In conjunction with the high rate of abortion in postwar Japan, there has been a marked increase in the number of persons who go to temples for memorial rites for aborted fetuses. This increase was at first little noticed, but from the mid-1970s it began to receive increased media attention and closer scrutiny. Commentators referred to Japan not only as an "abortion heaven" but also as experiencing a "mizuko boom." During the 1980s there was growing concern about certain aspects of this phenomenon—even though voices calling for a rollback of legalized abortion remain comparatively few. The charges of some of these critics will be looked at more closely in a later chapter.

Here a couple of things, however, can be noted. First, due to the decriminalization of abortion and wide public acceptance of it, there is no longer a need for women to be terribly cautious and clandestine about having had one. At the same time decriminalization has meant that it is no longer necessary to conceal Jizō's mizuko role under the guise of a cult

In 1968 a woman prays before inchoate, fetoid images in a portion of a traditional temple posted as dedicated to mizuko Jizō rites. (Tokyo.)

publically intended to enhance childbirth. Whereas once it was necessary or at least prudent to hang out the shingle of "safe childbirth" on images of Jizō, nowadays people can be more forthright. Cemeteries for mizuko memorials are labeled as such, and no one bothers to disguise the fact that it is almost exclusively aborted fetuses that are memorialized there. There is an openness about abortion that would have been inconceivable during the war years and unlikely during much of the Meiji period. Today many temples that offer such services, especially if they are virtually the raison d'être of such temples, are not at all loath to advertise in newspapers.

Second, it seems clear that the mainline Buddhist sects of Japan have slowly taken such rites under the umbrella of services they offer the general public. It seems not to have begun thus. As noted above, in the Edo and Meiji periods it was probably the local associations of women who, in devoting themselves to Jizō, found in such informal practice a mode through which they could—as prudently as possible—give ritual attention to aborted fetuses and children never allowed to live. Today, when the word *mizuko* has come—in the public consciousness at least—to refer almost exclusively to aborted fetuses, increasing numbers of mainline Buddhist temples are willing to provide such rites.

They caught on slowly. And it appears that they are reacting to the fact that for some time now, in response to rising abortion rates, unaffiliated institutions of a clearly entrepreneurial character jumped into the picture. These new, business-oriented "temples" tended not only to cash in—most literally—on the new public need but also to make the older temples unable or unwilling to meet a real needs of their parishioners. The priests of established temples were forced to worry when their parishioners called to ask why the family's traditional temple did not provide mizuko rites. This led, in turn, to anxiety about eventually losing parishioners.

Put in strictly business terms, the abortion boom had opened up a new market, and some newcomers on the field looked like they were ready to move in to capture all of it. Priests in the older, mainline Buddhist denominations had many qualms: they did not like the crassly commercial way the new temples sold their services, the advertisements they ran in public media, and the way they intimidated people by talk about tatari, or retribution, from mizuko. The Jōdo Shinshū, Japan's largest mainstream denomination, had originally hoped to take a firm stand against the provision of mizuko rites in its temples.

Yet there has been a fair amount of pragmatism of approach. And in one temple after another the mizuko rites—and small cemeteries for memorials—have been appearing. Not the older, generic Jizō but a Jizō explicitly labeled as having a special concern for jettisoned fetuses is being brought into the practice of the mainline Buddhist temples in Japan.

A Tokyo newspaper includes this advertisement, in which a temple claims to be unexcelled in northeastern Japan in its mizuko rites and ability to exorcize malign influences.

PART THREE

CONTEMPORARY ISSUES

Chapter 9

APOLOGY

> Yen Hui asked about Goodness. The Master said, He who
> can himself submit to ritual is Good.
> (Confucius, *Analects*)

> The one way to make bereavement tolerable is to make
> it important. To gather your friends, to have a gloomy
> festival, to talk, to cry, to praise the dead—all that does
> change the atmosphere, and carry human nature over
> the open grave. The nameless torture is to try and
> treat it as something private and casual.
> (G. K. Chesterton, *Lunacy and Letters*)

FUNERALS FOR NEEDLES

THE HISTORY surveyed in Part Two naturally shapes contemporary Japanese attitudes and practices with respect to abortion. Here, however, we need to look in detail at the concrete ways individuals deal with abortion in their lives—and at the kinds of debates and disputes that have arisen in today's Japan over those methods. The topic of this chapter is the ritualization of attitude with respect to aborted fetuses.

The central ritual for mizuko is of a type the Japanese call *kuyō*. The two words are frequently joined in the phrase *mizuko kuyō*. To explore kuyō, it is first of all important to see that on one level it is shared throughout the Buddhist world in Asia. The root concept comes from the Sanskrit term *pūjana*, which refers to those acts of ritual and worship through which Buddhists express their respect for the Buddha, the Teaching, and the Community. Gifts of flowers, incense, oil, food, and the like were ritually presented at Buddhist temples and shrines—and all of these activities were embraced by this concept. The major sutras of Buddhism are replete with descriptions of how kuyō is done and what kind of benefits accrue to the person who does it.

Gifts and ritual services, however, can also be dedicated to the dead. In fact even merit can be transferred to the dead. And this is, apparently, not an East Asian twist on the early tradition but one that can be found within the cultures—for instance, that of Sri Lanka—that take pride in being true to the earliest forms of Buddhism. In an important study, Richard F. Gombrich has shown that rituals for the dead, although doctrinally hard to reconcile with the earliest teachings of the Buddha, are nonetheless important to Sri Lankan Buddhists. These are instances of "Buddhicizations of practices . . . which afford some psychological relief from the oppressive doctrine of man's total responsibility for his own fate."[1] Ritual, in that sense, provides for human, emotional needs neglected by the more bare, orthodox tradition.

The notion of some kind of rites for dead relatives seems to have been part of Buddhism in all the cultures into which it penetrated. Careful observers of Japan have noted that the Japanese quickly became, for a variety of reasons, especially fond of this notion and extended it to all kinds of matters never before thought worthy of kuyō. Some go on to see the way the Japanese carry this out as a rather significant difference between them and others. They suggest it is a difference that non-Japanese do well to attend to closely if they wish to locate an aperture for looking deeply into Japanese values. Toward the end of his life, Hiroshi Wagatsuma, an anthropologist who spent many years living and teaching in both Japan and North America, wrote a little book in Japanese that he hoped might bridge the cultural gaps that sometimes lie behind international tensions. It is, I think, significant that Wagatsuma singled out the kuyō ritual as one of the things that, though readily understood by Japanese, might prove next to incomprehensible to Americans. In Wagatsuma's interpretation, the kuyō is a context where it is clear that Buddhist rituals had absorbed and retained very archaic forms and values.

If Wagatsuma thought it important to explain to the Japanese why this would be difficult for Western people to grasp, it would seem worthy of our attention. Perhaps the most striking instances are those—still very much practiced in contemporary society—in which Japanese will perform services of kuyō for clearly inanimate objects that have been part of their lives in some especially intimate way. What is important is that such objects are personalized and then ritually inducted into a state of "ease." A classic case to which Wagatsuma called attention is called *hari kuyō* or "the memorial service for needles." The heart of this ritual is an action performed by women who have collected all the old, dulled, and broken needles they have used at home. Having taken these to a Buddhist temple or Shinto shrine, the women will do the following—as narrated by Wagatsuma:

> The women pray that these needles may now enter into a deserved Buddhahood. There in the temple or shrine they pass these through a block of beancurd [tofu, an eminently soft substance]. In effect they say: "You needles have spent your lives doing hard work. You unstintingly gave of yourselves by again

and again going through tough pieces of cotton cloth—even suffering in such labors. Now lie down on this mattress of bean-curd and take your rest." In this way the women humanize their treatment of even a piece of metal.[2]

If there can be such a thing as a funeral for needles, this certainly is it.

I have been present at temple services where men and women who practice the Japanese tea ceremony bring forward the small bamboo tea whisks they have used for months or years to whip up tea into a broth for guests. These wisks are presented to the altar, addressed with words of thanks and appreciation for their good service, and then ritually burned—a kind of Buddhist "cremation" of a tea whisk. The list of objects given a ritual dispatch through kuyō is really quite long and includes not only sewing needles but also those used for innoculations. Old clocks, dolls, chopsticks, and pairs of spectacles are also treated through the kuyō ritual. Perhaps one of the most unusual—and new—ceremonies of kuyō was performed a few years ago when, in the Zōjō-ji temple in Tokyo, words of thanks were intoned to a collection of 200,000 brassieres that had been collected from their owners. Before these items of inimate apparel were properly cremated, the chorus of the Yokohama City University gave a rendition of Mozart's "Ave Verum Corpus," which, at least as I read Latin, means—appropriately or not—"Hail to the true body."

In such contexts it is clear that the ritual is one of thanks, not the expression of some feeling of guilt. There is not the slightest suggestion that the participants feel there is something slightly wrong or unseemly about their daily "use" of needles, brassieres, and tea whisks. Such clearly inanimate objects are being thanked as part of a self-reminder that even "things" are not to be heedlessly or wastefully used.

I suggest that the matter is a bit different, however, when the object of the ritual is an animal. Buddhists in medieval Japan, thinking of animals as bound up, along with humans, in the cycle of transmigration, had qualms about eating meat. Although those qualms have largely disappeared in modern times, there remains among some people a sense that animals ought—at least occasionally—to be thanked for the sacrifice of their lives. This, for instance, is the case with animals that have been used for laboratory experiments—animals that are at times memorialized in kuyō ceremonies.

Annually in Japan there is an autumnal rite of kuyō for eels. Through the medium of national television, each year presents select restaurateurs and their customers, people who love to eat eels, gathered by an altar while Buddhist priests intone the words of sutras to express thanks to the eels for having been so nourishing and for having such a delicious taste. Of course, in this—especially when the whole rite is projected to the nation via the nightly news—the Japanese tell themselves once again that their ties with antiquity are intact and that they as a people are not ingrates or irreligious, however much they consume eels with great relish most of the time. Since there is "life" in animals of this type, these rituals are not just matters of thanks. There is also an element of apology in them.

There is, of course, a great jump in gravity when a kuyō is provided for an aborted fetus. However much an individual may wish to "humanize" his or her relationship with household items or even with foodstuffs, there is something obviously different—categorically so—about the human fetus. This difference is one that, in fact, gains in significance when placed against the background of the thread of similarity running through all kuyō rites. That is, if many Japanese are concerned to state through ritual that even inanimate objects like needles and chopsticks are "humanizable" so as to express the intimacy of our relationship to them, it must be all the more so that fetuses are not only "humanizable" but even *human* in some real sense. If tea whisks, dolls, and research animals ought to be dispatched into their own kinds of "Buddhahood" in a proper way and with the right kind of rituals on their behalf, it is all the more true that fetuses require ritual.

This is to say that the underlying motive for kuyō for fetuses is significantly stronger than that for eels or research animals. These gradations are significant. If it is thanks in the case for needles, thanks mixed with a modicum of directed guilt with respect to eels, it has become almost exclusively guilt when fetuses are involved. And when guilt is present, the attitude of the "user" becomes more apologetic than merely appreciative. Kuyō, in fact, could be viewed on a scale of graduated seriousness as follows:

To needles, tea-whisks, and so on: thanks
To eels, laboratory animals: thanks/apology
To aborted fetuses: apology

These differentiations lie on a continuum.

This means that, at least in certain areas, the differentiation between gratitude and guilt is not very sharp in Japanese. Thanks shades off into guilt, and guilt easily becomes a kind of gratitude; the area of overlap can be considerable.

The Japanese practice of addressing apologies to aborted fetuses conforms well, in fact, with what scholars have discovered about the rather extraordinary role of apology in that culture generally, even in criminal proceedings. In an essay that brought forward some striking instances in showing how the Japanese legal system could get along with many fewer formal, punitive sanctions than our own, John O. Haley, in 1982, wrote, "Confession, repentance, and absolution provide the underlying theme of Japanese criminal process. At every stage, from initial police investigation through formal proceedings, an individual suspected of criminal conduct gains by confessing, apologizing, and throwing himself upon the mercy of the authorities."[3] Haley argued that in Japan apology constitutes an alternative "track" for dealing with crime and wrongdoing and that persons who apologize both expect and receive much more lenient treatment than otherwise would be the case.

Wagatsuma and Rosett pursued the cultural contrasts that must be figured into this difference in Japanese legal practices—pointing out, for instance, that "in the United States, the relative absence of recognition of apology may be related to the observed tendency of American society to overwork formal legal processes and to rely too heavily on the adjudication of rights and liabilities by litigation."[4] In fact, the contrast is often sharp. They noted, "Many Japanese seem to think it better to apologize even when the other party is at fault, while Americans may blame others even when they know they [themselves] are at least partially at fault."[5] The use of written apologies (*shimatsusho*) to the police is another widespread means of handling such problems.[6]

If there exists in Japan this cultural inclination to use apology widely and frequently to restore relationships and solve societal problems—a proclivity that extends deeply even into the realm of law—we need not be surprised to see the same thing coming into play when persons feel they have "wronged" a fetus and seek a way to deal with that problem. To restore homeostasis in this arena too an act of apology is expected to be effective. In this there is no structural difference between what is assumed to "work" in mundane interpersonal relationships and in the more metaphysical one between parents and a fetus aborted and dispatched to some world "beyond." Likewise, the practice of making out written apologies has a parallel here, since mizuko too are frequently addressed in brief letters of apology that are placed at temples dedicated to their memorialization.

Wagatsuma and Rosett also affirm that in the Japanese the differentiation between words of apology and words of thanks is often not sharp.[7] Conceptually too there often is overlap. But, as has been argued here before, conceptual imprecision often makes for ease of performance. Apology can overlap with gratitude. There is no great need to determine precisely whether one is addressing a guilt-presupposing "apology" to a mizuko or merely expressing "thanks" to it for having vacated its place in the body of a woman and having moved on, leaving her—and her family—relatively free of its physical presence.

Mizuko Kuyō

Today the mizuko kuyō can be performed in many different ways. It comes in a wide variety of sizes, types, and costs. And monetary cost, of course, is usually directly correlated to the elaborateness of the ceremony and whether religious experts—priests and the like—are to officiate.

The simplest rite of all is probably the one with the oldest pedigree— that is, the one carried out by local women who have organized themselves into a confraternity to take care of the local Jizō shrine or shrines. This involves a kind of perpetual care for a simple sculpture or sculptures at a junction of streets—or at a roadside. The care involves putting out flowers in front of the icon, washing it down from time to time, and lighting a few sticks of incense once in a while. These Jizō shrines, whose otherworldly protection extends both to deceased children and aborted fetuses, are as close as possible to whole communities. It takes very little effort for anyone with concerns about such departed children to stop and bow at such sites. In the Japanese countryside and even in the residential sections of a metropolis such as Tokyo, such shrines can be found in abundance; from time to time people of the neighborhood, most likely women, will be seen stopping for a momentary act of kuyō.

Also very simple will be the rite at the household shrine. Fairly often today the mizuko will be remembered as if it were merely another "ancestor"—although technically it is not. When fine distinctions are not made, the fetus, which did not precede the living, is treated as an ancestor and will be remembered along with them at the Buddhist altar in those households that have them. In homes a small icon of Jizō can be placed on the altar and reverential bows can be made to it. If a bit more pious and concerned for such things, members of the family may also recite the words of the "Heart Sutra"[8] or a prayer addressed simultaneously to Jizō and the invisible dead fetus.

The next level of complexity involves paying for a stone image of Jizō and having it properly enshrined at one of the many cemeteries specializing in this. Such cemeteries can, as noted above, increasingly be found connected to temples of the established Buddhist denominations. During the past couple of decades, however, there has—in connection with the "mizuko boom"—been a large growth in the number of independent temples that deal exclusively in mizuko memorializing; often such institutions have little or no antiquity and may even be regarded as semi-private *business* ventures. Their commercial aspects are patent. Persons who initially visit such places are often presented with stories of others who experienced tragedy when they "neglected" their mizuko, and such stories are soon followed by an outline of the temple's services and the fees charged. For a price, a concerned parent can have what in these cemeteries is tantamount to the "perpetual care" in American mortuary contexts. Periodic rites for the mizuko can be purchased—and it is not strictly necessary for the parent to be personally present on such occasions. The requiem then is vicariously performed.

Within the context of many established Buddhist temples, there is often a large Jizō icon or a set of six or more smaller ones bedecked with red bibs. There a parent can perform simple rites—largely bowing, observing reverential silence, lighting a candle, and maybe saying prayers or chanting. Some temples have an alcove filled with dolls and other items that in their own way relate to the departed child or fetus. Others have Jizō cemeteries or, in special instances, a collection of look-alike and rough-hewn stones that are designated as the Riverbank of Sai. Candles can be lit and coins deposited in such places. More and more, however, the mizuko kuyō is moving inside the temple as well. Many temples now have special days set aside for mizuko remembrance rites. Robed priests will then officiate, and the concerned parents will join a larger congregation of persons—the "parents" of mizuko—like themselves.

In fact, the mizuko rite now has an important role even outside of Buddhism; some of the "new religions" have made them a part of the panoply of services offered. Helen Hardacre vividly describes such a rite in the Oi church of Kurozumikyō, on the outskirts of Okayama City. In this case it is one offered to nonmembers:

> The woman making the request, invariably the one who would have been the mother of the child, comes to the church, and a minister prepares an ancestral tablet [*mitama bashira*] for each aborted or miscarried child, writing a name and approximate date on each slip of white wood. Initially this is placed on a small movable altar adjacent to the ancestral altar of the church. The church's ancestral altar is decorated with particularly colorful flowers and food offerings and with a large red and white paper streamer, representing a symbolic offering of clothes for the child. Before the ancestral altar, the ministers recite the Great Purification Prayer and read a *norito* to console the child's spirit, directing it to enter the ancestral tablet previously prepared. The officiating minister, who has donned a paper mask covering the mouth, and an assistant then move to a temporary altar on which the tablet rests. The officiating minister directs the spirit of the child to enter the tablet as the assistant intones a long "Ooooo" indicating the spirit's passage into the tablet. Then the tablet is removed to the ancestral altar, and all assembled offer *tamagushi* before it while music is played.[9]

Here, as in many of the new religions of Japan, there is mix of Buddhist, Shinto, and even Christian elements. Much of the terminology of the rite just described is Shinto; moreover in that context, according to Hardacre, the soul of the unborn has to be purified, because in abortion or miscarriage it has been polluted by contact with blood—a distinctively Shinto theme. The institution performing this kind of mizuko kuyō is, significantly, a "church" and its officiant a "minister."

This confirms the fact that the impulse to deal with abortion through a ritual such as this comes from deep roots in Japanese culture. Although the practice has historically centered around the figure of Jizō and the largely Buddhist kuyō rituals, it can with apparently little difficulty now enter into the religious context of the new religions. There is, it seems, a deeply sensed need for such rituals and, when abortion is practiced across denominational and religious lines, so too, it seems, will rituals emerge.

Perhaps one of the most fascinating questions is whether mizuko ritual will enter into Japanese Christianity—or whether it has already begun to do so. Japanese researchers have already noted what seems an undue interest in the mizuko ritual by Western Catholics residing in Japan.[10] Some of the very few studies of mizuko in English have been published in a journal that is based at Nanzan University, a Catholic institution in Nagoya. Although this does not necessarily reflect institutional or even editorial policy, it is at least interesting to note that these studies have moved from initial criticism to an enlarged "understanding" and contextualization of these rites.[11]

It is not unreasonable to expect that in Japan what begins as the Christians' effort to understand phenomena within Japanese culture eventually may, with great caution, be accepted into the Christian context itself. Many Protestants have done just that with respect to rites for ancestors: although since the Meiji period, many Protestants in Japan scorned the kuyō for ancestors as compromises with false religion, in recent years even foreign missionaries in Japan have, according to reports in Japanese newspapers, been exploring the importance of ancestor rituals for family coherence. That is, once the Japanese family is understood to be—in its basic structure—even stronger than that of the Christian cultures of the West, it seems to some wasteful not to make an accommodation to the practices that make it so.

Mizuko kuyō may, in time, prove to be a context wherein the Catholic Church's adamant opposition to abortion comes—at least in Japan—face to face with what some perceive to be the emotional and ritual needs of persons who, rightly or wrongly, have had abortions. If this happens in Japan, even non-Catholics will have reason to watch with great interest.

And perhaps the underlying question will then become: Is such a rite merely something that arose to fit the peculiar and idiosyncratic needs of one culture, that of Japan, or does it accord with more generally human needs?

BENEDICT'S BLUNDER

The essence of the rituals for fetuses is that they do something with and for the sense of guilt that people feel. To say that, however, might seem to contradict something that many people in the West think is true of the Japanese—namely, that they belong to a "shame culture" rather than to one characterized by a concern for guilt.

This conception of Japan has its origins in Ruth Benedict's *Chrysanthe-mum and the Sword,* a widely read book that has both assisted and bedev-iled the American attempt to understand Japan from the time of its initial publication in 1946. Benedict held that in Japan shame is the principal curb on deviant behavior and that the development of "conscience" is not part of a culture characterized by shame rather than by guilt. You can, she held, know the existence of a guilt culture by the role it allows for confession:

> We know [confession] brings relief. Where shame is the major sanction, a man does not experience relief when he makes his fault public even to a confessor. So long as his bad behavior does not "get out into the world" he need not be troubled and confession appears to him merely a way of courting trouble. Shame cultures therefore do not provide for confessions, even to the gods. They have ceremonies for good luck rather than for expiation. True shame cultures rely on external sanctions for good behavior, not, as true guilt cultures do, on an internalized conviction of sin. Shame is a reaction to other people's criticism. A man is shamed either by being openly ridiculed and rejected or by fantasying to himself that he has been made ridiculous.[12]

Soon after Benedict advanced it, experts on both sides of the Pacific found this distinction wanting.[13] Still it hangs on and is injected into a good deal of popular thinking about Japan—as, for instance, in the statements about Japanese culture found in *Shōgun,* the widely read 1975 novel by James Clavell.

Attitudes held by Westerners vis-à-vis a culture thought to be one that knows "only shame" tend to be strangely extreme—and *opposite* to each other. Some have held or hinted that since guilt is a defining characteristic of civilizations in which moral conscience has been refined, it must really be the cultures of the Judeo-Christian West that demonstrate such a char-acteristic of advanced social and spiritual evolution. Latching on to Benedict's characterization of Japan as a shame culture, there have been suggestions, therefore, that Japan still needs to evolve upwards into a culture like that of the West—either through actual Christianization, the missionaries' goal, or through a deep philosophical change that allows for the development of true "subjectivity." These are ways in which a "shame culture" tends to be viewed, either explicitly or implicitly, as being at a lower stage of development. The baldest and most embarrassing—for its racism—statement of this view was General Douglas MacArthur's claim that during the American occupation he had to treat the Japanese "like twelve-year olds."[14] Our relations with Japan are still marred, more than we like to admit, by such attitudes.

The other—actually opposite—attitude to Japan as a putative "shame culture" has been projective and affirmative. An illusion of Japan as a wondrously "guilt-free" sexual paradise was strengthened in the occupation period because, desperate for the wherewithal to support themselves, Japanese women worked in bars and consorted with American military personnel. Onto this, in addition, have been projected the notion of a Japan as guilt-free by virtue of never having been infected by the conscience burdens that are assumed to be unique to the Judeo-Christian heritage.

In fact, it appears that guilt is merely distributed a bit differently in Japan. Benedict's hypothesis about Japan as a shame culture has no serious adherents today among students of Japan—even though it has an afterlife in the popular imagination. And not only are feelings of guilt connected with abortions today but they have been for some time in Japan.

It takes no more than a look into the pages of *The Life of an Amorous Woman*, by the Edo writer Ihara Saikaku, to see an instance of guilt focused on sexual activities and the death of the mizuko that resulted. In this classic work of fiction, a prostitute confesses:

> One night as I lay gazing into the past through the window of my heart, calling to mind my various wanton doings, I seemed to see a procession of some ninety-five different childlike figures, each wearing its placenta on its head and each one stained with blood from its waist down. Standing before me they spoke in slurred and weeping tones: "Carry me on your back! Oh, carry me!" These, I thought, must be like women who had died in childbirth; for I had heard it said that they returned to earth in the form of spirits. But, as I gave heed, I heard each of the small figures cry bitterly, "Oh, cruel mother that you are!" Then I perceived to my grief that these were the children whom I had conceived out of wedlock and disposed of by abortion.[15]

Here, quite clearly, it is guilt that was operative and the activities of conscience that were at work.

All that we know of the Japanese kuyō for fetuses further supports the fact that guilt is involved. If nothing more than shame were present, it could easily be avoided by simply hushing up the fact of an abortion. By Benedict's own definition, where there are no eyes to frown and condemn there is no shame. In a hypothetical "shame culture," an abortion would be a matter of clandestine removal of the fetus (probably off in

Wood pallets on which parents write out apologies to their mizuko. (Asakusa, Tokyo.)

some distant town), the maintenance of utter secrecy about the matter to the whole of one's family and community, and then a life-long silence about it.

It is abundantly clear that this is not what happens in Japan. In fact, we find ourselves somewhat amazed at the *public* nature of open participation in the mizuko rituals. Actual family names are sometimes written on the amulets that record a kind of apology to the mizuko in some temples. In very public places, such as the great temple dedicated to Kannon in the Asakusa section of Tokyo, I have seen amulets dedicated to mizuko and bearing not only the names of the parents but written apologies directed to the child in another world. They have messages such as, "Please forgive us. We—your parents and siblings—are in your debt." In her important study of illness in Japan, Emiko Ohnuki-Tierney noted the same thing—that many carry an apology, *Gomen nasai.* She writes, "Most of them are signed by *haha* (mother). Some are signed by both the mother and the father, reflecting the recent trend toward more involvement by young fathers in childbearing and rearing. In a few cases the names and addresses are written, and in even fewer cases, the names of the entire family."[16] These are clearly addressed to fetuses that were deliberately aborted.

In contrast to "shame"—in which to be undetected is to be free—efforts directed toward dealing with guilt often involve making things *more difficult* for oneself, at least initially. The fact that the pain and discomfort of guilt are what is faced in mizuko rituals suggests that the involved persons think their behavior in the rituals proper, good, and even probably therapeutic for themselves.

This fits well, I believe, with understandings of the positive role of guilt that are emerging—or perhaps reemerging—in Western philosophy. After a period during which guilt was something of a whipping-boy in Western intellectual history, philosophers more recently have been evaluating it anew. No longer are there attempts to pinpoint a special sense of guilt as a telltale mark of Western civilization—for better or for worse. Likewise, although it should be recognized that power or profit sometimes propels outside persons or organizations to exacerbate another's guilt for their own ends, it does not seem that *all* guilt is caused in such ways.

Some philosophers, in fact, are once again having some positive things to say about guilt. If seen as resolvable, guilt is taken as having an appropriate role in studies such as those by Herbert Morris and Gabrielle Taylor. Their studies, however, key the concept not to some kind of transcendent law but to a person's relationship to others and to himself or herself. Guilt, in Morris's view, is bound up with an agent's sense of caring for others and with that agent's own sense of being such a person who cares. Thus, "Not being pained by the hurt done others would reveal an absence of care for them and an absence of care for oneself as a person identified as caring for others."[17] This can voluntarily lead to self-inflicted pain—of an important type: "By inflicting upon oneself something painful or by accepting its infliction on one, one thereby provides both oneself and the other party with a sign of the hurt one feels in having hurt the other. . . . When doubt has been raised about care and commitment, assumption of pain is a preeminent mark of their presence."[18] The sense of guilt and even some intentional self-inflicted pain, then, can be a sign *from oneself to oneself.*

Gabrielle Taylor too has been involved in reestablishing the necessary and even valuable place of guilt in human experience. Taylor not only analyzes these concepts with great skill but does so in such a way as to make clear that guilt is a constitutive of the human being's humanity. This means that the presence or absence of such emotions—and their relative depth or shallowness—are reflectors to that person of the kind of person he or she is. She writes, "The experience of an emotion of self-assessment is also a happening which changes the state of things. The change is in the view the agent takes of himself."[19] Thus, to dismiss these emotions too easily is to miss out, according to Taylor, on something that can bring to a person a good deal of his or her sense of what makes being a human being valuable. Personal pain but also drama are involved. Taylor continues: "Much will depend on what the agent makes of his experience. In trying to find out why he feels pride or guilt or shame on this or that occasion he may make discoveries about himself which may change his whole outlook and lead him to form a different and perhaps juster view of himself and of the life which he should lead."[20] There is, then, a good deal at stake. The choice is between making light of these things or, on the contrary, prizing them as indices to the self, to human worth, and to what is really valued.

In keeping with Gabrielle Taylor's analysis of guilt, I suggest that many Japanese who make ritual apology to an aborted fetus do so to retain their sense of their own humanity. As chapter 10 will show, there clearly are instances of people being badgered into exacerbated guilt over mizuko. Still, the majority of those who do mizuko kuyō may do so, at least in part, because they want very much to keep on believing that they are sensitive, conscience-controlled persons—even though in undergoing an abortion they have felt virtually compelled to do something that would seem to fly in the face of that self-assessment.

This is to say, the terrible fact of abortion makes it all the more important for the "parent" of the fetus to find concrete evidence that she—and sometimes he as well—still remains a person who cares and who has human feelings. The hardness of the fetus-destroying act makes the excavation of a fundamental softness in the actor a matter of crucial importance. The guilt, then, can be a welcome sign, a gratifying testimony to the perdurance of a humanizing sensitivity still at the center of the self. The Japanese have a very basic word for this softness; they call it *kokoro*. Very often tears will be the outward signal of its presence.

Rituals, especially rituals of guilt and apology, are often the forms that confirm the sense that, in spite of everything, the person that one wants oneself to be is *still intact*. They are the arena of self-assessment. In Japan it is simply assumed that such rituals are given by the culture; they are simply available there as forms (*kata*) into which the individual can enter in order to be reaffirmed. But this does not mean they are mere externalities—as if without also a deep personal introspection such rituals would have no value. As a matter of fact, the participation in ritual is itself a mirror that the person holds up to herself or himself to prove thereby that she or he "cares" enough to be participating. The rite is self-reflexive. To be in ritual is, as Confucius suggested, to already *be* in Goodness. As noted by David L. Hall and Roger T. Ames, in their superb exposition of Confucian thought, "Ritual actions are not only performed *by* people, but, because they actively evoke a certain kind of response, in an important sense they 'perform' people."[21]

SWEATERS, NOT LAWYERS

Persons in the West have trouble with this. Over recent centuries we have built into our own intellectual and social climate a many-layered set of objections and impatiences vis-à-vis both guilt and ritual. This puts us in a double bind in trying to understand this kind of practice in Japan. We expect that what is ritualized is likely to be concealing something nefarious. It *must*, we feel, be false. Ritual is suspect. Ritual is waste.

This is what is most likely to make things difficult for Westerners to see why Japanese who have had abortions are often quite willing to expend some of their valuable time and even make an outlay of cash to apologize to their mizuko. Perhaps the modern Western fantasy of finding a guilt-free culture or of turning oneself into a person no longer "burdened" by guilt is connected to the wish to have a culture without rituals. Our notions of what it means be rational and to be freed from the religious components in our own culture's past often include beliefs about an *economical* use of our time, our emotions, and our wealth. Guilt and rites do not fit well in such beliefs. Guilt has become an emotion many in our society are simply embarrassed to find in themselves.

What may be peculiar about the West is not that it had an unduly stressed concept of guilt but, rather, that in its modern phase it gave wide credence to the belief that guilt itself was and ought to be completely dispensable and there should be no need whatsoever for rituals in a truly rational society.

We will not find that in Japan—at least not to any comparable extent. And perhaps, then, we cannot really fault the Japanese for trying, sometimes a bit forcedly, to retain certain practices of the past, especially if such practices throw into relief the contrast with the West's rather rigid notions of what modernization means and what of the past is necessarily pared away to make room for it. The Japanese, to the dismay of some critics in the West, are sometimes quite willing to be less consistently "modern" or even eagerly postmodern. And if the model of a normative modernity is fixed, this will make much of Japan—including certainly practices such as the mizuko kuyō—look like kitsch or like pastische.

The practices of the past that the Japanese have intentionally retained cannot all be accounted for in terms of ideological manipulation. Many of the Japanese social customs that have been selected for retention are things that we need to view as more than merely interesting, quaint survivals but also as other than the camouflage used by a political ideology. Even when we have noticed that it is usually political conservatives who beat the drums most loudly for the preservation of past culture, we have not fully *explained* that preservation.

The retention of ritual is a case in point. The Japanese have simply never subscribed to the modern Western notion that ritual is in conflict with a truly economic modernization and with rapid economic development. The paring away of such "uneconomical" social etiquette has not proven to be a necessity in Japan. Large amounts of time and energy still go into such things.

The deliberate refusal to allow litigation to become a deep and pervasive cultural pattern is another. With a still relatively small ratio of lawyers to the total population, Japan in the eyes of many of its people functions fairly well—and with just about as much social justice as anywhere in the world, perhaps quite a bit more than in most of it. This is a boat that does not, many feel, need rocking. To train and pour in a higher percentage of lawyers would be to fix something not perceived as really broken. On the other hand, the *disadvantages* of a society given over to pervasive and deep litigation are all too obvious to the Japanese. The notion that where there is more law there is more modern efficiency is, in the eyes of many, one of the odder myths of the modern West.

The notion that religion is somehow inimical to modernization is another idea cherished by many Westerners but openly and emphatically rejected by a lot of Japanese. That is so even if the practice of religion costs money—sometimes a good deal of it. Individuals will often complain about the outrageous cost of religious funerals and the like; still they go on paying and praying. Emiko Ohnuki-Tierney correctly observes, "To the Japanese, who may literally throw ten-thousand yen or hundred-yen coins to deities and Buddhas when they go to shrines and temples, the commercial side of contemporary religious establishments is quite within tradition—they have always paid for religious services."[22]

Much of what is given seems, even to many in Japan, not quite necessary. Yet people go on doing it. The society, at least as judged by the sheer quantity of its religious activities, still thinks of religion as important in public and private life. The contrast with its Marxist-Maoist continental neighbor could not be sharper. But that contrast, many Japanese people will privately suggest, only shows that the wise culture is the one that does not get rid of the gods too quickly. The gods and Buddhas, they often nowadays say with a laugh, seem—when it comes right down to it—to have done their own part in making the Japanese rich.

In the kuyō for mizuko a number of these things come into focus. Guilt and rite are still present and used. My point is that this is precisely why the practice of the rites for the mizuko arose in Japan—and came in as *the* Japanese way of handling the moral dilemma posed by the practice of abortion. Such rites both express and tap into a deeply enculturated pattern of thinking and behaving. Such cultural "inventions" are not accidental.

The pragmatic retention of religion is involved here too. In essence the Japanese, seeing abortion as a moral problem, have brought that problem directly into the arena of religious practice and tried to work out their own solution there. It is a problem that has its legal dimension, but in Japan there is not the sense that the problem might be somehow *solved* in the domain of law and litigation. The courts are not usually where consciences are treated.

The existence of the old kuyō concept and its adaptability for memorializing the large number of fetuses aborted in modern times constitute the Japanese "solution" in another sense too. They make it possible for many Japanese to tolerate the practice of abortion and still think of themselves as moral and even as "sensitive"—both individually and collectively. Kuyō demonstrates that the practitioner and, collectively, the culture still have *kokoro*—the capacity to be moved. That is, through this ritual their moral options are not limited to either categorically forbidding abortion or, at the exact opposite pole, treating the fetus as so much inert matter to be dispensed with guiltlessly.

The mizuko ritual gave another alternative. Although it involved the discomfort of feeling guilty for a while, it also permitted the involved parent both to have the abortion and to retain a self-image as humane and caring. The presence of guilt was an index to the presence of such admirable emotions, and the performance of the rite was an enacted bodily expression of the same.

Abortion was in this way neither forbidden nor treated lightly. It is an act that by definition objectifies, instrumentalizes, and even on one level rends a relationship—the one of the parent and child—that is ordinarily the epitome of what ought *not* be objectified, instrumentalized, or rent. Everywhere the mother-child relationship is ordinarily the paradigmatic expression of intimacy, of emotional and bodily closeness, of noninstrumentalized life together.

This is probably why the mizuko kuyō bends over backwards on every level of its multiple meanings to reassert the reality of the *bond of emotional intimacy* between the parent and the deceased child. In many small ways, the rite says that the fetus was not considered a mere "thing" and ought not, wherever it is, to harbor the feeling that its now-distant parents regard it as a thing. The whole language of the ritual is to negate any suggestion of thingness, any hint that the child in question was objectified and instrumentalized.

Thus there is so much attention paid to kuyō rituals, why prayers are chanted to remind the fetus that "out of sight" on the Riverbank of Sai does not mean "out of mind," why pinwheels are placed next to the statue that serves both as Jizō and surrogate child, why sweaters are lovingly knitted to keep the masonry icon from catching cold, why money is paid to the temple for the sake of the deceased child's "educational" needs, why the fetus's siblings in "this world" are brought to the cemetery for introductions, and why there can even be the equivalent of "graveside" conversations about going together to see the film "E.T." Even when absurd, and when "kitschy" from the usual Western perspective, the *importance* of these things to those directly involved cannot be denied. Kitsch can easily come under criticism when we apply aesthetic standards, but these may not be appropriate here. To the degree that it becomes the tangible focus of sentiment that, at least to the person most directly involved, seems to prove anew that there is a "softness" deep down, the usual criteria of aesthetics are inadequate.

Chapter 10

MORAL SWAMPS

> Asia is the grave as well as the cradle of religions.
> (Edward J. Thomas, *The Life of the Buddha in
> Legend and History*)

LIQUID MORALS

IN *SILENCE*, his captivating historical novel about the dying days of
the first Catholic mission to Japan, in the early-seventeenth century,
Shusaku Endo portrays two Portuguese missionaries, themselves both
now apostate, conversing about what had gone wrong:

> "For twenty years I labored in the mission." With emotionless voice Ferreira
> repeated the same words. "The one thing I know is that our religion does not
> take root in this country."
> "It is not that it does not take root," cried Rodrigues in a loud voice, shaking
> his head. "It's that the roots are torn up."
> At the loud cry of the priest, Ferreria did not so much as raise his head. Eyes
> lowered he answered like a puppet without emotion: "This country is a
> swamp. In time you will come to see that for yourself. This country is a more
> terrible swamp than you can imagine. Whenever you plant a sapling in this
> swamp the roots begin to rot; the leaves grow yellow and wither. And we have
> planted the sapling of Christianity in this swamp."[1]

The implication here, of course, is not only that Christianity has a difficult
time in such a culture but that a kind of moral rot inevitably takes over in
it. Instances of moral terpitude in Japan have, in fact, been the theme of
many of the novels of Endo, who is not only one of Japan's best-known
writers but, because himself a Catholic who often writes about evil, someone often compared with Graham Greene.

I know of no way to compare or evaluate whole cultures in terms of the
degree to which moral perfidy has easy sway within them; everything
would seem to depend on the kind of measuring instrument being used.
By some yardsticks, Western nations could be shown, I suspect, to outdo
Japan in terms of producing evil. What interests me is not such an apparently insoluble problem of cultural comparison but one that is much more
specific. An important question needing to be addressed is exactly how

representative *Japanese themselves* perceive and judge the relationship between the Japanese ethos and the practice of mizuko kuyō as a practical way of "handling" the problem of abortion. Does the evolution of such a practice require a certain kind of religio-moral climate? And if so, is there something about it that Japanese themselves feel to be deserving of *censure*? That is, do they suggest there something morally "swampy" about their own religion or religious ethos that has given Japan the practice of rituals for aborted fetuses?

It goes without saying that persons and organizations that are categorically opposed to legalized abortion will answer these questions in the affirmative. For instance, even in Japan there is a religious organization, *Seichō no Ie*, the "House of Life," that holds that abortion should again be criminalized.[2] Its total membership is not large but is fairly vocal and organized for maximum political impact. It has roots in several religions, especially Christianity and Shinto. Its Buddhist component is, significantly, much more muted.

In at least some sense, the House of Life represents a contemporary reincarnation of that kind of neo-Shintoism that in the prewar period was unambiguously fecundist. It is the view of most adherents of this religion that the Japanese need to move toward making abortion illegal once again. Samuel Coleman writes, "Unlike other religious organizations in Japan the Seichō no Ie has matched its anti-abortion beliefs with political activities, including organizing mass petitions to the Diet [parliament] to restrict the Eugenic Protection Law and media events that have boasted of the participation of Diet members in the ruling Liberal Democratic Party."[3] In writings of Taniguchi Seicho, the head of the organization, the equality of fetal life with life forms outside the womb is stressed. The only difference is a matter of comparative size and the fact that the fetus is connected to the mother by an umbilical cord.[4] Later in this chapter some other aspects of the position and practices of this organization will be looked at.

By comparison most Buddhist organizations look relatively benign; at least they do not appear to threaten existing liberal abortion law. They include some advocates of a return to strict laws against abortion, but these are few and not so vocal. When the Buddhists are criticized for their practices with respect to abortion, the sharpest charges tend to come from persons who tend to base themselves in a Marxist or quasi-Marxist critique of *all* religions. Others criticize the very existence of the rites for mizuko, because they see such things as themselves creating an intensified emotional climate, in which persons already feeling guilt are likely to feel virtually compelled to take recourse in the mizuko rites—and pay accordingly.

A good example of this perspective is that of Ōta Tenrei (b. 1900), an obstetrician, the inventor of an IUD called the "Ōta Ring," and the author of numerous books on socio-medical problems, including an important study of the prohibition of abortion and its legalization through the Eugenic Protection Law.[5] Ōta is an advocate of liberal abortion laws, but he has strenuously opposed the practice of mizuko kuyō. In a book whose title means "Abortion is Not Murder," he writes,

> The degeneration of Buddhism is a public scandal. The kuyō for mizuko is evil. . . . All people have things in their past that they regret and for which they blame themselves. But we should avoid being hung up on such past events and should face the future. For most women the thing they most want to put out of their minds is their own past experiences of abortion. Thus to force them to remember again such bitter experiences, just like picking open old wounds, is extremely cruel and inhuman. When priests do such things in order to make money it is not really religion but the practice of an evil profession. . . .
>
> [In earlier periods in Japan] the people, except for those with power and wealth, eked out a miserable existence and for them abortion and even infanticide were necessary evils. Consequently they had very little feelings of guilt and seem not to have been frightened of retaliation from such mizuko. These were measures that simply had to be taken so that parents and older siblings of the mizuko could live and thus there was no reason for such terminated children to feel resentment for what was done to them. . . .
>
> It is very common in Japan that, when someone else has illness in the family or gives birth to a physically or mentally handicapped child, someone is sure to think they have put his or her finger on the cause by saying "This is bad karmic retribution coming from a dead ancestor" or "No one in that family has been paying attention to what I've been telling them about the ill-omened nature of this household." . . . In like fashion people will attribute all kinds of problems to the retribution [tatari] of a mizuko. It is human weakness to do so, but the fact that there are so many priests ready to make money by capitalizing on this weakness is what I take to be the really deplorable thing here.[6]

The point is that such practitioners of religion tend to prey upon guilt and human weakness and that to do so, especially when women have already suffered by having abortions, is cruel. From Dr. Ōta's perspective, it is not the widespread practice of abortion that reflects a Japanese moral swamp but the institutions—Buddhist and "degenerate" in his view—that feed on the guilt feelings of women. He does not, obviously, distinguish between guilt that might possibly be part of "self-assessment" and an unnecessarily exacerbated guilt. His is a classically "modern" critique of guilt as an emotion of weakness and of religion as, by definition, parasitic on it.

BUDDHIST CRITIQUES

Japanese Buddhists, especially those in the older, mainline denominations, have been worried by such criticisms. That worry stems, in part,
from the fact that Buddhists have no clear "position" on these matters.
Most of the temples in the mainline denominations did not provide
mizuko services until the mid 1970s, when it became clear that there were
new, enterpreneurial temples springing up and that such temples were
siphoning off adherents through the services offered for people who had
had abortions. According to priests in these mainline temples, they began
to provide such rites only when requests for them came from their own
parishioners, who otherwise would have gone elsewhere.

There were denominations that showed extreme reluctance, especially
the Pure Land and the True Pure Land. However, as Fujiyoshi Jikai, a
highly revered senior monk in the Pure Land denomination told me in
1988, "Pure Landers officially do not have this kind of service, but I will
not say it can *not* be found in the temples of our denomination." Thus
Buddhists in general, not just the entrepreneurial temples or those that
manipulate guilt through talk about retaliatory mizuko, are involved in
mizuko rites and now bear something of the sting of that public criticism
of it that has appeared.

This has led to soul-searching. What is interesting, however, is that the
problem as perceived by most Buddhists has not been over the morality of
abortion per se as over the propriety and morality of tatari, the notion
that the spirit of an aborted fetus is causing harm to its parents or siblings
still in this world. For instance, in July 1987 an entire issue of *Daihōrin*,
an interdenominational Buddhist periodical, was devoted to discussions
of tatari. At issue was whether the notion of retribution or revenge upon
the living from the side of the harmed or neglected dead was, in fact,
compatible with Buddhism. The opening statement of that issue read as
follows:

> Are the misfortunes and tragedies that fall upon a given family caused by one
> of its members that has died but exists in a state of unrealized Buddhahood?
> Does the spirit of a mizuko take its own revenge? One often hears these
> questions posed. People are asking: Is there really such a thing as retribution
> upon the living from the spirit of the deceased? Is it really necessary to take
> proper measures to get free from the influences of a malign spirit? What is the
> connection between fear of this and the periodic requiem rites with which we
> remember our ancestors in Buddhism? We, the editors of *Daihōrin* addressed
> precisely these questions to 43 persons, all of whom are themselves profession-
> ally involved in the "world of Buddhism."[7]

Because the opinions given were varied and in many ways represent the key issues in the debates over religion and abortion in Japan today, I here summarize some of the key positions as they are articulated in the special issue of *Daihōrin* devoted to the topic.

Fujiyoshi Jikai, the senior monk of the Pure Land denomination mentioned above, wrote from his temple in Kamakura:

> In India Shakyamuni had little regard for miracles and said next to nothing about spirits; his attitude was rather rational. But things changed with time, especially when in China Buddhism got implicated with ancestor rites. This led to attention to invisible beings. In Japan the priest Shinran [1173–1262], following Shakyamuni in this, held that prayers to and for the dead have little avail. However, I hear that among his followers today in the True Pure Land denomination there are temples which provide rituals for aborted fetuses [mizuko kuyō]. Doesn't this suggest that Japanese Buddhism is in a very sorry, decayed state? One might possibly be able to rationalize ancestor rites as a kind of "entry level" in Buddhism—with the expectation that persons should eventually get beyond them to what Buddhism really is.
>
> Even if there is this practice of rites for fetuses, the thing about which we should really be searching our consciences is whether we should be letting our country become a kind of "abortion heaven." It is said that nowadays making money in dealing with spirits is thriving, but I think it reprehensible that religious organizations are making big profits out of human ignorance and weaknesses. Today in Buddhism the whole notion of "skillful means" is getting twisted, used very loosely, and made into a justification for letting people do exactly what they please.[8]

Hanayama Shōyō, a professor at Musashino Women's College, provides the following viewpoint:

> In traditional Buddhist teaching, although one might be able to transfer some of one's good merit to another, the reverse was not true. That is, one person's grudges or hatred would not devolve on the destiny of another. On the principle that one's karma was one's own, the necessary thing was a self-scrutiny, not a concern about "retaliation" [tatari] from someone else.
>
> I want, however, to consider mizuko specifically. Although in the past mizuko were mostly the result of miscarriages or of being born dead—that is, involuntary—nowadays the great majority result from humanly induced abortions and are the result of parental will. In most ordinary people this is bound to lead to feelings of guilt and bad conscience. It is at times like this that someone often shows up saying: "Your misfortunes are due to the retaliation of a mizuko. You've got to do something about that—by way of kuyō rites."
>
> My proposal is that we start at the beginning and totally get rid of the causes for producing so many mizuko. If children are unnecessary we must bend every

effort to avoid their conception. And then in those instances where an unwanted child has still been conceived, the thing to do is to seek the counsel of
the clergy at one's own traditional family temple. By making the proper rites
for the dead there, one need not later be terrorized by others. In sum, I hold that
it is not really necessary to suffer worry over the retribution of spirits, but in
cases where one is really bothered by such things it is to a reliable priest that
one should go for counsel.[9]

Hiro Sachiya is one of the most popular journalists in Japan, and often
writes on topics related to Buddhism. His comment is:

> In a healthy-minded person there will be no fear of retribution from spirits. In
> fact, the so-called "retribution of spirits" is nothing other than what happens
> in a person's mind when he or she worries: "Does such spirit revenge exist or
> not? How can I escape such a thing? At least I've got to think about such
> possibilities." It's that very state of mind which *is* the revenge of spirit.
>
> In my view the belief in retaliating spirits is simply false Buddhism; it is even
> contrary to Buddhism. So if you are worried about such things, simply avoid
> counsel from someone foisting such beliefs on you. If you take the advice of
> that kind of person it will be like an intoxicated man trying to get help from a
> heavy drinker; both will die drunk.
>
> The next thing in getting free from such feelings of revenge is to refuse abso-
> lutely to use money for such a purpose. The notion that one can resolve such
> problems by payments is a direct contradiction of the compassion of the Bud-
> dha. Actions like that treat the Buddha like a money-minded merchant. It is
> everything that Buddhism is not.
>
> As a Buddhist I hold that the notion of such retaliation is a delusion. For
> people afflicted by such fears there is no instant cure. The thing needed is a
> day-by-day program for rectifying one's daily life. This is what Buddhism is all
> about.[10]

Matsubara Taido, a priest and chair of the Nammu Society, takes a
more sanguine view of the matter. Buddhism does include the notion of
karmic payments—rewards for good deeds and retribution for bad ones.
He finds value in "uplifting" the notion of tatari—and those who are in
its sway—into something higher and better. He employs an analogy:

> When the horticulturalist wants to produce a new kind of seedless grape he has
> to begin with grapes that have seeds. . . .
>
> Even though science makes progress there are lots of things it does not ex-
> plain satisfactorily to people. If people insist on using the notion of tatari to
> explain what is still unexplained, such a notion might help them to accept
> things at a certain level; then an effort can be made to educate the holders of
> such notions into the realization of higher religious forms.[11]

Iizawa Tadasu, a writer and member of the Japan Arts Committee, pulls no punches in attacking the money-hungry and manipulative methods of those who specialize in tatari. He uses a group of striking analogies:

> Within our legal code there are laws that forbid extortion and good people will not practice it. It is members of the Japanese mafia, the *yakuza*, who make their living extorting money from others. We ought to realize that religious practitioners who—merely for profit—push on others the need to worry about spirits have really sunk to making religion nothing more than a business. There is no difference between them and the yakuza. . . .
>
> During the European Renaissance there arose the practice of selling "indulgences" by the Catholic Church; persons who were sincerely religious denounced this practice and this actually was something that began the Protestant Reformation.
>
> We all read in *Newsweek* about the big scandals in America caused by televangelists and their use of the media. So it is clear that even nowadays the naive masses can be intimidated. Given the high percentage of television viewers in Japan, shouldn't we expect the money-mongering purveyors of religion to be using that medium here too? Has it not begun already?[12]

The focus here is on the nonexceptional nature of the Japanese—neither better nor worse than others—when it comes to reprehensible practices. The problem is not abortion but extortion.

Matsunami Kōdō, a professor at Ueno Junior College, deals specifically with the anxieties of people worried about tatari from mizuko. He shows a striking difference in attitude.

> According to the Buddhist scriptures the fetus in the womb is supposed to be cared for and brought safely into this world. . . . If, however, for the physical or mental health of the mother it is felt that an abortion is unavoidable, it is important that she not be simply nonchalant about the matter. As humans it is natural for us to want to say "I am sorry" or "Somehow I pray for your well-being in the other world." The person who just takes an abortion in stride with a that's-the-way-it-is attitude is someone whom we feel to be a bit cold and cruel.
>
> Because the law of karmic cause-and-effect is operative such persons may sooner or later feel that the revenge of the mizuko is getting to them. . . . So bothered, they will be easy prey for money-mad religionists who detect in such afflicted persons the desire for the quick-fix of their anguish by means of a money payment. Buddhist texts teach that, while we need to recognize the karmic law, we should not be preoccupied with the past. Simple offerings of incense and prayers for an aborted child will suffice. Then the important thing is to face the future positively.[13]

Stress is on avoiding both the pitfall of the attitude of cold indifference and that of a mental preoccupation with the past.

These are only six out of forty-three views provided from within the Buddhist community in the pages of *Daihōrin*, but they represent the spectrum of opinion there.

A Woman's Viewpoint

One of the striking things about *Daihōrin*'s special issue on tatari is that of the forty-three opinions offered from within the Buddhist community, apparently not one was from a woman. We cannot know whether this was an oversight on the part of the editors—who on other issues, it should be noted, often publish essays by women. Yet, in this striking absence of a female perspective in this instance there may very well be a reflection of the problem of the almost exclusively male authority structure in Japanese Buddhism.

Fortunately, there is an exceptionally well-informed and articulate woman who has, as a Buddhist, written on this topic. As a newspaper correspondent, Ochiai Seiko has been intimately concerned with the abortion issue. As the wife of a Buddhist priest in Tokyo, one affiliated with the Buddhist True Pure Land denomination, she knows temple life from the inside. For a variety of reasons, we need here to quote extensively from an important essay she wrote, which discusses abortion from her perspective as a woman and a Buddhist.

She begins her essay with the reconstruction of a telephone conversation between her husband and one of his parishioners wanting him to provide a rite for an aborted fetus. Since his particular school of Buddhism did not traditionally provide such rites, he is placed in a quandary: because he does not provide such a service, the person on the line threatens to affiliate with one of the disreputable mizuko temples.

This kind of predicament for priests such as her husband became increasingly common, she writes, in the late 1970s. The rise in anxiety about revenge from mizuko was part of a larger "boom" in *reikon*, "spirits" or "souls" of the kind that can possess other people. At that time the new entrepreneurial temples had begun to sell their services through newspaper ads. Consequently more and more of the mainline temples, some of which never did this kind of thing before, began to offer mizuko rituals. They felt forced into it.

Ochiai finds all of this to be quite repugnant:

It should not even be necessary to point out that the intention of Buddhism as taught by its founder, Shakyamuni, was not to provide rites for dead persons who are blackmailing the living by threatening reprisals. Such a deviation from original Buddhism happened during later history when priests, wanting to support their temples and their own livelihoods, began to provide memorial masses for the dead. This was the origin of what we call "funerary Buddhism."

Honest priests can conceivably make something positive out of funerals—by using them as contexts for counseling the lives of the living relatives in a good direction. But in the case of rites for mizuko nothing of that applies. People make excuses about being remorseful for their abortions but, since their real intent is to escape fetus reprisal, what they really want is an exorcism, something that derives from the perspective of Shinto and has nothing to do with Buddhism. Buddhism, in fact, originally denied the existence of "souls" or "spirits."

Japanese history shows that even after the introduction of Buddhism the sutras of that religion were chanted by the Japanese as if they were really just the same as the magical prayers used in Shinto for exorcism. This pattern was not broken until the epochal changes of the 12th and 13th centuries when great figures like Dōgen, Shinran, and Nichiren rejected the belief in souls. (Shinran even criticized the related belief in the emperor as the great national shaman.)[14]

This encapsulates the part of Ochiai's argument that provides a short historical overview. She goes on to critique the existing mizuko rites and offer some startling judgments about them and Japanese politicians:

When the weak members of present-day society attribute their troubles to the tatari of dead souls, they thereby turn their attention away from the real social reasons for their plight. All this fits into an old pattern shown by religion in Japan. The temples established to perform mizuko rites are no exception and in the process of how they are set up we can see the strategy of people with political power. As an example take the place known as the Purple Cloud Temple dedicated to Jizō [in Chichibu]. Its head-priest is a man named Hashimoto Tetsuma, a full-fledged member of the political right-wing. He retains a deep connection with the Liberal Democratic party—so much so that, on the day in 1971 when his newly built temple was dedicated, Satō Eisaku, Japan's Prime Minister at the time, along with a whole group of politicians, drove from Tokyo all the way out to Chichibu to attend.[15]

Ochiai analyzes the verbal and written statements from the Purple Cloud Temple. She finds in them disturbing references to the need to rethink the laws that permit abortion and also pejorative references to the *wūman ribu* (women's lib) movement as posing a big problem in Japanese society.

What Ochiai finds especially disturbing is the positive interactions between Purple Cloud Temple and the House of Life (Seichō no Ie), the organization in Japan that is pushing for the recriminalization of abortion. The temple's head priest has high regard for the other organization's president. Moreover, it seems that those among the membership of the House of Life who worry about revenge from a mizuko are often referred to the Chichibu temple as the right place to go for rites. Ochiai notes that the ideology of the House of Life derives from rightest positions held during World War II, that it is based on a nationalistic form of Shinto, and that in it there are open expressions of nostalgia for the Meiji Constitution and its prohibition of abortion. She continues,

> The House of Life hoists the flag of righteousness which reads "Respect for Life." Its claim that fetuses too are children expresses the tenor of the propaganda it repeatedly puts out in calling for a revision of what it regards as the "evil" Eugenics Law [that legalized abortion]. It increases its rhetorical power by drawing Mother Theresa into its cause. By contrast those of us who want to insist upon the right of women to have abortions often present arguments which seem to many to be unclear and weak.
>
> This is why the recent return to a strong belief in spirits can trigger the total collapse of the movement for [social and political] modernization in Japan.[16]

Ochiai then shows how persons concerned both for women's rights and for real religious values need to become more effective:

> In order to bring persuasive power back into our own movement we need to have a knowledge of what real religion is and we need to educate ourselves so that we can always detect the fakery of those who are purveying teachings about souls and spirits. Then no matter how cleverly specious are the arguments based on "respect for life" we—if we base ourselves on what Buddhism really is—will immediately be able to peel off and expose what is merely cosmetic in such things.
>
> Religious people will naturally want to protect "life" but when over that is laid the notion of "souls" what you get is nothing more than Shinto . . . and a nationalistic Shinto at that. We know it leads to the denial of individual rights.
>
> It should by now be easy for us to see that when people are shouting about respect for fetuses they care less for fetuses than for what they represent as potential laborers who will support the national ideology or as potential recruits into the military.[17]

Finally Ochiai puts the matter in bold terms:

> Buddhism has its origin in the rejection of any notion of souls. At the time of its origin there was a decisive disengagement from any notion that souls could cast spells and, as a result, people were taught to think of what they could do on their own strength and to think of what they could make of their own lives through their subjectivity. Shakyamuni taught these things and Buddhism got its start on them. We are not merely "souls" meant to be stored in Yasukuni, the national military shrine.

Of course we who are Buddhists will hold to the end that a fetus is "life." No matter what kind of conditions make abortion necessary we cannot completely justify it. But to us it is not just fetuses; all forms of life deserve our respect. We may not turn them into our private possessions. Animals too. Even rice and wheat shares in life's sanctity. Nevertheless as long as we are alive it is necessary for us to go on "taking" the lives of various kinds of such beings.

Even in the context of trying to rectify the contradictions and inequalities in our society, we sometimes remove from our bodies that which is the life potential of infants. We women need to bring this out as one of society's problems, but at the same time it needs to be said that the life of all humans is full of things that cannot be whitewashed over. Life is full of wounds and woundings.

In Japan, however, there is always the danger of mindless religion. There are also lots of movements that are anti-modern and they are tangled up with the resurgence of concern about the souls of the dead. I think we need to educate ourselves to see through the falsehoods of such organizations. At least if we women do not again want to be bringing our children as dead soldiers to Yasukuni Shrine, we do well to see through such lies.[18]

The indictment of the practice of tatari is much stronger and comprehensive here. Based as it is on the attempt in postwar Japan to reappropriate "original Buddhism" and that of medieval thinkers such as Shinran, it is very sensitive to the political and social ramifications of various positions on these matters. It insists on an ideational *gap* between Shinto and Buddhism on this matter and holds to the moral superiority of the latter. This statement also shows accute awareness of the nexus between government-sponsored fecundism and war in twentieth-century Japan.

THE EXORCISTS

The important issues just brought out deserve commentary. Discussions by Japanese Buddhists as to how they should deal with the problem of abortion in their society are, in fact, more charged and potentially divisive than they seem. Even within the forty-three opinions offered within the pages of *Daihōrin's* special issue there is a rather large problem always under the surface and something of which the authors are well aware.

It does not come in the shape—as in the West—of a pitched battle over whether or not abortion should be permitted within society. It is important to see that none of the forty-three Buddhists argues, as do the people in the more Shinto-oriented House of Life, that public access to abortion needs to be curtailed. The fact that Japan has become an "abortion heaven" is lamented by a couple of the authors, but nevertheless one of the striking features of the posture of Japanese Buddhists on this question is that there is no strong voice advocating return to strict laws that would criminalize abortion again. When the fact that all the *Daihōrin* writers on this issue were male is factored into this, the matter becomes ever more striking.

Their discussion, as noted in the previous chapter, focuses on the problem of reprisals from dead fetuses. And that question, in a way that would be totally surprising to Westerners, touches a *very* raw nerve. It is important to note carefully both what the Japanese Buddhists are *not* making into an issue, namely the access to abortion, and what they *are* seeing as problematic. Why does the topic of tatari generate so much discussion, even striking differences of opinion, among them?

In order to answer this we need a concrete example. One such example is provided in chapter 1, in the discussion of the Purple Cloud Temple. Here we will not only look at the example again but also look at it differently and much more critically.

At that mizuko cemetery in Chichibu, one can receive, as I did, a brochure offered as a guide to the perplexed but something that at the same time is a promotion for the services offered and a suggestion of their costs. Its title is "The Way to Memorialize One's Mizuko"; my translation of it forms the Appendix. Here the prose of the opening section of that document needs to be quoted to give an idea of what is going on. A parent who picks it up will read,

> The mizuko resulting from a terminated pregnancy is a child existing in the realm of darkness. The crucial thing that needs to be done for such a child is the provision of a full apology to it and the making of amends.
>
> In contrast to the child in darkness because of an ordinary miscarriage or natural postnatal death, the child discussed here is where it is because the parents took active steps to prevent it from being born alive in our world. If the parents merely were to carry out ordinary memorial rites but fail to make a full apology to their child, that mizuko will never be able to accept their act.
>
> Think for a moment how even birds and beasts, when about to be killed, show a good deal of anger and distress. Then how much more must be the shock and hurt felt by a fetus when its parent or parents have decided to abort it? And on top of that it does not even have a voice with which to make complaint about what is happening.
>
> It often happens that the living children of a person who has repeatedly had abortions will cry out in the middle of the night; a nightmare wakes up such a child and he or she utters the plea: "Father, Help!" or "Help me, Mommy!" Uncontrollable weeping or cries of "I'm scared! I'm scared!" on the part of such children are really from dreams through which their aborted siblings in the realm of darkness give expression to their own acute distress and anger. Persons who have any doubts about this explanation would do well to take a

look at two of our publications entitled "Mizuko Jizō Temple's Collection of
the Experiences of Departed Souls" and "The Medical Dictionary of Life."[19]

The text goes on to present no other options than that of setting up a Jizō
image at the Purple Cloud Temple. The implication is that only in this
way will the aborted child feel satisfied and the risk of retribution from
the fetus be averted.

The text makes no mention of the extenuating circumstances of life
that may have necessitated the abortion. It makes no attempt to present
any sympathy for the plight of parents. Instead all the emphasis is on the
fact that those parents have *willfully* sent such a child into the nether
realm where it now languishes. The text simply assumes that the fetus, at
no matter what stage it was aborted, had sufficient presence of mind to
feel anger at its parents and somehow now has the full consciousness of
a child able to comprehend and even mull over such things—to the point
of feeling resentment. Also the text makes much of the fact that what
occurred in the act of abortion is *unnatural*. Great stress is placed on that.

This is so because it taps into one of the oldest patterns of Japanese
cultural life. Rich documentation, from historial and literary sources, as
well as from the notes of anthropologists and sociologists working in
Japan, gives abundant evidence that the concept and cultural role of tatari
there is old and probably antedates all the written records we have. What
such materials suggest—and the point of special importance here—is that
from early times in Japanese culture there was a deep sense that persons
who had died "unnatural" deaths were virtually certain to feel tremendous resentment vis-à-vis the living and would, unless somehow pacified,
wreck havoc on the living. Thus they needed to be exorcized.

As mentioned earlier, the classic instance of this, one known to virtually every Japanese, is that of Sugawara Michizane, who was wrongfully
accused of treason and who then "haunted" his enemies until they made
restitution and made him into the god of learning. But this was not a rare
instance. Herbert Plutschow claims that most of the major yearly festivals
in Kyoto, so admired by visitors from the West, began at places specifically dedicated to enshrine the angry souls of persons wronged.[20] During the ancient and medieval periods of Japan's history, epidemics from
time to time killed many people and were attributed to the souls of an-
gered but still-powerful dead persons. Ignorant of bacteria, the people at
such times, with their kin dying right and left, frantically built shrines and
held festivals to placate such ghosts.

Tatari, then, has a long history and, some would say, a well-pedigreed
role in Japanese life. We should not, then, be totally surprised when we
find in the promotional literature for the Purple Cloud Temple a description of the mizuko's death as "unnatural" and its continuing attitude one

of deep resentment. What probably most shocks us in that document is the fact that its authors have seen fit to interpret the ordinary nightmares of live children as really the voices of mizuko crying out to their parents from the world of the dead. From our own more skeptical position, we might wonder why the perpetrators of this claim do not worry about disconfirmation of it simply by the fact that nightmares are not limited to children with mizuko siblings. It is noteworthy that the authors of the "memorial" do, in fact, apparently worry about counterexamples. They tell their readers to consult their other publications if in doubt. Besides, it can safely be assumed that persons who are ready to accept this promotional material are already deeply anxious about abortions and for that reason may be quite ready to believe what is given them.

The materials of Purple Cloud, to my knowledge, make no overt effort to associate the activities of the temple with *traditional* Buddhism. In that they differ from, for instance, a promotional book for mizuko services written by Archbishop Domyo Miura of Enman-in, a temple about five miles outside of Kyoto. The Reverend Miura, concerned that the values of rites for mizuko should become known even beyond Japan and be available to the entire world community, had a book of his translated into English. His *Forgotten Child: An Ancient Answer to a Modern Problem*, published in England in 1983, tells of the thousand-year pedigree of his temple, describes in detail the experiences of individuals whose lives were positively changed once they owned up to an abortion and cared for it with proper rites, and issues an open invitation to people of any faith or religion to take part. Abortion, he writes, has become a common human problem; what he and his temple can do is provide a way of dealing with it religiously. His book is, to my knowledge, the only publication in English about mizuko intended for an international readership.

Perhaps for that reason alone it deserves a close look. First it is worth noting that Archbishop Miura's temple is, on his claim, one in the Esoteric Buddhist tradition. Furthermore, of all the mainline denominations in Japan, those in this tradition have historically shown both the highest readiness to include mizuko rites and also the greatest ease in accommodating scenarios that involve tatari.

Archbishop Miura treads on slippery ground. On one level he uses language that denies an element of "curse." He writes of people who came to him with stories of misfortune.

> What is unmistakable [among them] is the high rate of illfortune that was found to plague those who had neglected to hold a memorial service for their *mizuko*. There may be some people who, seeing this phenomenon, put it down to a curse brought by the soul of the *mizuko*. There may be others who say it is a mere coincidence. However, when we see so many actual instances we

cannot ignore that there is something here which cannot be explained as a curse or a coincidence.[21]

Since it is, according to this, neither statistical happenstance nor curse, Miura attributes it to "the intricacies of the Buddhist concept of cause and effect." That is to say, it is karma that is operative here. He then goes on to specify twenty categories of symptoms whereby the fact of an unresolved mizuko problem can make itself known:

1. Just when they think their business is going well, it takes a turn for the worse. This pattern repeats itself.

2. No matter how much effort they make, they do not achieve the progress that their efforts seem to deserve.

3. Someone is always ill at home.

4. They do not enjoy good health, and with women, especially, they have back, shoulder or neck trouble.

5. Their children have accidents and hurt themselves, and cannot settle down.

6. They have children with emotional problems, or autistic children.

7. They suffer because of their children's violent behavior.

8. Their school results are not bad, but on the day of the exam they do not feel very well and so their dreams of getting into the college of their choice is [sic] not fulfilled.

9. When their children were toddlers they were lively, but suddenly they became listless, and they do not know what they are thinking about any more.

10. Their children are continually prone to illness, especially stomach or bronchial complaints, so they spend their time taking them in and out of hospital.

11. Their grandchild suddenly starts acting strangely and they think that he or she has mental problems.

12. Husband and wife do not seem to be compatible and now do not even talk to each other.

13. In their dreams, they have a vision of their child's face wanting to talk to them.

14. They often dream of candles—exactly the same number as the *mizugo* [mizuko] they have had.

15. They can never rid their ears of the sound of their baby crying.

16. When they were praying at their ancestors' graves or by the "butsudan" [Buddhist home altar], weird things happen one after another, such as inexplicable noises, or a memorial tablet falling over.

17. When they go to bed at night, it feels as if someone is there, though there is no one; they see the shape of a figure through the "shoji" (paper sliding door).

18. They are involved in road accidents.

19. Somehow they feel depressed and have no enthusiasm for doing anything.

20. They are frequently unhappy, an unhappiness which comes in cycles.[22]

This list itself is extremely interesting—especially in terms of how the majority of the troubles fall either on the mother or on the mizuko's siblings, about whom the mother is bound to be constantly anxious.[23]

What I want to pursue here, however, is how one is told by the Archbishop's book to *interpret* these things. Even though earlier the book had rejected the idea of a "curse," this is exactly what the text seems quickly to contradict when it declares, "Neglecting a mizuko without having a service for it is like trying to run or swim with a heavy weight attached. . . . A mizuko who has not had a service, or in other words whose life has not found rest, radiates its influence and seems to cause things to happen whenever possible."[24] Although the word tatari itself seems not be used here, the phenomenon as described is undoubtedly the same— except that a softer cushion of language surrounds it: the mizuko "radiates its influence and seems to cause things to happen whenever possible." Of course, what "radiates" here is understood to be malign.

Although the classical notion of karma is used, it is given a bizarre twist when the Reverend Miura writes, "If we analyze the influence of this from the standpoint of the laws of cause and effect . . . we find that the strongest direct influence exerted is on the other children of the same family—i.e. the brothers and sisters of the mizuko."[25]

Karma, which in Buddhist texts usually means that the effect of actions—either good or bad—are realized in the life of the person whose actions they are, is here construed as deflected off. Not the parents who caused an abortion but their other children bear the brunt of the mizuko's resentment and wrath. This is meant to make the parents themselves suffer via the emotional impact of seeing the suffering of their other innocent offspring. Although, as noted, the notion of positive "merit transference" has an old, if irregular, pedigree within Asian Buddhist practice, what is peculiar about this karmification of tatari, is that it is its opposite in two senses: it is negative rather than positive, and it is the impact of the dead on the living rather than vice versa.

The critical question then becomes: In this kind of construction has not Buddhism itself been completely subverted by the old Japanese notion of tatari and the need for ritual exorcism? Is the "Buddhism" here anything more than an empty shell?

Moreover, are these not obvious patterns of psychological manipulation? Even if a person, Japanese or otherwise, were to be totally indifferent to whether or not Japanese "Buddhism" was remaining true to the Buddhist tradition, the question of the fundamental morality of such practices remains. Especially Ochiai but, in fact, almost all the Buddhist writers about tatari in the pages of *Daihōrin* repudiate those temples—like Purple Cloud—that use the fear of tatari to coerce and cajole people. There is, they suggest, a wide deviation away from the Buddhist tradition in this kind of thing. They go on to suggest, however, there is also a wide deviation from what most people—whether Buddhists or not—regard as acceptable human behavior. This is why the sense that there is something very reprehensible in tatari refuses to go away.

Chapter 11

A RATIONAL, NATIONAL FAMILY

> It is, after all, quite possible to argue that
> abortion is beneficial for society.
> (Mary Gordon, *Good Boys and Dead Girls*)

> In the contemporary world it would be hard
> to find a family system more honored and more
> important in its authority than that of Japan. But
> abortion there has for long been easily available.
> (Robert Nisbet, *Prejudices: A Philosophical Dictionary*)

The Starving and the Chic

YOSHIDA KENKŌ was a Buddhist recluse and a man of exquisite taste—so much so, in fact, that his *Essays in Idleness*, of the fourteenth century, are often thought to be something of a template for Japanese preferences in both the arts and daily life. Conscious of things Chinese, he seems to have been concerned to define—without being jingoistic about the matter—how some of the preferences of the Japanese differed from the Chinese. What till now has gone unnoticed, at least to my knowledge, has been the importance of what he says about progeny in the following: "Things which seem in poor taste: too many personal effects cluttering up the place where one is sitting; too many brushes in an ink-box; too many Buddhas in a family temple; too many stones and plants in a garden; *too many children in a house.*"[1] The sense that overly abundant progeny are a sign of bad taste fits in well with what we know of the tenor of Kenkō's aesthetic. Tending toward what we in our century have sometimes called "minimalism," he disliked excess of any kind. Although a Buddhist, he wanted no plethora of icons in a temple. In spite of being a literary man to the marrow of his bones, he deplored an ink-box full of writing tools. Even "good" things are not good if too many in number.

When he, therefore, prizes the home with a limited number of children, he links the notion of reproductive restraint to his *aesthetic*. Whether Kenkō was merely giving expression to some existing Japanese preferences or actively shaping them, we have in his statement a clear linkage between "taste" and reproductive restraint. To be sure, the degree to which this preference was adopted among the general population has very much to do with whether having large or small families fit notions of economic viability for such families. Nevertheless, the notion of the "tastefulness" of reproductive restraint did seem to enter into Japanese social values. Moreover, it fits what demographic historians have been suggesting about families in the late-medieval or early-modern period showing a distinct *preference* for the family of limited size.

This is to draw out an implication of the important research on population in the Edo period reviewed earlier. As noted in chapter 6, although the threat of starvation was indeed the reason many rural folk limited the size of their families, others in that period did so in a rather straightforward attempt to maximize their personal wealth and the quality of their lives. Such important research has demonstrated, among other things, the problem with the customary claim of Marxist historians that practices of abortion and infanticide—that is, the mabiki of the Edo period—came about solely because an impoverished and oppressed rural population had no alternative but to limit the mouths to be fed. Mabiki, however much practiced among those portions of the population that were starving and desperate, was also taken up by much more well-off people in the cities and towns.

As noted, the official philosophy moved in the opposite direction. Confucianism, at least as understood in Japan, was uncompromisingly fecundist in its ideological position—a position, moreover, often presented as "rational" in a way that others were not. One of the claims of this study, however, is that officially sponsored programs of "rationality" are not always seen as such by the people being told to adopt them. Claims of superior "rationality" can be self-serving and ideological, and people—even common people—being asked to accept them at face value often know better than to do so.

To that degree commoners did *their own* own moral reasoning. And it appears that they did so in the mode of bricolage—without accepting either the touted higher morality or the superior rationality of the government's official Confucian teachers. And, it seems clear, in the formation of their own thinking about right and wrong, they were substantially aided by Buddhist concepts of transmigration and by the folk Buddhist beliefs about newborn infants being able to revert back to the domain of the gods and Buddhas with considerable ease. In the Edo period, much of this was being condemned by official Confucians as so much "superstition," but commoners realized it gave their thinking about progeny a flexibility not available in the official orthodoxy of the era.

Mabiki as a metaphor also contributed immensely. The notion carried over from the rice field to the city was that culling had an important cultural role—if not to enhance quantity then at least for the sake of quality. This also was a language tool in the resistance to the policies of fecundism.

George Lakoff and Mark Johnson refer to "metaphors we live by," in their book by the same name. If, as they claim, "the conceptual systems of cultures and religions are metaphorical in nature," we may be permitted to characterize this development in Edo ethics as the discovery of the metaphor that *"the family is a field."*[2] If farmers found that to select out weak or crowded rice seedlings enhanced the eventual yield, they could apply this knowledge to domestic reproduction as well. And if rural people could conclude that the culling of their progeny helped to stave off starvation, then urbanites and the inhabitants of small towns could rationalize to themselves the practice of mabiki to head off some future threat of economic disaster—or, more positively, to enhance existing wealth and its utility for the family in question.

This seems undoubtedly to have been at least a factor in the growing wealth of such people. We can tell it was, in fact, by the intensity of the neo-Shinto invective against mabiki; it is as if such writers knew the conceptual power of the metaphor they wished to expunge from the popular mind.

But common people saw mabiki as rational. It was what left "space" for siblings—and by extention the population as a whole—for living and growing. In the case of an unplanned pregnancy too soon after a birth, mabiki enabled a couple to space their children to greater advantage. For those who recognized that another pregnancy would deplete the body and energies of a mother, such spacing would indeed be like that in the rice fields where culling weaker shoots means more nutrients for the stronger ones. In a world where nutrients and energies reach natural limits, harvesting human resources to make a population strong and healthy seemed as justified as the operations of the farmer on his fields.

Moral judgments often flow not just from principles but also from what is deemed feasible, desirable, and linguistically managable. And, if we can judge by the transportation of mabiki language into the reproductive lives of urbanites as well, there probably was an element of practical aesthetics in this too. In the Edo period, the samurai class, with no wars to fight, had undergone an occupational redefinition, had become the age's moral teachers, and was committed to the values of Confucianism. The merchant class, by contrast, were under no such constraint. To some within this class, the intelligent use of mabiki in reproductive life would have made sense both in economic terms and in terms of good "taste."

We know that the urbanites of Edo wanted above all to be chic. In terms of family planning, what made eminently good economic sense also fit certain criteria of good taste. Although not the only aesthetic of the epoch, the "restraint" value articulated by Yoshida Kenkō would have had its own currency in this age, one that could be applied where it seemed to fit. To refrain from being overly reproductive would have looked not only economical but also tasteful to such people. To have "just enough" children made sense for multiple reasons.

Also, since it seems that women in merchant families had much more freedom and a greater role in decisions than their counterparts in the samurai class did, it makes sense too that they would have felt much less need to bend to pressures on them—even from their husbands—to have many children. In this sense they did not have to be as Confucian as the wives of the samurai teachers. Abortion was for them too a more available option, morally speaking. Aesthetic factors combined with ethical ones in this. According to Rodman, Sarvis, and Bonar, "The abortion question pertains not only to what is just but to what is possible. Women throughout history have submitted themselves to abortion when they perceived it to be preferable to other alternatives."[3] Infanticide too could be drawn into that realm of possibilities—and preferences.

What farming women did out of desperation city folk did as part of their way of gaining certain advantages for themselves—not just as individuals but as families. Both types of people, we can assume from the available evidence, turned to the concept of Jizō as protector of children and fetuses—for the whole complex of reasons suggested. To the extent that Jizō was a Buddhist bodhisattva, something of Buddhism remained a powerful intellectual and emotional resource for such people. This is why when neo-Shintoists began to push fecundism at the end of the Edo period, they attacked not only mabiki as a practice but also Buddhists for having an ethic that was, if not hostile, then at least lukewarm about the need for people to have as many children as physically possible.

EUROPE'S DISCARDS

It would be easy to see all this in the frame of a rather crass materialism, one which has material wealth in view and then merely goes out to draw to itself any religious practice it can to make itself look somehow moral. I think, however, that such a judgment would be both facile and unfortunate. There are several reasons for thinking this.

First, it must be recognized that, contrary to the long-assumed superiority of European and American religion and morality in these matters, recent historians have found what looks to be a very spotty record. In a remarkable recent study by John Boswell, we are made to see clearly that since the development of Christianity gave people the sense that abandoning children was the least objectionable way of disposing of them—in moral terms—this practice went on for many centuries, and at a very high rate. Moreover, this way of jettisoning unwanted children often meant that their deaths were merely postponed. Boswell, whose study focuses on the period from Roman antiquity to the end of the Middle Ages, concludes,

> Behind the walls [of hospices for foundlings] paid officials dealt with society's loose ends, and neither the parents who abandoned them nor their fellow citizens had to devote any further thought or care to the children. Even the foundling homes did not have to care for them for long. A majority of the children died within a few years of admission in most areas of Europe from the time of the emergence of the foundling homes until the eighteenth century; in some times and places the mortality rate exceeded ninety percent.[4]

Jacques Donzelot, in fascinating research based primarily on materials from France from the seventeenth to the nineteenth centuries, has studied how the policing of families increased even as did the means of philanthropy. Abandonment, especially of bastard children, was still widely practiced in the eighteenth century—but this eventually became a matter of concern only because it meant a loss of valuable workers: "The administration of foundling children was reproached for the appalling mortality rates of the minors in its care: ninety percent of these 'forces' died before having been made 'useful to the state.' . . . [They were seen as needed] in national endeavors such as colonization, the militia, and the navy, for which they would be perfectly suited owing to their lack of constricting family ties."[5] Thus philanthropy came with very mixed motives and rather shocking results.

There is a striking parallel between these European materials and what we saw earlier of the early-nineteenth-century neo-Shinto compulsion to view children—and fetuses—as so much potential workforce for state use. Attention will be returned to this point later on.

Here, however, we need to explore in a bit more depth what the comparison of Europe and Japan means in terms of the *morality* of comparative child disposition. Just as in Europe there were instances not only of abortion but also of infanticide, so in Japan there were cases of abandonment. During a journey in 1684, the celebrated poet Matsuo Bashō wrote about coming upon an abandoned child by a riverside and being moved by the plight of the child. In the end, however, Bashō blamed "heaven" rather than the parents: "How did this happen? Were you hated by your father, or were you shunned by your mother? No, your father did not hate you, nor did your mother shun you. All this has been Heaven's will. You have nothing but your ill fate to grieve for."[6]

Fairly often abandoned children were taken into Buddhist monasteries. Nevertheless, the overall *pattern* of preference differed in this matter, and it seems fair to say that mabiki was to Japan what abandonment had been in Europe.

Although comparative figures are unknown, it is significant that in both cases the mortality rates were extraordinarily high. With mabiki the rate was, by definition, 100 percent. The European practice undoubtedly varied with time and place. At its worst it reached, we are told, more than 90 percent and at other times was what many regarded as appallingly high.

Defenders of the European approach might say this is still a significant difference. Even more important, they would claim, is the fact that the Japanese parent who practiced abortion or infanticide was intentionally killing offspring, but the European who chose the route of abandonment was merely turning the child loose to an unknown fate—a matter that was, in religious terms, in "the hands of God" or like what Bashō calls "Heaven's will."

Yet there are reasons why the Japanese often opted for mabiki rather than abandonment, and it cannot be automatically assumed that those reasons were nothing more than self-serving. The total context must be examined. When Japanese in the late-medieval and early-modern periods chose to live within a moral framework that gave much more latitude for practices abominated in Europe, they did so, it would seem, out of a sense of compassion for the child—that is, because they felt it preferable to urge the fetus or the newborn back into the otherworld, from which point it could prepare for rebirth into this world at a more propitious time and place.[7]

It is good to recall that what we often call the morality of "the West" is far from univocal. Even our classical philosophers held views many would have trouble recognizing as the West's tradition. Aristotle, in his *Politics*, held that deformed infants ought not to be allowed to live, and Plato, in the *Republic*, went so far as to advocate destroying the children of inferior parents, even of persons past the ideal age for childbearing.[8] Their reasons were strictly eugenic and, as far as we can tell, not "softened" through the vision of something ultimately better for such infants.

The practitioners of mabiki in Japan, by contrast, held an essentially religious view. The Buddhist notion of transmigration, apparently planted on top of an indigenous Japanese belief in a kind of "recycling" of dead children, made this sensible to them. Because, as suggested in earlier chapters, their set of beliefs about the cosmos and how it works was rather different from that of the Christian people of Europe, the "liquidation" of children was *not an act of finality*. To facilitate a child's move backward into the realm of the gods and Buddhas was not to expunge the child. Religious metaphysics made the difference.

This did not mean that life in this world was not valued. It was. But whereas the Christian cosmology assumed a *one-time only* creation by God of a soul for each fetus and a strictly forward movement from that point on, the Buddhist one entertained the possibility of a wider range of potential moves—including backward and lateral ones. Analogies are never exact, but perhaps one from the world of games may help to show the difference here. Life as understood by Europe's Christians was invariably a forward movement—till death—and in that is not unlike the game of checkers. Japan's Buddhists, by comparison, saw life as a kind of ontological chess; its movements could be forward, lateral, or backward on the board. This opened up a wider range of possibilities.

FAMILY PRACTICE

It seems safe to say that people in Japan during these centuries felt freer than their European counterparts to take actions to control the entry or nonentry of children into this world. The Japanese, in the terminology of Europeans, were more ready to "play God" in this domain, whereas their European counterparts passively preferred abandonment and to let God be the terminator of unwanted life. Similarly, the Japanese were much more ready to engage in *family planning and engineering*. To them the family was not just something given by the gods or by fate but, on the contrary, that about which a whole variety of choices could be made. At the most basic level, these were choices about the number and sex of the children in a given family.

This point can be derived from what we know of the leveling of the population curve in mid Edo and the data we have about an uncannily balanced proportion of male and female children in families. All these data indicate that the basic structure and character of the Edo family, especially in the urban areas, was something not to be left to chance. In ways that Europeans had not yet begun to fathom, the Japanese were conceiving of families as a realm in which human planning was needed and desirable.

Here was the notion of a family constituted *only* of children whose presence in that family had been willed and planned. This means that the reasonably well-off Edo family—and quite possibly those of earlier periods as well—included only children in which the parents were mentally and emotionally prepared to make a considerable investment. Resources of all kinds—parental time, money for education, and emotion—were to be poured into such offspring. That is, these were children who had not only to be loved but also to be cultivated and honed. Mabiki practiced at

life's doorway involved a commitment to strong enrichment of those selected for life in the present. To cull was also to commit to an active
cultivation of those chosen for life.

Amazingly, the actual *effects* of this kind of family planning did not go
unnoticed by Europeans. In the sixteenth century Saint Francis Xavier
(1506–1552) observed, "Judging by the people we have so far met, I
would say that the Japanese are the best race yet discovered and I do not
think you will find their match among the pagan nations."[9] But even more
to the point was the written comment of François Caron (1600–1673),
who had served the Dutch East-India Company in Japan and did not de-
part that country until 1641:

> Children are carefully and tenderly brought up; their Parents strike them sel-
> dom or never, and though they cry whole nights together, endeavour to still
> them with patience; judging that Infants have no understanding, but that it
> grows with them as they grow in years, and therefore to be encouraged with
> indulgences and examples. It is remarkable to see how orderly and how mod-
> estly little Children of seven or eight years old behave themselves; their dis-
> course and answers savouring of riper age, and far surpassing any I have yet
> seen of their times in our Country.[10]

This was written, it should be noted, during the time when the practices
of mabiki were, it seems clear, becoming quite common. Perhaps many in
Japan had begun to think of abortion and even infanticide as "prices" to
be paid for the constitution of family members, the kind of family life,
and children that they wanted. And, if François Caron's judgment is accurate, we must understand that this effort was succeeding to a noticable
degree. He did not hesitate to say the results were better than anything he
had known in Europe.

Robert Nisbet, an eminent scholar of the Western tradition, boldly
makes precisely this connection in the epigraph that opens this chapter. In
making his own case for the availability and rationality of abortion, he
writes, "It would be hard to find a family system more honored and more
important in its authority than that of Japan."[11] When he says that abortion has "long been easily available" in Japan, we can note that Nisbet
probably was unaware of some of the facts looked at in chapter 8—
namely, that from the early Meiji period until 1945, the Japanese government was as repressive as any known in terms of proscribing abortion and
punishing those who dared to practice it.

Nevertheless, Nisbet is, I judge, essentially correct. The Japanese provide the prime historical example of a culture in which the widespread
resort to fertility control not only had no demonstrable negative impact
on family life but, on the contrary, seems in its own way to have contributed to an emphasis on pouring resources into one's children in a *qualita-*

tive fashion. Some potential children may have been "returned" to the place of gods and Buddhas, but those children chosen to live were given a great deal. What had been deliberately selected for entry into the family was then cultivated to a high extent. The notion of the quality family was at the heart of this.

At the same time such parents were not, to all appearances, forgetting their mizuko. And, if we can accept the view that a sense of guilt, when not abused, can be a positive factor in a person's self-assessment, then we can assume that those who did mizuko kuyō gained from it a reaffirmation of their own essential sense of compassion and humanity.

I do not mean to suggest that a grand or master plan was in place—and most surely not one as part of government policy. The evidence merely is that both peasants and townspeople devised ways of circumventing the ideologists' demands that couples increase the yield from their sexual unions. The methods of mabiki, although they could never be flaunted in the face of administrators, were available in the Edo period. And the remarkable result was a leveling off of the population without any heavy dependence on Malthus's so-called "positive" curbs on runaway population growth.

Local-level practitioners, for the most part women who had to keep fairly quiet about what they did, were the key factor. Important research by Honda Masuko has shown that in that era infanticide was probably most commonly carried out by a midwife—at least when the family in question could financially afford one. This midwife was referred to as the "woman who washes" the newborn. Pictures and documents of the time, brilliantly analyzed by Honda in her research, show that there was a motif of structural complementarity in the method. Just as the "woman who gives birth" does so by bringing forth an infant between her two legs, so to the "woman who washes" seems often to have "returned" an unwanted newborn by squeezing it between her own two legs. The space between the legs of a female was in one instance a channel *into* this world and in the other a channel *out of* it. The symbols, their complementarity, and—most importantly—their *reversibility* were meant to be exact. Euphemized as the one who washes the newborn, such a midwife had the awesome task of facilitating its "return" to the world of the gods and Buddhas.[12] The Japanese public, to all appearances, had fairly ready access to these techniques and took advantage of them.

There was, no doubt, a kind of "feedback" factor operative here. Edge-of-starvaion peasants discovered that through mabiki the family might remain alive. Persons in cities and towns realized that mabiki could mean an increase in wealth as well as a capacity to provide even better for the children they already had. This kind of reinforcement put the lie to the government's injunctions about mabiki as unqualifiedly wrong.

As suggested earlier, this becomes especially instructive when it is compared with what happened in China during roughly the same crucial time frame. In contrast to the Chinese, the Japanese not only achieved a virtual population plateau but also gained the experience of what that could mean in *direct benefits*—both materially and in less-tangible aspects of family life. As suggested, a case could be made that probably no aspect of the premodern experience of the two giants of East Asia provides a sharper contrast. Largely by learning how and why to resist fecundism, the Japanese put in place *the mechanisms and the mores* to keep its population within reason and under control.

Perhaps a difference in the way Buddhism developed in these two nations was a factor. In China, where the charges against Buddhists as being unproductive and otherworldly came relatively early, there was both an atmosphere of tension and, as scholars such as Kenneth Ch'en have shown, repeated periods of severe persecution.[13] Although in China the Buddhist monks were more consistently celibate than their Japanese counterparts, what we know of Buddhism among the lay population is that it easily became accommodated to the interest in fertility and reproduction. Already in the Sung period (960–1279) the figure of "White-robed Kwan-yin" had been made into the center of cultic activities to enhance women's fertility.[14] Likewise, from all we can tell, since China's Buddhists did not transform Ti-tsang into a figure like its Japanese counterpart Jizō—that is, protective of children and fetuses—there seems to have been no special Buddhist mechanism to aborb the emotional pain of those who practiced infanticide or abortion. Chinese Buddhists as Buddhists seem to have uniformly opposed any such practices.

If there was a kind of commoners' "wisdom" operative in the family-planning practices of the Japanese, the disastrous results that came from the historical *departure* from that wisdom, in effect, only reinforced its importance. That is, the period during which informal family planning was banned and criminalized—from the early Meiji period until 1948—was ultimately so painful for the common people that it, ironically, reinforced the public's sense that limited but qualitative families were of optimal importance. After 1948 the government, in effect, came to agree with that essential approach. In subsequent decades, the benefits—both material and otherwise—that have accrued from intentional population limitation have been so pronounced that it is further public proof of the wisdom of this approach.

Certainly, it would have been far better if in recent decades the same level of population stability had been accomplished through a wider and easier use of contraceptives, especially through legalizing the Pill, rather than through abortion as the chief means of birth control. The inability or refusal of the Japanese bureaucracy to legalize the Pill seems, to many at least, to have been unnecessarily cruel to women and has meant that for an unnecessarily long period Japan has been an "abortion heaven" when, in fact, the numbers of abortions could have been drastically reduced.

An attempt has been made here to show that, aside from the cruelty described in the narratives about retribution from fetuses and the pain suffered by women due to slow legalization of the Pill, over a long period in modern Japan, the steady realization of positive personal and familial benefits from birth-control practices reinforced their value. Both negative and positive *reinforcement* added to the public sense of this as wise policy. All of this has proven to be "rational" in an ad hoc kind of way—as a pattern found to be sensible rather than as one arrived at intellectually and as part of a comprehensive plan. It has not been the result of what social scientists often mean by the deliberate "rationalization" of society but the product of an uncountable number of small, often simply domestic, decisions.

TOCQUEVILLE IN JAPAN

One might be able to grant all of that and still find something fairly disturbing in the way mizuko rites have been developing in Japan since the 1970s. In fact, an important Japanese sociologist, Hashimoto Mitsuru, finds them exactly so. As part of a team of researchers studying the "mizuko boom" and its implications, he offers some preliminary observations in an essay the very title of which suggests his point: "Mizuko kuyō: Religion that Requires an Anxious Society." In this essay he is not concerned with how the mizuko rites might be related to abortion itself but, rather, with the significance of the fact that, at least in Japanese society, many people attribute a long list of medical, psychological, and familial problems to revenging fetuses. In other words, it is the social implications of the tatari problem that concern Hashimoto.

Believing this to be the kind of phenomenon within a society that must be watched and analyzed carefully, Hashimoto also takes it as an indicator of *larger* developments within the society as a whole. That is, not satsified with the simple explanation that the tatari pattern occurs because religious organizations drum up clients in order to make big profits, Hashimoto wants to know how this phenomenon in Japan is an index to the anxiety *peculiar to contemporary* society. People come to such temples, as noted above, with complaints about all kinds of bodily and familial problems—such as aching shoulders and children having problems with school exams—and seem happy to attribute these things to mizuko. But why? Hashimoto writes,

> It makes them especially anxious when they suddenly realize that they have encountered problems and unhappiness—inexplainable to them—that others

say they have not experienced. In their minds they feel intimidated by the thought that they themselves may have made a sacrifice of something really important just for the sake of the kind of happy life-style people nowadays are thought to enjoy. Or they feel anxious about whether or not the *excessively good* life style of the present can really continue. This kind of vague apprehension about the future is what turns them to doing memorial rites for things that happened in the past.[15]

Hashimoto finds people in such contexts eager to corroborate their own personal identity, but notes that Japanese tend to find such identity in odd ways. The quest to find out if one is being besieged by a revengeful mizuko is not unlike an interest in self-identity via astrology or—as in the case of many Japanese—by a system that classifies different personalities according to different blood types:

They are happy to entrust themselves to a "system" according to which things that happen can be attributed to outside causes such as these. That is, they cease trying to evaluate things in such a way that they will still be reasoning individual subjects. All that is then left of the notion that they as individuals have their own "subjectivity" is what they show in deciding *which such* "system" to choose to follow. And it goes without saying that such selections will follow whatever happens to be faddish at the time.[16]

Hashimoto sees this, in addition, as a Japanese variation of a pattern that Robert N. Bellah and his colleagues, in offering an interpretation of Tocqueville, had pinpointed as having happened in America. Hashimoto quotes from *Habits of the Heart*, an important study by Bellah and his colleagues:

"Our fathers only knew about egotism." Individualism is more moderate and orderly than egotism, but in the end its results are much the same: "Individualism is a calm and considered feeling which disposes each citizen to isolate himself from the mass of his fellows and withdraw into the circle of family and friends: with this little society formed to his taste, he gladly leaves the greater society to look after itself."[17]

The quoted phrases are from Tocqueville. To Bellah, this historically had led to the following: "The most distinctive aspect of twentieth-century American society is the division of life into a number of separate functional spheres: home and workplace, work and leisure, white-collar and blue-collar, public and private. . . . Domesticity, love, and intimacy increasingly became 'havens' against the competitive culture of work."[18]

This is the point of special interest to Hashimoto. He sees some aspects of this kind of development in religion as having taken place, if anything, even *earlier* in Japan. The concentration of religion in and on the family—that is, the "small society" in Tocqueville's and Bellah's terms—took place when the Japanese system of ancestor-reverencing funerary Buddhism was developed. This process, which he calls the "feminization" of Japanese religion, took place progressively from the fifteenth and sixteenth centuries on, first in the mass "healing movements" of that time and then even more in the development of Japan's "new religions," many of which were based on the experience of charismatic women, from the early-nineteenth century on.[19]

The rites for aborted fetuses, according to Hashimoto, fit right into this development. Just like the ancestral religion of Japan's past, such rites encourage people to attribute the *cause* of some misfortune or unhappiness to an already-dead member of the family. The only difference is that nowadays the disquieted or revengeful dead "ancestor" is, in fact, not an ancestor at all but an aborted mizuko.[20] Hashimoto's point is that the cause of a problem is still being sought within the anxious person's own family—that is, in the "small society" rather than in the large one, the public realm.

This, he contends, tends to deflect needed attention away from the real social and political ills in the "large" society. The person thinking his or her troubles come from a dead ancestor or an aborted fetus has a very narrow focus.

There is, Hashimoto suggests, something subtly political in all this. The pattern fits a bit too neatly into what he calls the "new conservativism" in Japan:

> The old conservative movements of the past had their reference point in the society at large but, by comparison, the new conservatism that is spreading through today's Japan seems to limit people's concern for the narrow world of everyday life and its commodities. It can even be said that this new conservatism, just as it values the rites for ancestors, also sees a positive role for things such as mizuko rites and fortune-telling. Conceptually these things may not be especially dangerous . . . but one needs to wonder whether this whole pattern will leave us much capacity to resist if and when we get dragged along in the force of some powerful [social or political] movement.[21]

These are the main points of Hashimoto's critique, probably the most penetrating and important one available.

Initially we may be surprised to find a sociologist seeing such a close parallel between practices and trends in America and those in Japan. Tocqueville's observations attributed to Japan, especially Japan of some time ago, may strike us as a bit of an anomaly—largely because we are so accustomed to thinking of him as having identified peculiarly American developments.

Nevertheless, Hashimoto would play down the surface differences. What interests him is the proclivity in both societies to draw religion down into an individual's more or less privatized realm. What the "islands of piety" were—and are—to Americans is what the ancestral or mizuko rites are to the Japanese: a "small society" that has become emotionally satisfying to individual participants and, therefore, allows them to turn their backs on the larger one. In cultures like those of Japan and America, religion in the twentieth century becomes a privatized, affective, and internal affair. In Japan the people who want you to join their new religious organization—a particular "small society"—may inquire of you whether or not the troubles of your life may be caused by the revenge of an unacknowledged and unmemorialized fetus in your past. In America the tract-dispensing person at your doorstep will ask if you are saved or really "washed in the blood."

One thing that worries Hashimoto, as it did the authors of *Habits of the Heart*, is that such a privatization and narrow channeling of religion means that people will leave the world of public affairs to take care of itself. Once the larger world falls out of the scope of things that concern the common person, it becomes something to be manipulated at will by the powerful—who will certainly use it to their own advantage. Without saying it in so many words, Hashimoto clearly intends to suggest that what can result from this is a nation of depoliticized sheep. Japan, he knows, had severe problems with that in its not too distant past.

Hashimoto clearly wants to get a grasp on very large trends. Whether the close parallels drawn between Japan and America are apt may be somewhat problematic. The nub of his critique is that when religion has become so privatized into the "small society" it has no more impact on public policy and the objective of creating a good society. To the extent that anxiety about revengeful fetuses and the way of handling them has become limited to private exorcisms at mizuko temples, his criticism seems wholly appropriate. Probably it should also be said that the development of this phenomenon in Japan during the past couple of decades has resulted in insufficient attention to the need to liberalize access to the Pill—and to the need to see if Japan's medical establishment may, in fact, be harming women by its own role in blocking such change in legislation.

On the other hand, Hashimoto's critique would seem to be primarily applicable to the entrepreneurs who peddle tatari narratives. It is more difficult to see it as calling into serious question the value of any kind of memorial rite at all for fetuses. That is, just as we may distinguish rites for ancestors from fears that those ancestors will otherwise retaliate, so we can imagine justified mizuko kuyō without the intimidation by the tatari-mongerers. There is no *necessary* connection.

Also, although Tocqueville was right to worry about trends in which the whole of public life would be collapsed in favor of the privatized events of the "small society," this should not mean there is no value in what goes on in the private sphere. To declare that would be to deny the legitimacy and the role—psychological or religious—of private rituals or rites conducted on the family level.

In fact in certain historical and social contexts, the private may sometimes be the *only* way of refusing to be co-opted by public policies that do not deserve adherence. As has been argued here, it was the evolution of the private practice of mabiki and the Jizō rites to absorb its pain that, in effect, permitted Japanese commoners to defy the fecundist ideology of the state—at a time in history when public defiance would have been suicidal. Moreover, the *cumulative* effect of the multiple but privatized acts of disobedience was such that the wisdom of this approach was authenticated on a case-by-case basis and, eventually, could be made public.

This is not to say that Hashimoto's observations do not bear watching. It is merely to suggest that there may be another side to the portrait he paints.

THREE POSITIONS IN PROFILE

Perhaps the best way to address the questions posed by Hashimoto's analysis is by seeing his view as within a *spectrum* that seems to have crystalized in Japan concerning the whole abortion and tatari problem. His view is very incisive and sophisticated, but needs contextualization. In order to do that we need first to lay out the differing postures as they relate to one another.

By this point it should be clear that, although Japan today does not debate the pros and cons of abortion in the same terms that we have been using in North America, there is a considerable division of opinion in Japan concerning abortion and religion. Although not an intensely heated debate or one that receives "front-page" coverage in the Japanese media, there is an interesting and important set of options present on these issues within Japanese society. By scratching the surface and analyzing what is found there we can detect certain patterns.

The positions constellate into basically three. Although there will be a certain fuzziness at the edges, an analysis of the materials translated and presented in the foregoing chapters suggests that these three positions become quite distinct and delineated. Shorthand terms are never totally satisfactory, even though they are sometimes needed. In this case they can be called, respectively, the liberationist, the neo-Shinto, and the Buddhist positions. After reviewing them, we will need to say why it is important that there are three, not merely two.

The position we might call "liberationist" is represented above in the writings of Ōta Tenrei and, to some extent, in those of Hashimoto Mitsuru. It is also the position frequently found in the writings of a number of persons involved directly in the movement for women's liberation in Japan.[22] Central to this position is the belief that the modernization of Japanese society is still far from complete and that the need to liberate women from many of the past's encumbrances is of paramount importance. Old structures of domination in society are oppressive and need to be removed.

A primary concern of persons with this view is that there be no reversal of legal access to abortion; the arrival at free access to abortion is part, an important part, of an ongoing struggle for freedom. That struggle is a socio-political one that, especially in Japan, involves not only an individual's enhanced subjectivity but also the use of that subjectivity to gain leverage against politically conservative forces that tend to use language about "family" and about "nation" to force individuals into submission. Another of the older patterns of domination that needs breaking is sexism; therefore those of the liberationist persuasion want—and work for— much greater coresponsibility on the part of males for contraception and the legalization of every kind of birth-control device, including the Pill.

Persons whose intellectual orientation is primarily liberationist will tend to be suspicious of most efforts to see abortion in religious terms. Some, but not all, within this position share the Marxist view of religion as an unnecessary superstructure; in some sense liberation involves dispensing with it. Those identified with this position will tend to view talk about "abortion guilt" as something to be either rejected or used with extreme caution; they feel that such talk can readily become manipulative. Women are, they claim, often victimized by such talk.

Proponents of the liberationist position are most adamantly opposed to the neo-Shintoists—in part because there always seems to be a rejection of the right to abortion implicit in what neo-Shintoists say and do. To liberationists, neo-Shinto views also smack of the political ideology of the first half of the twentieth century. Liberationists are ambivalent about the Buddhists—in part because the Buddhists are often ambivalent about them. Although most mainline Buddhists in Japan seem to support legalized abortion, the authority structure of their institutions is almost exclusively male. Inasmuch as Buddhist institutions are linked with the ancestor rites and language about "home" and "family values," some Buddhists within recent years have criticized the feminist movement. Even when not openly critical, their support for movements of social liberation—and especially the gaining of rights for women—seems often either nonexistent or halfhearted.

It is worth noting that although I label this position "liberationist," in Japan it often embraces liberal—mostly Protestant—Christians; for them, however, it seems to be the *social* implications of their faith rather than its theological vocabulary that matters in the public arena. They too are "liberationist" to the extent that they want a very strict separation of the state from all religious institutions. They regard the imperial institution with a certain suspicion—because neo-Shintoists often seem poised to re-Shintoize the state.

The second position in this profile is what I have dubbed "neo-Shintoist." It is, at least in Japan, as close as possible to an antithesis to the liberationist one. It is not accidental that some of the language used by adherents of the neo-Shinto perspective taps into that of the Kokugaku movement of the early-eighteenth and early-nineteenth centuries. In its public language, it makes much of "life." Movements such as the House of Life (Seichō no Ie), while officially syncretist, are in much of their basic vocabulary and political agenda neo-Shintoist.

People of this persuasion also tend to use the word "sin" (*tsumi*) and "evil" (*aku*) fairly often when referring to abortion—in preference, for instance, to "suffering" (*ku*) or "sadness" (*kanashimi*), terms much more common in Buddhist circles. The stress is on abortion as an deep affront to a set of religious values rather than as a point at which the pain of the human condition—including that of the "parents" of a mizuko—is clearly seen and felt.

Significantly, within this position there are no doubts about the metaphysics of the afterlife, even that of fetuses. Mizuko are, it is confidently asserted, in a limbo of suffering. Readily envisioned as having the complete consciousness of an older child, such children in limbo—*Sai no kawara*—are desperately in need of being recognized. Not only that, but neo-Shinto has little difficulty with the notion that such souls need to be exorcized. It is important to note that this position tends to be realist and even fundamentalist: souls, gods, limbo, and revenge issuing from beings in another world—all are *real* entities. They are, that is, not interpreted as being, at bottom, only psychological categories.

As seen in the text of "How to Memorialize a Mizuko," the retribution from dead mizuko is concretized; religious leaders of this persuasion tend to see and present themselves as shamanic "seers" who can discern exactly how tatari moves from a mizuko to its parents or live siblings.

Political sympathies and connections here are decidely to the right, perhaps even the far right, of the spectrum; many neo-Shintoists are openly critical of—and opposed to—what they call "womens's lib." Importantly, it seems that even when their institutions provide mizuko pacification rites, there is frequent reference to legalized abortion as a great *shame* in Japanese society. There are either open statements or subtle hints that Japan would be much better off if abortion were not so readily available, perhaps not even legal.

Persons within this position are also likely to be worried about the future "purity" of the Japanese ethno-racial strain. They increasingly bring up the "problem" of there being too many foreigners—especially workers at menial jobs—in the Japan of today. Growing affluence and high educational levels make the performance of many laboring and service jobs unattractive to younger Japanese and, precisely because labor-seeking employers increasingly use aliens to do such tasks, the number of such aliens, especially from South and Southeast Asia, has increased dramatically. This brings in not only the problems of a non-Japanese "under class" but increased demands by such laborers for appropriate rights.

To many political conservatives this is the direct result of the Japanese themselves having failed to be as reproductive as they need to be. Foreign laborers would not been needed if Japanese women had produced more children and if, in essence, the efforts to minimize population growth had not been so successful.

To a number of persons with this view, the culprit is the easy access to abortion. They see Japan's racial purity threatened. Sometimes exhibiting traces of xenophobia not unlike that in the old Mito school, this perspective on the presence of many foreigners in Japan and their increasing employment interprets all this as a worm that will eventually, unless stopped, eat away at the Japanese soul.

This position, as should be clear, not only shows anxiety about the "Japaneseness" of the Japan of the future but has representatives eager to take political steps to recriminalize abortion. If in the future there were to be a more pervasive anxiety about the purity of race on the Japanese islands, such anxiety could conceivably fall into the agenda of this kind of neo-Shinto. In that case Japan's debate would certainly be concerned with the legality of abortion itself. Representatives of Japan's women's movement, it should be noted, sometimes express fears that things may already be moving in this direction.

The third position, which may be called "Buddhist," is probably most commonly found in the temples of the mainline denominations. From some perspectives it gives the appearance of looking like either a combination of the other two or a position that sits on a fence between them. It has this dual appearance partly because, although religious, Japan's Buddhists for the past hundred years have been trying to bring their views more in line with what is assumed to be the "myth-free" views of Shakyamuni and the earliest Buddhists. They reject belief in a single, all-powerful God. As for the multiple "gods" of traditional Japanese belief, many of the mainline Buddhists regard them as a quaint folk belief. So too the notion of "souls," something emphatically rejected by the Buddha, fits uneasily in their intellectual posture. Yet these temples gain considerable income by funerals and memorial services, and their parishioners, at least, believe in family members' having "souls." The gap between what the clergy know about "original Buddhism" and what their parishioners believe is often thought to be covered in terms of the doctrine of *hōben*, the accommodation of truth to real conditions.[23]

Mainline Buddhists want to think of fetuses as "life" in some sense but are often very reluctant to project that into clearly defined terms. As the essays in the pages of *Daihōrin* show, for them the critique of tatari has become the crucial matter—not only because the practice seems patently manipulative and immoral but, perhaps of equal importance, because such a critique helps them to stake out a distinctively "Buddhist" position for their adherents.

Abortion is a necessary locus of pain and suffering in contemporary society—obviously for the fetus but also for its "parents." Buddhist language about abortion regards it not so much a "sin" as a concomitant of human foolishness (*gu*). Guilt is taken as a natural and, if not exacerbated, potentially positive emotion when there has been behavior that, however necessary, has also harmed another being. Thanks and guilt tend to overlap. Compared to neo-Shintoists, there is much greater ease reinterpreting the medieval terminology into distinctly modern and psychological categories—something that, in fact, Buddhists have been forced to do for some time.

Although some mainline Buddhists have trouble with language about "liberation" and express concern about the sexual mores of the single (*shingaru*) life-style, they are also moved to show compassion to women pregant with unwanted fetuses. To that degree they tolerate, and make moral space for, abortion. Concerning women, the Buddhist tradition gives mixed messages: the bulk of it attributed an inferior position to women in the order of things, yet medieval Japanese thinkers such as Dōgen and Nichiren saw that stance as un-Buddhist.

The mainline Buddhist position—and its ambiguities—finds articulation in most of the essays on tatari in *Daihōrin*. Perhaps more clearly representative, however, of a position by a Buddhist woman is that of Ochiai Seiko. She scores what she sees as loathsome in the tatari manipulations. She too sees a fetus as "life," but she also sees the need at times to take life, out of compassion for the woman bearing it. Ochiai, who writes strongly about the need for Buddhism to be active in the further modernization of society, clearly represents an actively "liberationist" Buddhism, which has some affinities, in fact, with the position defined above as "liberationist."

Are there analogues to these positions in the West? It would appear so. The first two positions, the liberationist and the neo-Shintoist, are perhaps most easily correlated with counterparts in parts of Europe and North America. The posture and language of the liberationist viewpoint is fairly universal and, in fact, reflects the existence of a high degree of informational exchange among feminists around the world. The political vocabulary used resembles, quite naturally, that of the "pro-choice" position on abortion in the West. The fact that the "pro-life" movement in the West most resembles Japan's neo-Shinto position should be no surprise. Both overtly bring not only their social views but also their "God talk" into the public arena; the fact that the Christian pro-lifers are monotheist and the neo-Shintoists polytheist seems to matter relatively little. In both, religion is forefronted, the central determinant. Both refer often to "life" and the need to protect it at all costs. Both also tend to envision fetal life as more sentient and far more cognitively aware than most scientists would take it to be. The excruciating pain of fetuses is vividly envisioned and portrayed; the psychological pain of women is not. Moreover, as will be shown in the next chapter, talk about "retribution" is important in *both* orientations. Political conservatism, vocal opposition to the movement for women's liberation, references to deity, and concern to curtail or even criminalize abortion—these are the common to both.

Although by this point the reasons should be fairly clear, it is significant that what we here call the "Buddhist" position on these matters has no easily identifiable functional equivalent in Western societies. Although certain liberal Protestant denominations and groups and some Jewish ones may have views that approximate these, there remain rather striking differences.

The Buddhist orientation is rather distinctive on a couple of points that are worthy of note. For instance, the Buddhist posture permits—and even encourages—language about the fetus as human life in some sense but refuses to draw the conclusion that, therefore, abortion is disallowed. It avoids the dualizing dilemma often found in the American and European abortion polemics: namely, that of feeling compelled either to think of the fetus as life equivalent to that of a fully formed young child or, alternatively, as so much inert matter or "tissue." On the one hand it is not "LIFE!" and on the other it is not just "AN UNWANTED PREGNANCY!"

This is an extremely important point and one obscured by the polemics of the current debate in the West. The practical benefits of this position are likely to be very real. The natural feelings of a woman—or even a man—toward a developing fetus need not be denied or repressed. If a woman has an impulse to regard what is inside her uterus as a "child," that need not be negated. At the same time, precisely as her condition is taken to be one involving pain, she is permitted to see her way clear to a relative release from that pain by way of abortion. The presence of a "child" in the womb does not forbid that.

In mainline Japanese Buddhism, at least in its modern form, there is some uncertainty—even confusion—about the *specifics* of what happens to a given personality after death. There is a general willingness to admit that exact knowledge is impossible. This is so concerning fetal life, too.

The notion of an aborted child temporarily in some kind of liminal state—even if not the vividly imagined Riverbank of Sai—is still often held. The main point, however, is that parents are encouraged to believe that their aborted child will continue to have life, even good life, in some sense. And, since in that case the child will be much more "happy" than if it had entered into a family where it was not especially wanted, the preference here becomes clear. This may be the "good" that can be located even in the pain of having a mizuko.

That, of course, is to suggest that abortion can in this way be made a part of thinking about *familial strength*, a frequent concern of Japan's Buddhists. A woman's right to abortion then is not incompatible or even in tension with somewhat conservative views concerning the family. This means, for all practical purposes, that while mainline Buddhists resist the notion that an unmarried woman should feel free to have her "own" child, the inclusion of abortion as part of measures to strengthen nuclear families is generally accepted. Abortion may be part of what ensures the intelligent spacing of children and the quality of their education. Unwanted children are one of the greatest tragedies. The fragmentation of the family as a structure is resisted—in the sense that having a child is not an individual's inherent "right." The distance of the Buddhists from the neo-Shintoists on one side and the liberationists on the other is clear.

Mizuko rites, as long as they are not accompanied by the tactics of tatari, are interpreted by many as having a potentially positive and therapeutic effect. The sense of guilt as being part of an affirmation of a person's essential humanity—defined as *kokoro*—is strongly present. Simple rituals and even the payment of some fee are not incompatible with such a need.

In sum, in such a context of interpretations and actions, the fact of having an abortion is not incompatible with "strong" family life. In that sense Nisbet's claim about the Japanese and abortion is essentially correct. This benefits Japanese national life to the degree that any strong family system does. When children are genuinely wanted and are the subject of intense parental and social care, the society *as a whole* functions well. The premise is that the nation is only as good as its basic family system at any given time.

Chapter 12

CROSSOVERS

> Highest good is like water. Because water excels in benefiting
> the myriad creatures without contending with them and settles
> where none would like to be, it comes close to the way.
> (*Tao Te Ching*)
>
> Solidarity has to be constructed out of little pieces.
> (*Richard Rorty*)

COMPASSION

THE QUESTION naturally and rightly needs to be asked: What, if anything, of the Japanese practices can—and, more importantly, should—make the journey from there to American or European cultures?

It is by now a truism that we live in an age of swift cultural interchange. And we exchange, more than we sometimes realize, not only the wares and commodities of material culture but ways of doing things—and the ideas implicit in them—as well. With its introduction to Japan, Christianity certainly intensified concern for certain public-policy issues there. In the 1970s and 1980s, increasing numbers of Catholic monks, both in Europe and America, have found spiritual value in augmenting their own meditative traditions with the techniques of Zen.

Centers for Buddhist practice, especially out of the Tibetan, Theravada, and Zen traditions, can be found in various locations throughout the West. It is natural, then, that persons engaging in such exercises, when personally faced by the problem of abortion, would want to know what a "Buddhist" approach might be. The approach of various teachers will undoubtedly differ due in part to differences in the Asian traditions from which they derive. Yet it is clear that for some Western people practicing Zen, at least some aspects of the mizuko rite have already been adopted. An interesting question then arises, as it does in all intercultural exchange: What has been taken, what has been left behind, and what has been adapted into something fairly innovative and experimental?

Robert Aitken has provided an important exploration of these questions. Aitken was an American civilian who found himself in a detention camp in Japan during most of World War II; it was there that he learned to practice Zen meditation. His study of that tradition continued after the war, and since 1959 he has led the Diamond Sangha in Hawaii, where today he serves as *roshi*, or master, in the tradition of Japanese Zen. Also an author, his books include *The Mind of Clover: Essays in Zen Buddhist Ethics*. His discussion of abortion is straightforward and comes, importantly, early in that book on Buddhist ethics—namely, at the point where he writes about the First Precept, the one that deals with killing. There he writes about practicing compassion and peace in the pattern of the bodhisattva, in which the virtue of compassion has a high place. However, there are difficulties:

> There are many personal tests of this practice, from dealing with insects and mice to questions about capital punishment. Perhaps the most intimate and agonizing test is faced by the women considering an abortion. Over-simplified positions of pro-life and pro-choice do not touch the depths of her dilemma. Usually she experiences distressing conflict between her sexual/reproductive drive and the realities of her life: social, economic, and personal—and indeed, she faces such realities for any child she may bring to term. I have known women who said they were not upset at having an abortion, but I would guess that they were not sensitive to their own feelings at that particular time. Perhaps distress shows up in their dreams. Surely self-awareness is never more important.[1]

It is worth taking note of Aitken's sense that neither the pro-life nor the pro-choice position is likely to encompass the whole of the problem faced by the woman involved. He then suggests that a Buddhist position will, at least in some sense, be carved out a bit differently than *either of the options* commonly taken to be the only alternatives in our debates.

Aitken also acknowledges the value of embracing the experience of abortion within a ritual. He continues,

> In Japanese Buddhism, there is a funeral service for the *mizuko* ("water baby," the poetical term for the fetus). Like any other human being that passes into the One, it is given a posthumous Buddhist name, and is thus identified as an individual, however incomplete, to whom we can say farewell. With this ceremony, the woman is in touch with life and death as they pass through her existence, and she finds that such basic changes are relative waves on the great ocean of true nature, which is not born and does not pass away.[2]

There are important things to be noted about this—since Aitken has not only introduced the mizuko rite into his discussion of abortion but also, it would appear, reinterpreted it in significant ways.

First, he sees the ritual as analogous to what we in our culture already know of funerals—that is, as a way of "saying farewell." He writes that in Japan the fetus is given a posthumous Buddhist name, but this is so it can be "identified as an individual, however incomplete."[3] What the rite accomplishes, then, is a "definition" of the status of the fetus and that definition is somewhat complex: "like any other human being" but still "incomplete."

That, it seems, is both an accurate description of the facts and very much in accord with the understandings of the early Buddhists. Whether it is what *Japanese* Buddhists have historically most often meant by these things, however, is more of a problem. Aitken appears to be bringing into sharp clarity certain matters on which Japan's Buddhists have waffled for centuries. That is, he insists that a ritual such as this is fundamentally *for the sake of the bereaved*. It deals with parental guilt. Mizuko rites are not to be thought of as effective in changing the *status of the dead*—such dead conceived of as still somehow alive and involved in an otherworldly journey about which we on this side can know nothing.

This distinction seems subtle but is, in fact, deep and crucial. A lot hangs on it. Significant too is Aitken's reference to the mizuko as "passing into the One." If the fetus has gone on to be united with the "One," we know at least that this refers to a state of being that is not only complete but also benign. To think of it in this way is very different from conceiving of a fetus as moving to the Riverbank of Sai or any other "dark" realm, from which, if it so wishes, it can effect acts of revenge on persons still alive in our world.

The difference is that Aitken sees the kuyō rite as benefiting the mental state of the bereaved. Here, much more clearly than in the case of most Japanese funerary Buddhism, is executed a decisive move away from picturing "souls" as needing Buddhist requiem masses to release them from pain. Aitken, in effect, pushes things back to the orthodoxy of earliest Indian Buddhism and at the same time moves it in a more "modern" direction. Significantly, he never hints that a mizuko rite can change the ontological status of the fetus. It is then all the more true that it does not affect a supposed "anger" the fetus may feel toward its parent.

It is the woman and, if involved, a wider community of the confused and bereaved that appears to concern Aitken. The whole ceremony, he writes, is to put the woman "in touch with life and death as they pass through her existence" so that she can realize that "such basic changes are relative waves on the great ocean of true nature, which is not born and does not pass away." These are heady concepts—but also, it would appear, a rather direct account of Buddhist teaching.

Compassion becomes the key term. Aitken explains the nature of his own counseling: "[A woman] is likely to feel acutely miserable after making a decision to have an abortion. This is a time for compassion for the woman, and for her to be compassionate with herself and for her unborn child."[4] Here the rite also has a role of saying "it is over" and, in so doing, is meant to reduce the need for an unnecessarily *protracted* sense of guilt.

Aitken sees dreams as places where, even when otherwise denied, a woman's bad feelings about the abortion are often likely to surface. It is, of course, the "bad feelings" that surface in dreams—not, as in the propaganda of Purple Cloud Temple—the "anger" of a mizuko reaching out from the other world to this one. What Aitken writes here seems to fit the experience of others. Sallie Tisdale, in one of the most powerful appraisals of the pain and complexity of abortion available, writes of her experiences as a nurse in an abortion clinic. Without changing her conviction that such clinics are necessary in our time, she writes,

> I have fetus dreams, we all do here: dreams of abortions one after another; of buckets of blood splashed on walls; trees full of crawling fetuses. I dreamed that two men grabbed me and began to drag me away. "Let's do an abortion," they said with a sickening leer. . . . I woke from this dream barely able to breathe and thought of kitchen tables and coat hangers, knitting needles striped with blood, and women all alone clutching a pillow in their teeth to keep the screams from piercing the apartment-house walls. Abortion is the narrowest edge between kindness and cruelty. Done as well as it can be, it is still violence—merciful violence, like putting a suffering animal to death.[5]

Tisdale's writing about kindness and mercy as having a narrow edge comes close to what Aitken writes about abortion as the most agonizing test of the bodhisattva's vow to practice compassion.

TATARI IN AMERICA

Many Japanese Buddhists have begun to show that they feel there is something profoundly wrong with a Buddhism that has used or even tolerated within itself notions of revenge-bearing "dead souls." Even more feel disgust vis-à-vis the crass monetary gain some enterprising temples or pseudo-temples have sought to extract from the guilt feelings of women who have had abortions. The manipulative aspects of tatari scenarios are patent. A housecleaning of such concepts and practices seems, to many of them, very much in order.

In that sense, I suspect, Robert Aitken's adaptation of the mizuko rite pushes it even one step farther in a positive direction. Not only is the Gordian knot of retaliatory souls broken once and for all but the whole meaning of the ritual is directed toward meeting the empirical emotional needs of a parent rather than some imagined metaphysical needs of a fetus thought to be a completely formed child off in some other, dark world. The real problem to be dealt with, as articulated by this American Buddhist, is the pain of what is often called the "post-abortion syndrome" of the women, not a fetus's otherworldly journeys.

By stating this, however, there is no intent to leave the impression that linking the notion of retaliation to religious belief is exclusively or peculiarly Japanese. It is true that Westerners will tend to find something peculiar in the notion that a fetus, bearing a grudge against parents or siblings, is mentally set and then physically—or *meta*physically—equipped to carry out reprisals against them. What large numbers of Japanese, especially when distressed, find credible in the notion of tatari from dead ancestors or dead mizuko is simply not something that can be easily believed by persons in the West. Therefore, there may be reason for Westerners to explore—in keeping with the sociological analysis of Hashimoto Mitsuru—whether there is something pathological in the mizuko "boom" that occurred recently in Japan.

Nevertheless, the idea that reprisals might occur within specifically *religious* contexts is very well known in the West. For example, the Old Testament, shared by Jews and Christians, not only portrays Jahweh as willing to retaliate but represents this as a positive aspect of the Deity's being. The opening verse of Psalm 94 reads, "O Lord, thou God of vengeance, thou God of vengeance, shine forth." Isaiah 34:8 promises the people that their Lord has "a day of vengeance." In the New Testament, vengeance is something that God will inflict on those who do not know him and do not obey the Gospel of the Lord Jesus (1 Thess. 1:8).

Still, it is probably Romans 12:19 that defined things for the Christian West: "Beloved, never avenge yourselves, but leave it to the wrath of God; for it is written 'Vengeance is mine, I will repay, says the Lord.'" The point here, of course, is that vengeance is the prerogative of the Deity, not of human beings.

These passages are quoted not to make a general—and even gratuitous—comment about a certain "sameness" in religions but to call attention to something quite specific and related to arguments about abortion. In the history of Europe, there was an especially deep fear of retribution from God for sexual behavior judged to be sinful. James A. Brundage points out that in the second half of the thirteenth century a new level of hostility against homosexuals "may have stemmed in part from fear that their presence may trigger a salvo of divine wrath against the whole community."[6] Likewise in fifteenth-century Venice, with more than a third of the population killed by the Black Death, the unusually severe searching out and punishment of sexual offenders may have been premised on "the theory that sexual licentiousness had brought the disaster on the community."[7]

It is worth recalling the existence of this Western notion of a justified divine revenge or reprisal if we are to make any sense of the numbers of religious people in America who are convinced that the legalization and permitted practice of abortion here is certain to call down some kind of *vengeance* from God on the entire nation. The tatari envisioned in our culture is not from a fetus against its parents or siblings but from the Creator of all life, and it is directed *collectively* at a people that is permissive in terminating life. Jerry Falwell, for instance, writes, "[Abortion is] America's national sin. I might say that Adolph Hitler brought the wrath of God upon Germany for the destruction of 6 million Jewish lives. I would agree with the Roman Catholics and many of our friends nationwide that the 10 to 12 million little babies who have died in this country since *Roe v. Wade*, January, 1973 Supreme Court decision have brought the wrath of God upon this nation."[8]

Others, some of whom have been involved in physically obstructing the operations of abortion clinics, are even more emphatic and concrete. In 1989, the *Los Angeles Times* reported, "Randall Terry, the leader of Operation Rescue, preaches that God is love—absolutely—but God is also fire, and unless America repents for abortion, it will suffer his fury. The consequences could be economic collapse, plague, drought, famine, or even military intervention from an outside aggressor."[9] And it is not incidental that, while president, Ronald Reagan's major written statement against legalized abortion was entitled "A Nation at Risk."

It is not inappropriate to see such writings as, in fact, a notion of tatari. Of course, there are differences. The Japanese who fear reprisal from a fetus see it coming on individuals, siblings, or families, while the Americans who speak and write about God's vengeance believe that it will be directed at their whole nation. Still, in both cases the fact of abortion stirs up a deep fear that abortion involves the crossing of a definitive ethico-religious line, one that cannot be crossed with impunity.

In the American case, the fear of divine reprisal against the entire nation seems to deepen whenever pro-choice advocates seem ready to play down or deny the experiences of emotional distress and guilt in persons who have had abortions. Such statements are then interpreted by the pro-life as indications of a kind of moral "hardening"—postures that are sure to speed and intensify God's vengeance.

The element of deep fear in the minds of the pro-life people may be much more real than the advocates of choice recognize. There is among the latter a tendency to slight it as merely "irrational." The problem then is that such a level of fear impels people into powerful, dramatic actions—directed against laws, organization, clinics that perform abortions, and the people involved. Under the banner of "the Right to Life," ironically, human lives can be taken. That seems simply irrational to the advocates of choice, but the matter probably ought not be dismissed so easily. What seems obvious is that abortion can touch off powerful feelings of revulsion and fear in many people.

To recognize that, however, is not to say that such fears have precedence over other matters—or that the rhetoric of retribution, as coming either from fetuses or from God, may be allowed to hold sway over the lives of persons who do not accept it. The problem for those who reject such rhetoric or the particular kind of religious thinking behind it, however, is one of taking adequate cognizance of the fear and anxiety in the others. To treat such fear as merely "irrational" does not eliminate it—or its impact on society and public policy.

Up the Slippery Slope

One of the arguments against legalized abortion is based on a belief that abortion is only the prelude to much more serious "crimes" in and against society. Those who argue that way say that however bad abortion itself may be, one of the worst things about it is that it dulls the public conscience vis-à-vis intentional killing. We will, the argument goes, gradually become so inured to taking the life of fetuses that soon enough we will feel comfortable putting deformed or handicapped infants to death. This argument, when its rhetoric becomes high-pitched, sees legalized abortion as putting a whole society on the road to Hitler's atrocities. Persons whose language then gets inflamed will, on occasion, even deride their opponents as "femi-Nazis."

What is viewed as a downward plunge of public morals is traced by some as having begun earlier, namely, with the wide use of contraceptives. The public acceptance of contraception—about which there was once, after all, much wider reservation and ecclesiastical objection than now—it is claimed, made people prepared to accept abortion. That, in turn, is readying our society—so the argument goes—for a new phase in our ethical insensitivity, one in which it begins to tolerate infanticide, especially in cases where physical or emotional handicap may make a given child undesirable. Each stage of moral and emotional depravity leads to a deeper one.

This is sometimes called a "slippery slope" argument. It is based on the premise that just about the only force operative in the moral life is a kind of gravitational pull: once a person or society crosses a certain moral boundary, ethical sense gets dulled and there soon follows a pellmell plunge to the bottom, to the deepest kind of turpitude. To many of those who pursue this argument, holding the line on abortion has become a "last chance" for America. Therefore, Christians have a duty to preserve society from a slide into total "paganism." This is why the battle over abortion is so crucial to them.

Robert D. Goldstein has already suggested some of the problems with the "slippery-slope" argument—among them that it is, "at best, speculative and unsupported by cross-cultural comparisons with societies that have for decades allowed legal access to abortion."[10] His analysis seems correct, and we should note how the comparative data from Japan would appear to make that case even stronger. For instance, an argument advanced in chapter 11 was that the availability of abortion may have strengthened the Japanese family. It surely has not destroyed it—in spite of a *very* high abortion rate.

We may even go farther. Japanese society, we might justifiably claim, can be seen as moving *up* the so-called slippery slope. The point is not that Japan is an example of what others must do but that there is nothing necessary about ratcheting downward on the moral ladder. For instead of going from contraception to abortion to infanticide, Japan has—for whatever reasons—historically gone in the *opposite direction*. In the Japanese case, it seems incontrovertible that the term mabiki included infanticide and that the killing of newborns was a fairly widespread practice in the past, demonstrably so between the seventeenth and late-nineteenth centuries. We have seen that even Japan's foundation myth includes an episode in which a defective child was deliberately "returned" to the waters—and that the parents were, at least in the text, not censured for that act. This is certainly not to say that people felt simply "free" to kill children at will—as if this were not a moral and religious problem. It is only to note that, at least in comparison with Europe, there was more latitude and probably also a higher incidence of infanticide in Japan.

This changed considerably during the past one hundred years. And the most important fact is that it changed most especially after 1948, when abortion was finally legalized. That is to say, whereas earlier infanticide had been fairly common in Japan, the legalization of abortion was accompanied by a public turn *away* from infanticide as a means of controlling births. This was, I would claim, a major step *up* the putative slippery-slope.

The second step, it can be argued, is in process right now, and it involves the substitution of contraceptives for abortion as the preferred birth-control method. In the Japanese case, there has been a period—unnecessarily protracted—during which abortion has served as what Samuel Coleman calls the "major method of contraception," but that is gradually being supplanted by readily available condoms, IUDs, vasectomies, and the possibility of widespread use of the Pill in the near future. In fact, since it has been the women's movement in Japan that has led the uphill fight to gain ready access to the Pill, it must also be said that those involved in it have been a moral force in moving away from dependence on abortion and toward a much fuller use of contraceptive means. To that degree, it has been largely the concerned women of Japan who have been moving their nation up the so-called slippery slope.

The important point is that once contraception is sufficiently available to make recourse to abortion less and less needed in Japanese society, the rate of abortion should decrease dramatically. In that case Japan could become able to remove its unfavorable reputation as an "abortion heaven." In addition, that major change would mean that Japan had, over a historic progression, moved not only from dependence on infanticide to reliance on abortion but, after that, from abortion to contraception.[11]

To say this is not to deny that societies or subsocieties can sometimes become inured to morally objectionable practices. A real wariness about our own society coming to countenance the "removal" of the handicapped is justified. However, taking abortion as *the* sole or crucial index for judging whether a whole society is plunging down the moral ladder should be suspect.

In saying that Japan has in some sense moved "up the slippery slope," the point is *not* that Japan in some total sense shows moral progress. I am not arguing for some kind of evolutionary track operative in the realm of societal ethics, one on which the Japanese are doing better than we are.

The point I am making is much more modest. It is simply that the Japanese case provides us with a strong counterexample to claims concerning moral collapse as the inevitable consequence of legalized abortion. When I claim that on this issue the Japanese seem to have moved *up* the so-called slippery slope, this is not part of an attempt to take the moral pulse of whole societies but merely to suggest that no one can assume that abortion necessarily precipitates a downward plunge.

BEYOND FECUNDISM

One of the oppressive elements in the history of modern Japan seems to have been the severe pressure that the increasingly centralized government and its bureaucratic organs placed on family life and especially on women. The pressure was both legal, in terms of abortion's being illegal from the early Meiji period until 1948, and psychological, via the creation of a social climate in which each family was pressured into producing children as an expression of its patriotism and loyalty to the imperial institution. The Japanese bedroom was expected to be a kind of factory for the manufacture of soldiers and laborers. Women were to be maximally productive of sons and daughters who could and would serve the centralized state.

We have tried to show that, although to differing degrees, Japan's religions were sucked up into the ideology of production and reproduction for the sake of the state. The claim made here was that much of what happened in the late-nineteenth century and the first half of the twentieth was the playing out of the dynamics—as well as the eventual tragedy—of a neo-Shinto religious vision of Japan and its future. Although they dragged their feet on occasion, Buddhists during the period of fascist control fell in line with this vision. Since the neo-Shintoists had long held and insinuated that Buddhists were not sufficiently committed to maximum reproductivity, many Buddhists bent over backwards to prove their compliance.

When placed within the larger history of the world's religions, however, the neo-Shintoists seem to have been merely a heavily ideologized version of something found with great frequency. Human history seems to be full of perceived links between religious practice and human reproductivity. Fertility goddesses and phallic gods can be found in virtually every archaic tradition. Even though historically some cultures refused to be iconographically overt in their expressions of fertility as religiously important to them, the notion that *piety and fecundity are linked* was a notion that remained strong. Moreover, it often seems to have intensified when those perceived as hostile seemed to threaten the people—and religion—in question. In chapter 2, for instance, it was noted that in today's Sri Lanka this notion surfaces among Buddhists who worry about their own land and their own religion being threatened by too many non-Buddhists on that island.

Thus, for example, the God of both Jews and Christians, we are told, at the beginning of time issued the following command to Adam and Eve, "Be fruitful and multiply, and fill the earth and subdue it; and have dominion over the fish of the sea and over the birds of the air and over every living thing that moves on the earth" (Gen. 1:28). The Hebrew Bible has multiple cases of stated links between religious faithfulness and the production of abundant progeny; God explicitly tells Noah to be fertile and promises Abraham that his sons will be as many as the sands of the seashore.

Jeremy Cohen has demonstrated the rich interpretative tradition of this text, including that of Yavnean sages who believed that God sponsored reproduction because through the making of humans God saw his own image reflected, the whole reason for the creation.[12] This implied a ban on onanism, on any type of autoerotic behavior, and on marriage to women deemed incapable of childbearing. Cohen notes, "The rabbis repeatedly frowned on any sexual practice that did not aim toward conception."[13] It appears that only in the Hellenistic period, with the spread of ascetic practices among pagans, Jews, and eventually Christians, was there an "exclusion of sexual reproduction from the sphere of fundamentally important human activities."[14]

This was the only major interruption in a history of largely fecundist assumptions. And in Christianity, although there was a brief period of nonmarrying due to the expected early return of Christ, the stage was set for marriage to be valued again as important for populating the earth.

The germ of that can already be seen in the Epistles, where Paul writes, "Woman will be saved through bearing children, if she continues in faith and love and holiness, with modesty" (I Tim. 2:15). The message is there, and it is that piety and progeny are deeply connected.

The *submessage* is almost always there too; it is that the deity will give his people enough sons and daughters so they will be able to conquer needed lands and fight effectively against their enemies. This forging of a link between whatever is deemed "right" religion and fertility, so pervasive in human history, is what I have called fecundism. Although most overt in those religions that use the reproductive organs as icons and as objects of veneration, fecundism is not limited to them. It is found wherever people believe or are taught that high reproductivity shown by a specific tribe, nation, or religious group is viewed as desirable—and is assisted—by their deity.

It was argued earlier that Buddhism made a break, however uncleanly and at times ambiguously, with that notion. Buddhism is a system of thought within which fecundity has no *intrinsic* connection to what is thought religiously important. While in principle opposed to all homicide, Buddhists are for the most part not committed to natalism and certainly not to fecundism. Moreover, a deep difference on this score between the Buddhists and, for instance, the major thrust of neo-Shinto in Japan comes out clearly in what has been described in chapter 7 as the "debate" over abortion and infanticide in early-nineteenth-century Japan.

It should be made clear that I am not claiming that the Buddhists were collectively *precocious*—that twenty-five hundred years ago they somehow foresaw a world in which the threat of overpopulation and the rapid depletion of resources would be critical problems. They did not, we can be sure, have ecology and demography in mind when they articulated their vision of the monk who avoided making progeny and whose whole mode of life was reduced to the barest of essentials. The Buddhists' reasons for separating their notion of the religious path from existing forms of fecundism had to do with their idea of what it meant to have a sharply focused religious quest. Children were simply seen as hindrances to that.

That should not, however, prevent us from deriving new significance—a kind of secular significance, as it were—in the move to break with fecundism. That is, we may be at a time in human history when it has become obvious to many people that a good part of religion has been too long and too deeply co-opted by our biological and tribal instincts. One of the reasons, in fact, that religion as a whole became suspect in the eyes of many people in the modern era is that they became aware of how pervasive has been humanity's efforts to construct gods in the image of the constructor—that is, as the kind of projection Ludwig Feuerbach, in

1841, had declared religion to be. Causasians made their gods white. Semites made them semitic. And males made them male. And whenever racial or ethnic struggles were involved, both sides assumed the deity would be a staunch ally—if asked and propitiated in the right way. And long before they engaged in actual battle against one another, whole tribes and nations undertook programs of production and of *reproduction*, activities that they claimed to be the "will" of the god or gods.

When Japan's neo-Shintoist theologians, writing in the 1830s and 1840s, insisted that the Japanese kami desired a Japan that "bustled" with people and had explicitly given men and women sexual organs meant to be used for maximal production, they were merely saying what the theologians of this kind of "tribal" religion have said all over the world for many millennia. Data from a wide spectrum of religions show that virtually each of them has a deity or deities that, in a way fitting its own tradition, encourages the select tribe or nation to reproduce in goodly numbers. On this there is nothing unique about Jahweh's telling the ancient Jews to do so or about accounts of the Japanese kami feeling good when the Japanese are fertile. To this degree there is a thread of striking similarity running through many of the world's religions. And it is for that reason also suspect—in the eyes of many.

We recognize it immediately in what the Reverend Pat Robertson declared while campaigning to be America's president. The *New York Times* reported what Robertson had been saying to anti-abortion groups in 1987 in the following way:

> Pat Robertson, the Republican Presidential hopeful, said today that Government policy should encourage the birth of more American children to pay future bills and to stave off the decline "of our culture and our values." [Otherwise] Western nations would be extremely vulnerable to threats from other ideologies. "At current rates . . . our share of the world population—I'm talking about the entire West—will come in 100 years from 33 percent of all the people in the world to 7 1/2 percent." "That not only means that we no longer have any dominance in the world, but our culture and our values will at that point be squeezed out . . . and we as a nation [will be] extremely vulnerable as well as our allies in Europe."[15]

So fecundism becomes the agenda—to protect Western values, to pay the bills of the future, and to make sure that America and its European allies will not be "vulnerable."

It is not hard to hear echoes of the neo-Shinto rhetoricians—and perhaps even distant drumrolls—in this. The agenda involves the preparing of enough population to fight future wars, sons and perhaps also daughters born in goodly numbers so that, even if they return home on slabs and stretchers, there will be others to take their places. Although Robertson did not explicitly say that such a policy is "the will of God," there may be such implications in his reference to the need to protect "our culture and our values."

Such ways of conceptualizing the deity—as a supernatural partisan of "our" cause or "our" culture vis-à-vis those of others—is, many today sense, nothing more than idolatry in the mind. In fact, the rise of secularism in the modern world, so bemoaned and castigated by the religious right—whether Protestant, Catholic, Jewish, Muslim, Buddhist, or whatever—is, much more than its detractors admit, due in part to a growing sense of revulsion against such motifs of tribal idolatry that have long been, and remain, in so many religions. They feel that true religion, whatever else it may be, cannot possibly be *that*.

It may be that in seeing things this way the modern secularist is—in his or her own way—recapitulating something of the ancient Buddhists' sense that religion rightly conceived is unconnected to fecundism. Needless to say, this does not mean that people with this view are really crypto-Buddhists. Nor, to be sure, does it mean that our own culture would have to be transformed into a Buddhist one in order to gain freedom from fecundism. It is merely to suggest that there may be *contemporary utility* in what had once been an effort to separate religion from the notion that the deity takes special delight in the proliferation of "our" kind of people.

There is no reason why a practical critique of fecundism cannot be made using a variety of resources, some of them secular and some of them having roots in the West's own religious traditions. After all, in Christianity and Judaism too there are strong suggestions that religion ought to be other than a collective egotism marching under the name of God. If we could carry out such a many-sided critique of fecundism, we might be able to derive more benefit from our secularity and be much less embarrassed by our religions.

SOLUTIONS

Nakatani Kinko is an expert on criminal law. In 1970, she writes, she attended a legal-issues conference in West Germany. It became the catalyst for her deepened interest in abortion law. This was because she was shocked to hear Western scholars debating at great length about the *exact day of the soul's entry* into the fetus according to Christian doctrine—and how pinpointing that event seemed somehow crucial to the whole matter. She writes, "For me as a Japanese involved in the study of criminal law the debate conducted within this framework of thought seemed beyond belief. I fully realized at that point that when it comes to abortion the history and way of thinking of us Japanese and the people of the West is very, very different."[16]

There are also persons in the West, it is worth noting, to whom the focus of that particular conference would have seemed just about as absurd as it did to Nakatani. Yet even if we ourselves might have trouble entering into such a debate with seriousness, we *are* able to recognize the mentality that assumed the abortion question might be somehow solved by answering a technical question and then fashioning law to fit that answer.

In this basic *approach* there is, as Nakatani intuited, something very Western. Even if we cannot share the theology and metaphysics of the debate she observed in Germany, we continue to conduct our debates as if there were simple and "right" answers to issues as complex as this. We also, like the conferees, tend to believe that with such answers we will be able to fashion good law. We will then, we tend to think, be able to decide whether abortion is "right" or "wrong."

Or, when the struggle becomes pitched, we define our positions in stark terms. This means avoiding ambiguity and disapproving of ambivalence in those we count as our allies. Thus the battle over abortion turns into one between the "rights of a woman over her own body" and the "right of a fetus to live." Large and complicated positions are reduced to *single* points of focus, points that make legalized abortion "right" to one side and "wrong" to another.

Neither side can or will recognize even a modicum of truth in the other's position. If this, in fact, tends to be a characteristic of the Western—or at least American—way of approaching this issue, it does contrast quite sharply with one found in Japan. With her characteristic ability to get to the core of such matters, Takie Sugiyama Lebra writes,

> The Japanese are used to sayings like: "Even a thief may be 30 percent right" and "To hold a grudge against others is not good, but to do something that arouses a grudge in others is just as bad." The Japanese tend to hold everyone involved in a conflict responsible for it. The Anglo-American compulsion for a court trial that determines one person guilty and the other innocent is in remarkable contrast to the Japanese ideal that mutual apology and compromise be attained between the parties before the conflict attracts public attention.[17]

This accords well with details of matters looked at in earlier chapters—for instance, the impulse to make apology to a fetus and the unwillingness to depend on legislation to "decide" the rightness or wrongness of such complex issues.

It is not by accident that the complex body of differences that separate one side from the other in the American debate over abortion have settled into rival claims over interpretation of the *law*. Appeal to the Constitution and its interpretation become the place where everything lies. The focus of one side is on the *right* to life while that of the other is the *right* to choice and privacy. Both sides hope—or fear—that the entire "abortion war" will be won or lost by past or future legislation. But, aware only of how pitched their battle must be, both sides seem oblivious to the *commonality* in their rhetoric.

To say this is not to minimize the awesome power of laws to have an impact on our lives, even on the most private aspects of them. The point to be noticed, simply, is that we may have built ourselves into a very tight box. We have become a people who cannot think beyond legal solutions to our societal problems—or apart from public actions and reactions designed to effect law. Our range of cultural, societal options thereby becomes impoverished. Flexibility is lost.

This loss of flexibility also means we have moved farther away from the American tradition of pragmatism—pragmatism that is increasingly difficult to find when the rhetoric is as heated and heavily ideological as it has become. The point here is that although the West's tradition includes a heavy dependence on legal frameworks for addressing problems, there is—at least in the American context—also a tradition of pragmatism.[18] And pragmatism, especially as a social philosophy, will make us wary of ideologies—both of the left and of the right. The pragmatist is concerned about what may be happening to community and social solidarity when opposing participants in public debate are insisting on total victory. That is, although he or she is intensely interested in finding solutions to specific social problems, if social solidarity has been sacrificed, it has not been a real solution at all.

In American life the protracted struggle over abortion has rapidly become a face-off between two heavily ideologized agendas in pursuit of clear-cut victory. There is little sense that an entire nation's need for solidarity should also be factored in.

The gain to us in looking hard at how the Japanese have dealt with this problem could come, perhaps, in the form of a stimulus to us to reappreciate the importance of pragmatism. In some sense, especially when contrasted with the neo-Shinto and liberationist positions on abortion, it is the Buddhist position that articulates a kind of societal pragmatism.[19] It forefronts the need for a solution but, importantly, one that does not tear the social fabric apart. Community matters.[20]

Also, if we compare the Buddhist position with that of neo-Shinto and of liberationism, it seems clear that it does not so readily become ideologically driven. In fact, it shows a certain wariness vis-à-vis both the transformation of religion into ideology and an ideology that is utopian. Although this wariness is connected to Buddhists' interest in not rupturing the social fabric, there is also a sense that ideologists tend to portray either the past or the future in unrealistic and unrealizable ways. Jeffrey Stout makes an apt and interesting comparison: "Pragmatists can refuse metaphysical comfort because they adopt a Buddhist-like attitude toward incoherent desires that add nothing but disappointment to life. That is, they try to extinguish such desires."[21]

If the Buddhists of Japan have somehow come into possession of ways to handle abortion that seem less disruptive to society than our own, this is because over time they have put together a practical "response" to this problem. What is noteworthy is that their response has indeed been hammered together out of bits and pieces. Some of these are doctrinal, some come from folk religious roots, some are metaphors that are linguistic enablers, and some involve strategic silences—that is, not making declarations about what cannot be known.[22]

The formation of this position, then, is an unusually *open* case of moral bricolage. And perhaps because it is pragmatist about such things, that mode of pasting together the pieces of a moral stance is not deemed inadequate or lacking in rationality. Japan's Buddhists lodge their objections against the abuses of the tatari-mongerers but, as we have seen, do not seem ready to jettison the tolerant approach to abortion that they themselves have forged over time.

Some advantages in this should be clear. This view makes abortion permissible but, at the same time, makes unnecessary any denial of strong emotions a woman might have about her fetus as life and even as a child. In short, there is no need to reduce the options to "inviolable life" or "an unwanted pregnancy." A third option—perhaps a middle way between the others—is opened. That is, a woman is free to acknowledge any feelings of bonding that have developed within herself. Such feelings need not bar her from deciding to have an abortion.

In addition, of course, this high degree of pragmatism allows for close attention to the education and welfare of children. It prioritzies the well-being of real children in this world over putative children in other worlds. It contributes directly and substantially to what the Catholic observers in sixteenth-century Japan noted about good life conditions and behavior of such children. And it contributes as well to what Robert Nisbet pinpointed as the Japanese possession of what may be the strongest family system in the world.

CONCLUSION

THERE IS NO easy way either to sum up what has been written about here or to tuck away what may still be loose ends. Perhaps the best way to close down is to open up—that is, by enlarging the scope of considerations somewhat. I will try to do that by commenting on two matters. The first has to do with how we think of Japan, and the second constitutes a note about abortion and our earth.

I expect that, among those things that will shape the reactions Westerners might have to the phenomenon of mizuko kuyō, one factor bound to be present will be our own perplexity concerning just how "alien" Japanese social practices really are. As our involvement with Japan deepens on many fronts, our curiosity and sometimes even our consternation deepens. Although I began this study hoping that something I could call "Japan" could throw some light on features of our culture's ongoing debate about abortion, that project became complicated by my growing recognition that "Japan" too is something about which our own culture has increasingly entered into discussion, even debate. So although I began thinking of Japan as the stable pole and of "abortion" as the contested arena, I came to see that this topic is really one in which *two contested items* come together.

The fact is that Japan still—or, more accurately, *again*—shows a capacity to throw us into a quandary. During most of the Cold War, Americans, for a variety of reasons, tended to regard Japan in a non-adversarial way—that is, as a country that, however strange its old ways had been, was progressively becoming more and more like us. And it was, we assumed, becoming so in a way that would position it comfortably within the company of what we wished to regard as our "client states."

Americans, however, have been caught up short. And what has surprised us, I suggest, is not just the strength of the economic power Japan has rapidly gathered but also the perception that Japan is unusually successful *as a society*. Moreover, because this awareness comes at a time when Americans have increasing worries about the direction and success of their own society, the "otherness" of Japan becomes not merely a matter of curiosity but one of implicit challenge, even of threat. Simply by virtue of its seeming "successes" in a world in which comparisons come quickly and almost automatically, Japanese society impinges on our own lives whether we want it to or not. It is not just the economic power but the fact that Japanese children excel in school, that Japanese city streets are safe even in the dark, that people do not go homeless, and that employment is high. The comparisons—implicit or explicit—force us to be caught up in a debate about "Japan" that is more intense than it has ever been since the days of World War II.

That debate is intensified because there exist, probably for the first time, experts on Japan who are willing to state that our own society would do well to *learn from Japan*. This kind of advice has increasingly spread along a variety of fronts. For instance, one of the "lessons" many commentators and public officials drew from Chalmers Johnson's widely read *MITI and the Japanese Miracle* was the need for a deeper and more direct involvement by the American government in the formation of industrial policy and growth—on the Japanese model.[1] Likewise, Thomas P. Rohlen's *For Harmony and Strength*, while objectively depicting the effective mechanisms of cooperation within enterprises and institutions in Japan, stimulated debate concerning the "importability" of such mechanisms, especially because they were obviously already being put in place to some degree within Japanese-managed companies in North America.[2] Discussions of "learning from Japan" in this domain appeared frequently in the American public media. In his *Taking Japan Seriously*, Ronald Dore explicitly argues for the applicability of Japanese modes to Great Britain and the United States.[3]

Then Merry White, in her *Japanese Educational Challenge*, focused for the West the implications of Japanese achievements in the world of education.[4] Certainly the American debate over ways to improve the quality of education has been greatly stimulated by what many have called the "lessons" to be gained from Japanese ways. David H. Bayley's *Forces of Order* brought out the effectiveness of Japanese policing methods and to some American communities suggested the value of implementing Japanese methods of "policing" by means of closer, on-the-beat-type relationships between the police and their communities.[5] It is no surprise that delegations of American law enforcers subsequently went on fact-finding trips to Japan to see what could be learned there.

Discussions of law and legal processes have not been unaffected. While American observers are surprised to learn of the low percentage of attorneys in Japanese society and the governmental regulation of that number, American scholars of Japanese law have been impressed with the actual effectiveness of its procedures. J. Mark Ramseyer and Minoru Nakazato have shown how those processes provide a high level of compliance with the laws while at the same time needing a much lower rate of recourse to the court.[6] And in his *Authority without Power*, John Owen Haley explains the historical process through which the Japanese, while focusing on correction rather than on exact determination of guilt, have achieved low recidivism rates and an ever-declining crime rate. Moreover, reacting against a kind of cultural relativism that would suggest that Japanese accomplishments have relevance only for themselves, Haley writes, "Cultural explanations tend to be equally, albeit more subtly, ethnocentric by quarantining the Japanese experience and denying its relevance outside of Japan's peculiar cultural setting."[7] The implication here too seems to be that Japan provides a context from which we ourselves might well glean new insights and methods.

To be sure, there are persons in the West, even scholars of Japan, to whom the notion of "learning from Japan" is, almost by definition, repugnant and objectionable. This attitude, no doubt, has a variety of causes, some of which are quite openly ideological. While it is true that neither the automatic superiority of Japanese practices nor their easy importability ought to be assumed, it is contrary to the norms of good science to assume automatically that there is no need or reason even to *explore* the utility of something that seems to be working well elsewhere.

And Japanese ways of dealing with abortion, I wish to advance through this study, deserve exploration by us in greater depth and detail. It would seem clear that Western societies would want to avoid—and probably could quite easily avoid—the kind of patent abuses that arise from the notion that a fetus can and will wreak vengeance on its parent. No doubt there would also have to be a conscious concern to ensure the existence of other kinds of safeguards against abuse.

However, it is not, I think, insignificant that Westerners who have lived in Japan—including persons who are Christian—have increasingly come to the view that there is an appreciable level of psychological and spiritual sanity in the practices of mizuko kuyō and that aspects of these practices should be introduced into Western society and the ambit of the West's religious modalities. Although, given the official positions of the Roman Catholic Church on abortion, there is a reluctance to articulate such things overtly, a growing number of Catholics in Japan, I am told, have an interest in exploring what of the mizuko kuyō could be transferred into Christianity. There are also, it appears, members of the clergy who share this interest, and this all seems to arise from a sense that the churches that condemn abortion wholesale have in many instances proven unreasonable and impractical.

This supports, I suspect, the view that the debate about learning from Japan ought also to include a careful, balanced, open look at how abortion is dealt with there. For Americans to join in that debate might prove to be very profitable—especially since, as now seems to be the case, discussions of abortion in the United States threaten to remain deadlocked, divisive, or both. One of the salient features of the Japanese approach appears to be that it has enabled that society to avoid the kind of social division and disruptions we have been absorbed in for decades now. To the extent that it contributes to social solidarity rather than to fracturedness, the Japanese approach is eminently pragmatic.[8]

When persons are inclined to view religious phenomena, symbols, and language as nothing other than ideology, the mizuko phenomenon in Japan will be seen as precisely that. Such a reductive path will take the practices depicted in this book as *nothing other* than clever manipulations, ploys for gaining monetary profit, and forms of religion in the service of conservative politics. My point is not that such abuses will not occur. This study has shown that in Japan, as in other places, the grief and guilt of individuals is often misused by unscrupulous persons and organizations. Such misuses surely deserve public censure.

But if that is *all* that we see, we will have missed something. We will have lost the chance to explore the possibility that rituals such as those for mizuko may have a positive therapeutic function.[9] Our studies should remain, I suggest, open to the possibility that metaphors, symbols, and rites—some of them often religious in nature—often will seem indispensable to a given society in dealing with and solving its intellectual, moral, and social problems. In this perspective there is no need to judge such a society against one assumed to be able to operate without metaphor and on a basis of "rationality" alone.[10]

For us such a way of thinking about how to deal with abortion will, as I have argued, involve new configurations of thinking about morality. But any society, to the extent that it is interested in the practical *resolution* of its problems, will necessarily deal with its intellectual and moral dilemmas by means of bricolage. Its efforts to solve its ethical problems will do well to be informed by pragmatism.

Concerning abortion—and some other issues as well—American society often seems less in touch with its pragmatic tradition than it profitably could be. Too often this problem appears to have been dealt with only in terms of two ideologies diametrically opposed to one another. These then become two sets of ideas without a detectable capacity to allow for compromise between them. Japan's approach, although initially so different from our own that it almost looks incomprehensible and bizarre, is in fact very *pragmatic*. And it has kept the society from flying apart over the issue. To the extent that a concern for social solidarity is intrinsic to the pragmatist's approach, it should come as no surprise that Japan has garnered certain—but not all—of the benefits of pragmatism as a public philosophy. And ironically that is a philosophy once thought by Americans to be rather specially their own.

. . . . .

Finally, a comment about abortion and population. In one of her incisive essays about America's abortion dilemma, Mary Gordon writes,

We must be realistic about the impact on society of millions of unwanted children in an overpopulated world. Most of the time human beings do not have sex because they want to make babies. Yet sex has, throughout history, resulted in unwanted pregnancies. And women have always aborted. One thing that is neither hidden, mysterious, nor debatable is that the illegality of abortions will result in the deaths of women, as it always has.[11]

There are at least three points of importance in this paragraph, points on which I will expand.

Japanese history provides no exception whatsoever to the universal rule that, when prohibited, abortion kills women. Although it is feasible that a pill such as RU-486 will make it possible to jettison an unwanted fetus more easily than with current mechanical methods, the pro-life movement in North America will undoubtedly do what it can to keep such chemical abortifacients illegal. And if that movement succeeds, the need to resort to more dangerous methods will, just as Gordon suggests, result in deaths—deaths that are completely unnecessary. In Japan one of the things that will bear close watching is whether or not such chemical means become readily available. The monetary profit that the medical profession makes by providing abortions may make that difficult. Since there has been such resistance there to the availability of the Pill as a form of contraception, there may be a similar refusal to license and legalize a pill that itself performs abortions.[12] My argument that abortion has become relatively accessible in Japan does not negate the fact that things could be made *much* easier for Japanese women than they are and that the responsible involvement of men in contraception is of crucial importance.

The second point worthy of comment is Gordon's reference to "the impact on society of millions of unwanted children." Here is probably an area wherein the Japanese materials could be most instructive. I have argued that one of the reasons the Japanese legalized abortion is that it promotes their goal of making sure that the children who are born are also *maximally wanted*. Achieving this has meant the rejection of fecundism and a societal switch to thinking about children in terms of the quality of their lives. The "having" of a child is never merely equivalent to giving birth to it.

The tangible benefits of this policy can be readily shown. By UNICEF's account, infant mortality in Japan is, along with that of Sweden and Finland, the world's lowest; that of the United States climbs yearly. Japanese literacy is 99 percent compared to 80 percent in the United States. The school dropout rate is only 6 percent compared to 30 percent. Drug episodes and crimes of rape remain statistically very few. Children in Japan's cities do not live in fear of their lives because of lethal weapons in the hands of adults and other children.

And children in such a society do very well. Merry White writes, "The challenge inherent in the Japanese school is a clear demonstration of the power of cultural consensus and of being true to one's roots. If we want to borrow anything from the Japanese, it is paradoxically the attention they devote to their own paramount cultural property: the improvement of children's lives."[13] Here is where the trade-off seems to have taken place. The historical development in Japan of an emphasis on the family *as planned*—with abortion in that picture when necessary—has also made possible this kind of emphasis on the quality of children's lives and education.

Lastly, there is Gordon's passing reference to "an overpopulated world." It is perhaps for the sake of such a world that the critique of fecundism—and the impact of fecundism on our abortion debates—is most urgent. If the United Nations's projections are correct, the world's population will have doubled, perhaps tripled, by the end of the next century.

Bill McKibben, whose *End of Nature* cogently argues for urgent measures to keep us from incrementally destroying our planet as a habitable place, specifies what is needed in practical terms. In phrases that sound as if they could have come from the texts of the earliest Buddhists, he writes of the need to eschew utopianism but also to condition ourselves so that "our desires are not the engine." The key thing is that "we would have to conquer the desire to grow in numbers."[14]

To carry this into our debates about abortion would mean that this worldwide and *panhuman* problem—namely the livability of our planet—would have to be factored in as well. The reversal of the fecundism to which humankind has become habituated, then, is not just of benefit to women but to everyone. The preservation of a woman's right to decide matters of momentous importance to her is not the only criterion that should be used in arguing for legalized abortion.

Perhaps what McKibben refers to as "the desire to grow in numbers" is biologically programmed into us. In prehistoric times it may in fact have facilitated the physical survival of the human race. But on top of that biological impulse, at least in many cultures, various kinds of religious ideas have been placed, which, in essence, turned reproductivity into a mode of being godly. The multiplication of one's kind became both an index of divine favor and, it was often assumed, a way of receiving such favor.

Although there would seem to be little we can do to offset the biological component in our desire to grow in numbers, we should be able to have more success in dealing with those religious ideas and motifs that have, in fact, become inimical and even hazardous to our human future. With so much at stake, it would increasingly seem the morality of fecundist religion needs to be brought under close scrutiny and criticism. Perhaps what the world needs to meet the looming crisis is an approach that is both more rational and more religious than that.

APPENDIX

"THE WAY TO MEMORIALIZE ONE'S MIZUKO"

(Translation of Promotional Brochure of Shiun-zan Jizō-ji)

1. The mizuko resulting from a terminated pregnancy is a child existing in the realm of darkness. The principal things that have to be done for its sake are the making of a full apology and the making of amends to such a child.

In contrast to the child in darkness because of an ordinary miscarriage or by natural death after being born, the child here discussed is in its present location because its parents took active steps to prevent it from being born alive in our world. If the parents merely carry out ordinary memorial rites but fail to make a full apology to their child, their mizuko will never be able to accept their act.

Think for a moment how even birds and beasts, when about to be killed, show a good deal of anger and distress. Then how much more must be the shock and hurt felt by a fetus when its parent or parents have decided to abort it? And on top of that it does not even yet have a voice with which to make complaint about what is happening.

It often happens that the living children of persons who have repeatedly had abortions will in the middle of the night cry out "Father, help!" or "Help me, Mommy!" because of nightmares. Uncontrollable weeping or cries of "I'm scared! I'm scared!" on the part of children are really caused by dreams through which their aborted siblings deep in the realm of darkness give expression to their own distress and anger. Persons who are not satisfied with this explanation would do well to have a look at two publications of the Purple Cloud Villa; these are entitlted *Mizuko Jizō-ji's Collection of the Experiences of Departed Souls* and *The Medical Dictionary of Life.*

2. The next thing to do in remembering the mizuko is to set up an image of Jizō on the Buddhist altar in one's own home. That will serve as a substitute for a memorial tablet for the mizuko. Such a Jizō can do double service. On one hand it can represent the soul of the mizuko for parents doing rites of apology to it. Simultaneously, however, the Jizō is the one to whom can be made an appeal in prayer to guide the fetus through the realm of departed souls. Such Jizō images for home use can be obtained from the Purple Cloud Villa but can also be purchased at any shop specializing in Buddhist art and implements. As long as one performs this worship with a pure heart it is bound to have a positive effect.

Some prices follow. Jizō images made of metal are either 3,000 yen for silver ones or 4,000 yen for gold. Add 1,100 yen to the price of either of these if home delivery is desired. These are prices as of September 1984.

3. Inasmuch as the Jizō image on the Buddhist altar also does double duty as a memorial tablet for a terminated fetus, it is allowable—after asking permission of the Jizō—to give it a place on the altar lower than the memorial tablets for one's parents and ancestors. Also it does not matter greatly whether it is to the right or the left on the altar.

4. The next thing of importance is to set up a stone Jizō image either in the cemetery of the Mizuko Jizō Temple or at one's own family temple. Such will serve as substitute for a grave-stone for the aborted child and will constitute an eternal, ongoing ritual of apology and remembrance. Such action will undoubtably have a good effect—a fact shown in things published in our monthly periodical "The Purple Cloud." The expenses involved in setting up a stone Jizō Buddha at our place are fully detailed in our publication "Concerning the 10,000 Jizōs." If requested, we will be pleased to send it.

5. The following pertains to the number of images needed if a person is the parent of more than one mizuko. One of each on the home altar and in the cemetery will suffice if all the mizuko were produced by a single couple—whether married or not. If, however, the father of a later mizuko was different than an earlier one—and, of course, also had a different family registry—separate Jizō images will be required. An exception to this could be made if a woman were to discuss this candidly with her second husband and get his permission. Then it would be just as in the case of a woman bringing along into her second marriage the children begotten in an earlier one. In such a case if she requests that the deceased ancestors understand the situation, it is allowable for all her mizukos to be collectively remembered with a single image.

6. When at your home altar you are giving a daily portion of rice and water offering to your deceased ancestors be sure to include the mizuko too—and let them know of their inclusion. Also pray for the well-being of your mizuko in the other world. Do this by standing before the Buddhas there and reciting either the Heart Sutra or the Psalm to Jizō used at the Jizō cemetery in Chichibu. In addition to that, if as an ongoing remembrance of your mizuko you write out in longhand a copy of the Heart Sutra once a day, you will at some point along the way receive the assurance that your child has most certainly reached Buddhahood. Until you receive such an assurance you should continue to perform these rites of apology and remembrance.

7. To make amends for the fact that you never had to pay anything for the upbringing and education of a mizuko you should give to the Buddha every day an offering of 100 yen for each of your mizuko. However, if you have had as many as ten terminated pregnancies, there may be hardship in laying out 1,000 yen every day; in such cases it is permissible to give only 300 or 500 yen—or even to give more or less depending on one's income. This is an expression of apology to the child for not having given it a love-filled upbringing. Therefore, you should put your love into these acts of remembrance, not being stingy with your time and resources. Once you get into the habit of thinking how much easier it would be simply to make a 10,000 yen contribution once a month, you are missing the whole point. It is far better to put a daily offering on the altar every day and then on a special, designated day pay a visit to the Jizō Temple at Chichibu and make a contribution to the temple. Alternatively, you could do it while making the 88-temple pilgrimage on the island of Shikoku or the pilgrimage to the 100 Kannon sites in western Japan.

8. When a person has awakened to the value and importance of remembering mizuko, one gains a much deeper faith and makes efforts to live as a bodhisattva, setting one's mind to performing at least one act of goodness each day. Also

vowing to go on pilgrimage to Shikoku or the Kannon sites is an excellent way to be total and thoroughgoing in one's act of apologizing to and remembering the mizuko. It is important to be of a mind to do more than enough; to be of the opinion that one has already done plenty is just the kind of attitude that evokes a bad effect.

9. Children that are miscarried, born dead, or die shortly after being born differ, of course, from those whose lives are cut short by being terminated by their parents. Nevertheless, they too are mizuko and, when one gives consideration to his or her responsibility for the fact that these too did not enter life successfully, it would seem good to provide them too with mizuko rites just as one would in the case of aborted fetuses.

10. Households whose members think about the seriousness of karmic laws related to abortion are also households which can take advantage of such occasions in order to deepen the faith of those within them. By continuing to perform adequate rites of apology and memorial, such persons later are blessed with the birth of fine, healthy children. Or, as an extension of good fortune, there are many instances of people really thriving. Some persons find that their own severe heart diseases are cured or that the rebelliousness of children or neuroses go away. When on top of all that there is increased prosperity in the family business, there is good cause for lots of happiness.

Why not find out more about this by simply paying a visit to the Jizō Temple in Chichibu?

NOTES

CHAPTER 1
BEHIND THE GREAT BUDDHA

1. Kannon, a figure originally known in India as Avalokiteśvara, was initially male. Over time its iconography underwent a progressive feminization, so that today many think of it as the Buddhist "Goddess" of Mercy.

2. The child-monk was common in medieval and early-modern Japan, especially because orphaned children were often sent into monasteries for care. Artistic and iconographic representations of them were prized. Innocence, holiness, and charm were seen combined in such figures.

3. See essays in Sakurai Tokutarō, ed., *Jizō shinkō* (Yūzankaku Shuppan, 1983); Ishida Mizumaro, *Jigoku* (Kyoto: Hōzōkan, 1985), 236–54; and Ogura Yasushi, "Ojizōsan to kodomo: hitotsu no bunka henyō," *Hikaku bungaku kenkyū*, no. 48, 74–94.

4. Shundo Tachibana, *The Ethics of Buddhism* (London: Curzon Press, 1926), 81. Texts refer to *brunahatiya*, "killing a fetus."

5. In the years immediately after World War II, the self-criticism of many of Japan's Buddhists often led to such a conclusion. An especially strong censure from within was Watanabe Shōkō, in his *Nihon no bukkyō* (Iwanami Shoten, 1958).

6. Jeffrey Stout, *Ethics after Babel: The Languages of Morals and Their Discontents* (Boston: Beacon Press, 1988), 74. Stout, objecting to Lévi-Strauss's attribution of this only to so-called primitive peoples, writes, "We are all *bricoleurs* insofar as we are capable of creative thought at all" (p. 74).

7. Stout, *Ethics after Babel*, 75.

CHAPTER 2
A WORLD OF WATER AND WORDS

1. In this I find much value in the arguments presented by George Lakoff in his ongoing studies of metaphor. See, for instance, his *Metaphors We Live By*, co-authored with Mark Johnson (Chicago: University of Chicago Press, 1980), and his *More Than Cool Reason: A Field Guide to Poetic Metaphor*, co-authored with Mark Turner (Chicago: University of Chicago Press, 1989).

2. For the underlying basics of this medieval Buddhist cosmology, see Paul Mus, *La lumière sur les six voies: tableau de la transmigration bouddhiques* (Paris: Travaux et Mémoires de l'Institut d'Ethnologie, 1939), and my *Karma of Words: Buddhism and the Literary Arts in Medieval Japan* (Berkeley: University of California Press, 1983), 26–59.

3. Murasaki Shikibu, *The Tale of Genji*, translated by Edward G. Seidensticker (New York: Alfred A. Knopf, 1977), 1:85.

4. Hiro Sachiya, "Mizu to hi, soshite chi," in *Risō* 614 (July 1984): 83–88.

5. An accessible version of the "Fire Sermon," as translated from the *Maha-*

Vagga, is in Henry Clarke Warren, *Buddhism in Translations* (New York: Atheneum, 1969), 351–53.

6. *Bhavisyottara-purana* 31, 14, as quoted in Mircea Eliade, *Patterns in Comparative Religion*, translated by Rosemary Sheed (New York: Sheed and Ward, 1958), 128.

7. Gen. 1:20–22. For the fascinating history of the interpretation of this text within both Jewish and Christian communites, see Jeremy Cohen, *"Be Fruitful and Increase, Fill the Earth and Master It": The Ancient and Medieval Career of a Biblical Text* (Ithaca, N.Y.: Cornell University Press, 1989).

8. D. C. Lau, trans., *Tao Te Ching* (Baltimore: Penguin Books, 1963), 128.

9. Ibid., 64. On the importance of this kind of symbolism in Taoism, see especially N. J. Girardot, *Myth and Meaning in Early Taoism* (Berkeley: University of California Press, 1983).

10. See, for example, Lowell Bloss, "The Buddha and the Nāga: A Study in Buddhist Folk Religiosity," *History of Religions* 13:1 (August 1973): 36–53; E. R. Leach, "Pulleyar and the Lord Buddha: An Aspect of Religious Syncretism in Ceylon," *Psychoanalysis and the Psychoanalytic Review* 49:2 (1962): 80–102; and S. J. Tambiah, *Buddhism and the Spirit Cults of North-east Thailand* (Cambridge: Cambridge University Press, 1970), esp. 109ff.

11. Richard Gombrich and Gananath Obeyesekere, *Buddhism Transformed: Religious Change in Sri Lanka* (Princeton: Princeton University Press, 1988), 267.

12. Ibid., 270–73.

13. Donald Keene, trans., *Essays in Idleness: The Tsurezuregusa of Kenkō* (New York: Columbia University Press, 1967), 163, 166.

14. Eliade, *Patterns*, 188.

15. Gaston Bachelard, *Water and Dreams: An Essay on the Imagination of Water*, translated by Edith R. Farrell (Dallas: The Pegasus Foundation, 1983), 183. A brilliant use of Bachelard's water meditations by a modern Japanese philosopher is Sakabe Megumi, *Kamen no kaishakugaku* (Tōkyō Daigaku Shuppankai, 1976), 34ff.

16. *Nihon-kokugo daijiten* (Shogakkan, 1975), 18:553.

17. Takahashi Bonsen, *Nihon jinkō-shi no kenkyū* (Sanyūsha, 1941–1962), 347.

18. Donald L. Philippi, trans., *Kojiki* (Tokyo: University of Tokyo Press, 1968), 51. Philippi holds to the eighth-century pronunciation of *piru-go* for leech-child. Original text is in Aoki Kazuo et al. eds., the *Nihon shisō taikei: Kojiki* (Iwanami Shoten, 1982), 23.

19. Takahashi Bonsen, *Nihon jinkō-shi no kenkyū*, 348.

20. Iwai Hiroshi, "Nihonjin to mizu no shinsō-shinri," *Risō* 614 (July 1984): 89–99, and esp. 93.

21. Philippi, *Kojiki*, 49. Original text in Aoki, *Kojiki*, 21.

22. W. G. Aston, trans., *Nihongi: Chronicles of Japan from the Earliest Times to A.D. 697* (Rutland, Vt.: Charles E. Tuttle, 1972), 95. Original text in Sakamoto Tarō et al., eds., *Nihon koten bungaku taikei: Nihonshoki* (Iwanami Shoten, 1967), 168.

23. A survey by prefectures of these practices and the beliefs accompanying them are in Onshi-zaidan-boshi-aiikukai, ed., *Nihon san-iku shūzoku shiryō-shūsei* (Dai'ichi Hoki Shuppan, 1975), 159–77.

24. Chiba Tokuji and Ōtsu Tadao, *Mabiki to mizuko: kosodate no fuōkuroa* (Nōsangyōson Bunka Kyōkai, 1983), esp. 31–38. The common words are *kaeru/ kaesu*, *modoru/modosu*, and combinations thereof.

25. Chiba and Ōtsu, *Mabiki to mizuko*, 24.

26. Terauchi Daikichi, a writer who is also a Buddhist priest, notes that the records of his temple show that until recently there was ritual simplicity and no use of *kaimyō* for such infants. See his "Gendai no mizuko jizō," in *Jizōsama nyūmon*, Daihōrin-Henshūbu, ed. (Daihōrinkaku, 1984), 92–93. On *kaimyō* and ancestral rites as a way of putting distance between deceased ancestors and the living, see Robert J. Smith, *Ancestor Worship in Contemporary Japan* (Stanford: Stanford University Press, 1974).

CHAPTER 3
SOCIAL DEATH, SOCIAL BIRTH

1. The key works are Arnold van Gennep, *The Rites of Passage* (Chicago: University of Chicago Press, 1960); Mircea Eliade, *Rites and Symbols of Initiation: The Mysteries of Birth and Rebirth* (New York: Harper and Row, 1958); and Victor Turner, *The Ritual Process: Structure and Anti-Structure* (Chicago: Aldine, 1969).

2. See especially Walter Edwards, *Modern Japan through Its Weddings: Gender, Person, and Society in Ritual Portrayal* (Stanford: Stanford University Press, 1989).

3. David W. Plath, "Where the Family of God Is the Family: The Role of the Dead in Japanese Households," *American Anthropologist* 66 (1964): 300–317, quotation from 312.

4. Culture, as Robert J. Smith has repeatedly noted, really matters, perhaps especially when studying Japan. See his "Something Old, Something New—Tradition and Culture in the Study of Japan," *The Journal of Asian Studies* 48:4 (November 1989): 715–23.

5. Robert J. Smith, *Ancestor Worship in Contemporary Japan* (Stanford: Stanford University Press, 1974), 41, and Herman Ooms, "The Religion of the Household: A Case Study of Ancestor Worship in Japan," *Contemporary Religions in Japan* 8:3–4 (1967): 201–303.

6. Here I use "ontological," a term usually found in discussions of philosophy, to refer to the social processes that accompany dying and being born and to the "amount" of existence assumed at each stage.

7. Kuroda Hideo, *Kyōkai no chūsei; shōchō no chūsei* (Tōkyō Daigaku Shuppankai, 1986), esp. 185–230.

8. Ibid., 228. Kuroda's views on this are essentially in agreement with Chiba and Ōtsu, *Mabiki to mizuko*, 143–83.

9. Ariyoshi Sawako, *Kōkotsu no hito* (Shinchōsha, 1972), translated by Mildred Tahara as *The Twilight Years* (Tokyo and New York: Kodansha International, 1984).

10. A sense of transmigration into animal and other species was found especially in the late-classical or early-medieval period. See my *Karma of Words*, 26–59.

11. On the medieval connection—fostered by Buddhist texts—between play,

the sacred, and Buddhist realization, see *The Karma of Words*, 54ff. This connection was important throughout the medieval period. The Edo monk-poet Ryōkan (1757–1831) epitomized it in both his verse and his much-celebrated delight in playing games with local children. See Burton Watson, trans., *Ryōkan: Zen Monk-Poet of Japan* (New York: Columbia University Press, 1977).

12. Elaine Pagels, *Adam, Eve, and the Serpent* (New York: Random House, 1988), 52.

13. John T. Noonan, Jr., "An Almost Absolute Value in History," in *The Morality of Abortion: Legal and Historical Perspectives*, Noonan, ed., (Cambridge, Mass.: Harvard University Press, 1970), 15.

14. Chiba and Ōtsu, *Mabiki to mizuko*, 144.

15. Michael Cooper, *They Came to Japan: An Anthology of European Reports on Japan, 1543–1640* (Berkeley: University of California Press, 1965), 60.

16. Chiba and Ōtsu make a good case for these practices having begun well before the Edo period—that is during the time when Xavier and others were in Japan. See *Mabiki to mizuko*, 49.

17. Robert Nisbet, *Prejudices: A Philosophical Dictionary* (Cambridge, Mass.: Harvard University Press, 1982), 42–43.

18. See Takeda Chōshū, *Sosen sūhai* (Kyoto: Keiraku-ji Shoten, 1982), 20ff.

19. Yuasa Yasuo, *Nihonjin no shūkyō-ishiki* (Meicho Kankōkai, 1958), 90–91.

CHAPTER 4
JIZŌ AT THE CROSSROADS

1. Lafcadio Hearn, *Glimpses of Unfamiliar Japan* (Boston and New York: Houghton Mifflin Co., 1894), 1:43, 44, n. 2.

2. M. W. de Visser, *The Bodhisattva Ti-Tsang (Jizō) in China and Japan* (Berlin: Oesterheld and Co., 1914).

3. James Bissett Pratt, *The Pilgrimage of Buddhism and a Buddhist Pilgrimage* (New York: The Macmillan Co., 1928), 497–500.

4. Principal sources for my discussion of Jizō are Manabe Kōsai, *Jizō bosatsu no kenkyū* (Kyoto: Sanmitsudō Shoten, 1960) and *Jizōson no kenkyū* (Kyoto: Fusanbō Shoten, 1960); Hayami Tasuku, *Jizō shinkō* (Hanawa Shobō, 1975); Sakurai Tokutarō, ed., *Jizō shinkō*; Ishida Mizumaro, *Jigoku*, 236–54; and Ogura Yasushi, "Ojizōsan to kodomo: hitotsu no bunka henyō," 74–94. The number of spurious, forged texts on Jizō in Chinese is discussed in Manabe and Hayami.

5. Joseph M. Kitagawa, *Religion in Japanese History* (New York: Columbia University Press, 1966), 85.

6. Yuasa, *Nihonjin no Shūkyō-ishiki*, 104.

7. Ibid., 105.

8. Ironically—but consistent with what Yuasa claims—Kūkai himself became an object of great veneration after his death, even though he had failed to establish Dainichi Nyorai as such. See Joseph M. Kitagawa, *On Understanding Japanese Religion* (Princeton: Princeton University Press, 1987), 182–202.

9. See de Visser, *The Bodhisattva Ti-Tsang*, and Stephen F. Teiser's important

study, *The Ghost Festival in Medieval China* (Princeton: Princeton University Press, 1988), 186–88.

10. Hayami, *Jizō shinkō*, 19ff.

11. See my *Karma of Words*, 26–59, and my "Hungry Ghosts and Hungry People: Somaticity and Rationality in Medieval Japan," in *Fragments for a History of the Human Body*, Michel Feyer et al., eds., part 1 (New York: Zone Books, 1989), 270–303.

12. The extent of this even in urban Tokyo is impressive. See Miyoshi Tomokazu, *Musashino no jizō-son* (Yūhō Shoten, 1972).

13. The iconographic history is graphically shown in Matsushima Ken, *Jizō-bosatsu-zō* (Shibundō, 1986).

14. Valuable translations of some of these are provided by Yoshiko Kurata Dykstra, in her "Jizō, the Most Merciful: Tales from *Jizō Bosatsu Reigenki*," *Monumenta Nipponica* 33:2 (summer 1978): 179–200.

15. D. E. Mills, trans., *A Collection of Tales from Uji: A Study and Translation of Uji Shūi Monogatari* (Cambridge: Cambridge University Press, 1970), 153–54.

16. Hayami, *Jizō shinkō*, 158. Hayami, it should be noted, takes this early child-identification motif as disproving the claim of Yanagida Kunio that Jizō is merely another version of the indigenous Japanese roadside deity Dōsōjin.

17. For reasons why the notion of indigenous cultures as a kind of "sieve" that filters out unassimilable elements is problematic in the history of Buddhism, see my *Buddhism: A Cultural Perspective* (Englewood Cliffs, N.J.: Prentice-Hall, 1988), 8–9.

18. Moriya Katsuhisa, "Jizō-e," in *Edo jidai no minkan shikō*, Haga Noboru, et al., eds., (Yūzan-kaku Shuppan, 1984), 96–97. See also Sakurai Tokutarō, "Honpō shamanizumu no henshitsu katei: toku ni jizō-shinkō to no shūgō ni tsuite," in *Jizō shinkō*, Sakurai, ed. (Yūzankaku Shuppan, 1983), 229–53.

19. Chiba and Ōtsu, *Mabiki to mizuko*, 29, 49. Individual instances of abortion were, it is said, recorded already in writings by Kiyohara Motosuke in the tenth century and in the *Eiga monogatari* of the eleventh. See Tsuboi Hirobumi, *Ie to josei: kurashi to bunka-shi* (Shogakkan, 1985), 433.

20. Yuasa, *Nihonjin no shūkyō-ishiki*, 113ff.

21. Tanaka Gen, *Kodai nihonjin no sekai: bukkyō juyō no zentei* (Yoshikawa Kōbunkan, 1972), 202–36. On the anti-Buddhist climate of Meiji Japan, see especially James Edward Ketelaar, *Of Heretics and Martyrs in Meiji Japan: Buddhism and its Persecution* (Princeton: Princeton University Press, 1990)

22. Yuasa, *Nihonjin no shūkyō-ishiki*, 115.

23. Robert Borgen, *Sugawara no Michizane and the Early Heian Court* (Cambridge, Mass.: Harvard University Press, 1986), 307–36.

24. Jacques Le Goff, *The Birth of Purgatory*, translated by Arthur Goldhammer (Chicago: University of Chicago Press, 1981), 220 ff.

25. Ibid., 336.

26. John Ciardi's translation of Dante's *Divine Comedy*, 7.28–33, as quoted in Le Goff, *The Birth of Purgatory*, 336.

27. W. Y. Evans-Wentz, ed., *The Tibetan Book of the Dead* (New York: Oxford University Press, 1960). Amidist Buddhists in both China and Japan elimi-

nated or at least abbreviated the time spent in the intermediate state—via promise of immediate rebirth in the Pure Land of Amida.

28. There is, I believe, some evidence for this, and I hope to expand the attention to this topic on another occasion.

29. Leon Hurvitz, trans., *Scripture of the Lotus Blossom of the Fine Dharma (The Lotus Sutra)* (New York: Columbia University Press, 1976), 38–39.

30. Although the etymology of the word *sai* is contested and difficult to pin down, Gorai Shigeru suggests that it may originally have been written with a Chinese ideograph meaning "boundary." See his *Ishi no shūkyō* (Kadokawa, 1988), 236.

31. Also known as Kōya. See Joseph M. Kitagawa, *Religion in Japanese History*, 81.

32. Manabe, *Jizōson no kenkyū*, 79–89.

33. My translation of a text in Manabe, *Jizō bosatsu no kenkyū*, 225–27.

34. Manabe, *Jizōson no kenkyū*, 208–13.

CHAPTER 5
EDO: AN ERA IN VIEW

1. Watsuji Tetsurō, "Sakoku: nihon no higeki," in *Watsuji Tetsurō Zenshū*, Abe Yoshinari et al., eds., 15 (Iwanami Shoten, 1978.); see also my "Haikyo ni tatsu risei: sengo gōrisei ronsō ni okeru Watsuji Tetsurō no iso," in *Sengo nihon no seishinshi: sono saikentō*, Tetsuo Najita et al., eds. (Iwanami Shoten, 1988), 112–44.

2. Ronald P. Toby, *State and Diplomacy in Early Modern Japan: Asia in the Development of the Tokugawa Bakufu* (Princeton: Princeton University Press, 1984).

3. Olof G. Lidin, *The Life of Ogyū Sorai, A Tokugawa Confucian Philosopher* (Copenhagen: The Scandanavian Institute of Asian Studies Monograph Series, no. 19, 1973), 9.

4. I will here and in subsequent chapters often conflate Confucian and neo-Confucian perspectives. This is not to negate the important differences between them on a number of issues, but merely because, at least to my knowledge, there is no discernible difference between them in this period on questions having to do with reproductivity.

5. Uesato Shunsei, *Edo shoseki-shō-shi* (Meicho Kankōkai, 1965), 45–51. Both in the number of publications and in number of published pages, Buddhist works were far larger than any other category.

6. Japanese scholarship for some time now has been much less skewed on this issue than its American counterpart. See especially the texts in Kashiwahara Yūsen and Fujii Manabu, eds., *Nihon shisō taikei: kinsei bukkyō no shisō* (Iwanami Shoten, 1973).

7. Herman Ooms, *Tokugawa Ideology: Early Constructs, 1570–1680* (Princeton: Princeton University Press, 1985), 14 and passim.

8. Ketelaar, *Heretics.*

9. Tamamuro Taijō's calculation as noted in Kitagawa, *Religion in Japanese History*, 164.

10. Martin Collcutt, "Buddhism: The Threat of Eradication," in *Japan in Transition: From Tokugawa to Meiji*, Marius B. Jansen and Gilbert Rozman, eds. (Princeton: Princeton University Press, 1986), 146, n. 3.

11. James H. Sanford, "The Abominable Tachikawa Skull Ritual," *Monumenta Nipponica* 46:1 (spring 1991): 1–2.

12. Japanese scholarship on this remains largely dependent on one pioneering work, Moriyama Shōshin's *Tachikawa jakyō to sono shakaiteki haikei no kenkyū* (Rokuyaen, 1965).

13. An important attempt to see connections, however, is Kanaoka Shūyū's *Satori no himitsu: rishugyō* (Chikuma Shobō, 1965).

14. Sanford, "Skull Ritual," 3–4.

15. James H. Sanford, *Zen-Man Ikkyū* (Chico, Calif.: Scholars Press, 1981), 187. For excellent translations of Ikkyū, see also Sonja Arntzen, *Ikkyū and the Crazy Cloud Anthology: A Zen Poet of Medieval Japan* (Tokyo: University of Tokyo Press, 1986).

16. See my *Karma of Words*, 54–57, 69–79.

17. James A. Brundage, *Law, Sex, and Christian Society in Medieval Europe* (Chicago: University of Chicago Press, 1987), 474ff.

18. For an overview of this in modern scholarship, see Hashimoto Mineo, *"Ukiyo" no shisō* (Kodansha, 1975). On reasons why the historical change in the term must be seen from within Buddhist logic, see 94ff.

19. Ihara Saikaku, *Some Final Words of Advice*, translated by Peter Nosco (Rutland, Vt.: Charles E. Tuttle Co., 1980), 133.

20. This objective was, of course, even more easily realized when the monk's sexual partner was a male. Thus the history of some temple monks having homosexual relations in Japan was a fairly long one. This too was satirized by Saikaku; see Paul Gordon Schalow, trans., *The Great Mirror of Male Love* (Stanford: Stanford University Press, 1990), esp. 219ff.

21. Brundage, *Law, Sex, and Christian Society in Medieval Europe*, 9.

22. Kanaoka, *Satori no himitsu: rishugyō*, 189ff.

23. Tamamuro Taijō, *Nihon bukkyō-shi: kinsei kindai hen* (Kyoto: Hōzōkan, 1950), 155ff.

24. Tamamuro Taijō, *Sōshiki-bukkyō* (Daihōrinkaku, 1963), 128–30.

25. Stanley Weinstein, "Rennyo and the Shinshū Revival," in *Japan in the Muromachi Age*, John Whitney Hall and Toyoda Takeshi, eds. (Berkeley: University of California Press, 1977), 331–58.

26. This underlies the monumental work of Futaba Kenkō, *Kodai bukkyō shisō-shi kenkyū: nihon kodai ni okeru ritsuryō bukkyō oyobi han-ritsuryō bukkyō no kenkyū* (Kyoto: Nagata Bunshōdō, 1962).

27. See my *Buddhism: A Cultural Perspective*. 56–62.

28. Hori Ichiro, *Folk Religion in Japan: Continuity and Change* (Chicago: University of Chicago Press, 1968), 98–99.

29. J. R. McEwan, *The Political Writings of Ogyū Sorai* (Cambridge: Cambridge University Press, 1969), 103–4.

30. Ibid., 105.

31. Sorai's advocacies appear in the late-nineteenth century to have become literal policy. As part of the persecution of Buddhism during that period, Ichiki

Shōuemon (1828–1903) was "in the forefront of the collection of temple bells for their use in cannon-making." Ketelaar, *Heretics*, 55.

32. Georges Bataille, *The Accursed Share: An Essay on General Economy*, translated by Robert Hurley, 1 (New York: Zone Books, 1988), 109.

33. Actually within much of Confucianism ritual was prized as having great importance.

34. Although their approaches differ greatly, the two major works in English are H. D. Harootunian, *Things Seen and Unseen: Discourse and Ideology in To-kugawa Nativism* (Chicago: University of Chicago Press, 1988), and Peter Nosco, *Remembering Paradise: Nativism and Nostalgia in Eighteenth-Century Japan* (Cambridge, Mass.: Harvard University Press, 1990).

35. Matsumoto Sannosuke, "Bakumatsu kokugaku no shisōshiteki igi: shu toshite seijishisō no sokumen ni tsuite," in *Nihon shisō taikei: Kokugaku undō no shisō* (Nihon Shisōshi Taikei), Haga Noboru and Matsumoto Sannosuke, eds. (Iwanami Shoten, 1971), 633–61.

36. For the evidence on this, see my "Zen and the Art of Dealing with Zen and the [Literary] Arts," *Journal of Japanese Studies* 11:1 (winter 1985): 152–69.

CHAPTER 6
EDO: POPULATION

1. Engelbert Kaempfer, *The History of Japan Together with a Description of the Kingdom of Siam 1690–1692*, translated by J. G. Scheuzer, 3 vol. (Glasgow: James MacLehose and Sons, 1906), 2:330.

2. Hayami Akira, "The Population at the Beginning of the Tokugawa Period," *Keio Economic Studies* 4 (1966–1967): 19.

3. Gilbert Rozman, *Urban Networks in Ch'ing China and Tokugawa Japan* (Princeton: Princeton University Press, 1977), 77.

4. Diagram by D. Eleanor Westney and Samuel J. Coleman, in *Kodansha Encyclopedia of Japan* (Tokyo: Kodansha Ltd., 1983), 6:224.

5. Hayami Akira, "Population Changes," in Jansen and Rozman, eds., *Japan in Transition*, 288; see also James I. Nakamura and Matao Miyamoto, "Social Structure and Population Change: A Comparative Study of Tokugawa Japan and Ch'ing China," *Economic Development and Cultural Change* 30:2 (1982): 262.

6. By "bedroom" I mean to stress the private nature of the decision; I do not mean to suggest decision by a couple. Many were likely private decisions by women alone.

7. Robert Y. Eng and Thomas C. Smith, "Peasant Families and Population Control in Eighteenth-Century Japan," *Journal of Interdisciplinary History* 6:3 (winter 1976): 423.

8. Susan B. Hanley and Kozo Yamamura, *Economic and Demographic Change in Pre-Industrial Japan, 1600–1868* (Princeton: Princeton University Press, 1977), 317.

9. Ann Bowman Jannetta, *Epidemics and Mortality in Early Modern Japan* (Princeton: Princeton University Press, 1987), 5.

10. Ibid., 200.

11. See Eng and Smith, "Peasant Families"; Hanley and Yamamura, *Economic and Demographic Change*; and Thomas C. Smith, *Nakahara: Family Farming and Population in a Japanese Village, 1717–1830* (Stanford: Stanford University Press, 1977). Most of the early evidence of abortion and infanticide was provided in Takahashi Bonsen, *Nihon jinkō-shi no kenkyū*.

12. Chiba and Ōtsu call attention to this in *Mabiki to mizuko*, 29ff.

13. Cooper, *They Came to Japan*, 200.

14. Ibid., 58.

15. See my "Hungry Ghosts and Hungry People," which touches on famine conditions reaching the capital in the late-twelfth century.

16. Smith, *Nakahara*, 147.

17. Eng and Smith, "Peasant Families," 424ff. Hanley and Yamamura have found a larger gap between the sexes in permitted births.

18. Lloyd de Mause, "The Evolution of Childhood," in *The History of Childhood* (London: Souvenir Press, 1976), 1–74. See also Peter C. Hoffer and N.E.H. Hull, *Murdering Mothers: Infanticide in England and New England, 1558–1803* (New York: New York University Press, 1981).

19. V. G. Kiernan, *The Lords of Human Kind: Black Man, Yellow Man, and White Man in an Age of Empire* (New York: Columbia University Press, 1969), 27.

20. Hanley and Yamamura, *Economic and Demographic Change*, 266.

21. Eng and Smith, "Peasant Families," 444.

22. Thomas Robert Malthus, *An Essay on the Principle of Population and a Summary View of the Principle of Population*, Anthony Flew, ed. (New York: Penguin Books, 1979), 106.

23. *Nippo jisho [Vocabulario de Lingoa de Iapam]* original of 1603 reprinted by Iwanami Shoten, 1960, 294. An important discussion of this is in Sasaki Yasuyuki, ed., *Nihon no kogoroshi no kenkyū* (Kōbundō, 1982), 40–50.

24. Malthus, *An Essay*, 208.

25. Ibid., 207.

CHAPTER 7
EDO: POLEMICS

1. In addition to the essay in Kashiwabara and Fujii, eds., *Kinsei bukkyō no shisō*, see also the chapters on Edo, in Imai Jun and Ozawa Tomio, eds., *Nihon shisō ronsō-shi* (Perikansha, 1979).

2. Tetsuo Najita, *Visions of Virtue in Tokugawa Japan: The Kaitokudō Merchant Academy of Osaka* (Chicago: University of Chicago Press, 1987), 178.

3. Imai Jun, "Kinsei bukkyō no mondaiten," in *Nihon shisō-shi kōza: kinsei no shisō*, Furukawa Tetsushi and Ishida Ichirō, eds., 1 (Yūzankaku Shuppan, 1976), 266.

4. See J. Victor Koschmann, *The Mito Ideology: Discourse, Reform, and Insurrection in Late Tokugawa Japan, 1790–1864*. (Berkeley: University of California Press, 1987), 31ff.

5. Ketelaar, *Heretics*.

6. George A. De Vos, *Socialization for Achievement: Essays on the Cultural Psychology of the Japanese* (Berkeley: University of California Press, 1973), 263.

7. See Fukunaga Katsumi, *Bukkyō igaku jiten* (Yūzankaku Shuppan, 1990), 204–22.

8. Translated from text in Chiba and Ōtsu, *Mabiki and Mizuko*, 82. Although it does not deal with this point, Najita's *Visions of Virtue* is the best source on Nakai.

9. Masao Maruyama, *Studies in the Intellectual History of Tokugawa Japan*, translated by Mikiso Hane (Princeton: Princeton University Press, 1974), 289.

10. I do not mean to suggest that a *modern* scholar may not simultaneously derive significance from the Confucian tradition and articulate a position countenancing abortion—as, for instance, David B. Wong does quite skillfully in his *Moral Relativity* (Berkeley: University of California Press, 1984). This does, however, require bold new types of moral bricolage.

11. Herman Ooms, *Charismatic Bureaucrat: A Political Biography of Matsudaira Sadonobu, 1758–1829.* (Chicago: University of Chicago Press, 1975), 57.

12. Matsumoto Sannosuke, "Bakumatsu kokugaku no shisō-shiteki igi," 642.

13. Suzuki Shigetani, "*Yotsugigusa*," in Haga and Matsumoto, eds., *Kokugaku undō*, 236–37. Intense rivalries within this school may have led to the assassination of Suzuki in 1863. See Haga Noboru, *Bakumatsu kokugaku no tenkai* (Hanawa Shobō, 1963), 90ff.

14. Miyauchi Yoshinaga, "*Toyamabiko*," in Haga and Matsumoto, eds., *Kokugaku undō*, 358.

15. Miyahiro Sadao, "*Kokueki honron*," in Haga and Matsumoto, eds., *Kokugaku undō*, 293–94.

16. Ibid., 297.

17. Harootunian, *Things Seen and Unseen*, 301.

18. Ibid.

19. Jennifer Robertson, "Sexy Rice: Plant, Gender, Farm Manuals, and Grassroots Nativism," *Monumenta Nipponica* 39:3 (autumn 1984): 234–60.

20. See William W. Kelly, *Deference and Defiance in Nineteenth-Century Japan* (Princeton: Princeton University Press, 1985); Stephen Vlastos, *Peasant Protests and Uprisings in Tokugawa Japan* (Berkeley: University of California Press, 1986); and Anne Walthall, *Social Protest and Popular Culture in Eighteenth-Century Japan* (Tucson: University of Arizona Press, 1986).

21. Tsuboi Hirobumi, *Ie to josei: kurashi to bunka-shi*, 433ff.

22. Vinaya texts, in *Sacred Books of the East*, 13 (1881): 235.

23. *Suttavibhanaga Vinaya* 3:3, as quoted in G. P. Malalasekera et al., eds., *Encyclopedia of Buddhism* (Ceylon: The Government Press, n.d.) 1:138.

24. Ibid., vol. 3, 128.

25. Ibid., 129.

26. Institute of Population Studies of Chulalongkorn University, ed., *Thailand's Continuing Fertility Decline*, paper no. 40 (Bangkok: Professional Publishing Co., n.d.); see also T. O. Ling, "Buddhist Factors in Population Growth and Control: a Survey Based on Thailand and Ceylon," in *Population Studies* 23:1 (March 1969): 53–60.

27. Ling, "Buddhist Factors," 57–58.

28. Ibid., 60.

29. John A. Miles, Jr., "Jain and Judeo-Christian Respect for Life," *Journal of the American Academy of Religion* 44:30 (1976): 453–57.

30. Yokoi Kiyoshi, "Sessei no yuetsu," in his *Mato to ena: Chūseijin no sei to shi* (Heibonsha, 1988), 119–44.

CHAPTER 8
SEX, WAR, AND PEACE

1. Kano Masanao, *Senzen "ie" no shisō* (Sōbunsha, 1983) 38ff.

2. Carol Gluck, *Japan's Modern Myths: Ideology in the Late Meiji Period* (Princeton: Princeton University Press, 1985), 265; see also esp. 187ff.

3. Jacques Donzelot, *The Policing of Families*, translated by Robert Hurley (New York: Pantheon Books, 1979).

4. E. H. Norman, "The Restoration," in *Origins of the Modern Japanese State: Selected Writings of E. H. Norman*, John W. Dower, ed. (New York: Pantheon Books, 1975), 185.

5. Kano Masanao, *Senzen "ie" no shisō*.

6. Mikiso Hane, *Modern Japan: A Historical Survey* (Boulder, Colo., and London: Westview Press, 1986), 179.

7. Sharon L. Sievers, *Flowers in Salt: The Beginnings of Feminist Consciousness in Modern Japan* (Stanford: Stanford University Press, 1983), 183–84; see also Jan Bardsley, *Writing for the New Woman of Taishō Japan: Hiratsuka Raichō and the Seitō Journal, 1911–1916*, Ph.D. diss., University of California, Los Angeles, 1989.

8. Yanagida Kunio, "Kokyō nanajū-nen," *Teihon Yanagida Kunio shū*, supplementary vol. 3 (Chikuma Shobō, 1964), 21.

9. Kimura Hiroshi, "Mabiki no jizō ema," *Minkan* 269 (July 1965): 82–83; see also Chiba and Ōtsu, *Mabiki to mizuko*, 65ff.

10. Chiba and Ōtsu, *Mabiki to mizuko*, 67.

11. Ibid., 77–78.

12. Miyata Noboru, "Sei-shinkō no shomondai," *Gendai shūkyō* 1 and 2 (summer 1975): 114–26.

13. For a critical treatment of Yanagida, his background in Kokugaku, and ideology in the rise of folklore studies in Japan, see Harootunian, *Things Seen and Unseen*, 413ff.

14. See Michael Czaja, *Gods of Myth and Stone: Phallicism in Japanese Folk Religion* (New York: Weatherhill, 1974); Yanagida, in *Teihon Yanagida Kunio shū* 27:280–81. See Hayami Tasuki, *Jizō shinkō*, 158ff., for problems with Yanagida's view on this matter.

15. Although it does not mention Jizō, this "national character" type of interpretation is classically illustrated in John C. Pelzel, "Human Nature in the Japanese Myths," in *Personality in Japanese History*, A. M. Craig and D. H. Shively, eds. (Berkeley: University of California Press, 1970).

16. Aoyanagi Machiko section in Tsuboi Hirobumi, ed., *Ie to josei*, 430. Con-

cerning a village woman and Kishimojin, see Robert J. Smith and Ella Lury Wiswell, *The Women of Suye Mura* (Chicago: University of Chicago Press, 1982), 93.

17. Definitions according to Takie Sugiyama Lebra, in her *Japanese Patterns of Behavior*, 136.

18. Robert J. Smith and Ella Lury Wiswell, *The Women of Suye Mura*, 88.

19. Thomas Havens, "War and Women in Japan, 1937–1945," *American Historical Review* 80:4 (October 1975): 916–20.

20. Ibid., 927.

21. Ibid., 928.

22. Joseph M. Kitagawa, *Religion in Japanese History*, 202–4.

23. John W. Dower, *War Without Mercy: Race and Power in the Pacific War* (New York: Pantheon Books, 1986), 295–99.

24. Osamu Dazai, *Return to Tsugaru: Travels of a Purple Tramp*, translated by James Westerhoven (Tokyo and New York: Kodansha, 1985), 151–52. Original published in 1944 as *Tsugaru*.

25. The original has *kanbatsu* for "thinning"—although *kan* is the same character as *ma* in mabiki: "space" between plants, trees—or babies. See Osamu Dazai, *Tsugaru* (Shinchō Bunko, 1951), 156.

26. Perhaps the swift, emphatic rejection of "thinning" by the local person is Dazai's way of showing how sensitive people in northernmost Japan were about their reputation—based on fact—for being the locale not only of greatest poverty but also of the most extensive use of abortion and infanticide.

27. Thomas K. Burch, "Induced Abortion in Japan under Eugenic Protection Law of 1948," *Eugenics Quarterly* 2:3 (September 1955): 144.

28. Samuel Coleman, *Family Planning in Japanese Society: Traditional Birth Control in a Modern Urban Culture* (Princeton: Princeton University Press, 1983), 100–108.

29. Ibid., 37–38.

30. See Sandra Buckley, "Body Politics: Abortion Law Reform," in *The Japanese Trajectory: Modernization and Beyond*, Gavan McCormack and Yoshio Sugimoto, eds. (Cambridge: Cambridge University Press, 1988), 205–17.

31. Coleman, *Family Planning*, 3.

32. On the history and issues involved in this, see a dissertation in process by Kozy K. Amemiya, Department of Sociology, University of California, San Diego.

CHAPTER 9
APOLOGY

1. Richard F. Gombrich, *Precept and Practice: Traditional Buddhism in the Rural Highland of Ceylon* (Oxford: Clarendon Press, 1971), 242.

2. Wagatsuma Hiroshi, *Nihonjin to amerikajin: koka ga Ōchigai* (Nesuko, 1985), 138.

3. John O. Haley, "Sheathing the Sword of Justice in Japan: An Essay on Law Without Sanctions," *The Journal of Japanese Studies* 8:2 (Summer 1982): 269.

4. Hiroshi Wagatsuma and Arthur Rosett, "The Implications of Apology:

Law and Culture in Japan and the United States," *Law and Society Review* 20:1 (1986): 464.

5. Ibid., 472.

6. Ibid., 488–92. See also David H. Bayley, *Forces of Order: Police Behavior in Japan and the United States* (Berkeley: University of California Press, 1976), 134ff.

7. Wagatsuma and Rosett, "The Implications of Apology," 473ff.

8. Known as the *Hannya shingyō* in Japanese. An English translation in my *Buddhism: A Cultural Perspective*, 82–83.

9. Helen Hardacre, *Kurozumikyō and the New Religions of Japan* (Princeton: Princeton University Press, 1986), 151.

10. See Hashimoto Mitsuru, "Fuan no shakai ni motomeru shūkyō: mizuko kuyō," *Gendai shakai-gaku* 13:1 (1987): 42.

11. In sequence these studies, all in the same journal, are Anne Page Brooks, "'Mizuko Kuyō' and Japanese Buddhism," *Japanese Journal of Religious Studies* 8:3–4 (September–December, 1981): 119–47; Hoshino Eiki and Takeda Dosho, "Indebtedness and Comfort: The Undercurrents of *Mizuko Kuyō* in Contemporary Japan," *Japanese Journal of Religious Studies* 14:4 (December 1987), 305–20; and Bardwell Smith, "Buddhism and Abortion in Contemporary Japan: *Mizuko Kuyō* and the Confrontation with Death," *Japanese Journal of Religious Studies* 15:1 (March 1988), 3–24.

12. Ruth Benedict, *The Chrysanthemum and the Sword: Patterns of Japanese Culture* (Boston: Houghton Mifflin Co., 1946), 223.

13. An early critic in Japan was Watsuji Tetsurō with his 1949 evaluation of Benedict's book; see *Watsuji Tetsurō zenshū* 3:355–67. Gerhard Piers and Milton B. Singer, in their "Shame," criticized the shame-culture hypothesis; see reprint in Herbert Morris, ed., *Guilt and Shame* (Belmont, Calif.: Wadsworth Publishing Co., 1971), 147–54. George De Vos in 1960 refuted Benedict, in his "The Relation of Guilt toward Parents to Achievement and Arranged Marriage among the Japanese," *Psychiatry* 23 (1960): 287–301. A fine symposium on the history of concepts of sin and guilt in Japan is found in the journal *Nihon shisō-shi* 12 (1979).

14. John W. Dower puts this in context. See his *War Without Mercy*, 303.

15. Ihara Saikaku, *Kōshoku gonin onna; kōshoku ichidai onna*, Higashi Akio, ed., (Shogakkan, 1985), 350. English translation by Ivan Morris, *The Life of an Amorous Woman and Other Writings* (New York: New Directions, 1963), 194. I have altered Morris's English text in one phrase—rendering *hasu no hagasa* as "wearing its placenta on its head" rather than "wearing a hat in the form of a lotus leaf." Placenta is more correct in this context. Guilt associated with mabiki and mizuko shows up often in modern Japanese literature. One of the most compelling stories, set in the northeast and detailing the sufferings of a midwife who carried out mabiki on a wide scale, is "Michinoku no ningyōtachi" by Fukazawa Shichirō, first published in 1979. Lynne Kutsukake graciously shared her fine translation of this story with me, and I look forward to its publication.

16. Emiko Ohnuki-Tierney, *Illness and Culture in Contemporary Japan: An Anthropological View* (Cambridge: Cambridge University Press, 1984), 79.

17. Herbert Morris, *On Guilt and Innocence: Essays in Legal Philosophy and Moral Psychology* (Berkeley: University of California Press, 1976), 101.

18. Ibid., 106.

19. Gabrielle Taylor, *Pride, Shame, and Guilt: Emotions of Self-Assessment* (Oxford: Clarendon Press, 1985), 15. I am grateful to Herbert Morris for directing me to Taylor's work.

20. Ibid., 16.

21. David L. Hall and Roger T. Ames, *Thinking through Confucius* (Albany: State University of New York Press, 1987), 274. The impact of this aspect of Confucian thinking on Japan was probably deep. Nevertheless, Ogyū Sorai, although a Confucian, was so preoccupied with uneconomical "waste" that he could not see how Buddhist ritual could also be an act that "performs" people.

22. Emiko Ohnuki-Tierney, *Illness and Culture*, 144.

CHAPTER 10
MORAL SWAMPS

1. Shusaku Endo, *Silence*, translated by William Johnston (Tokyo and New York: Kodansha Int., 1969), 236–37.

2. The official translation into English is "House of Life, Wisdom, and Abundance."

3. Coleman, *Family Planning*, 64.

4. Ibid., 63

5. Ōta Tenrei, *Datai kinshi to yūsei hogohō* (Keieisha Kagaku Kyōkai, 1967.)

6. Ōta Tenrei, "Mizuko kuyō no zaiaku," in his *Chūzetsu wa satsujin de wa nai* (Ningen no Kagakusha, 1983), 48–52.

7. Unsigned editorial, "Rei no tatari aru ka?" *Daihōrin* 54:7 (July 1987): 92.

8. Fujiyoshi Jikai, "Bukkyō ni okeru reikon sūhai ni tsuite," *Daihōrin* 54:7 (July 1987): 104–5.

9. Hanayama Shōyū, "Hontō no shinkō o motsu," *Daihōrin* 54:7 (July 1987): 107–8.

10. Hiro Sachiya, "*Hotoke* o Shinjite ikiru," *Daihōrin* 54:7 (July 1987): 108–9.

11. Matsubara Taidō, "Tatari o ikasu," *Daihōrin* 54:7 (July 1987): 125–26. Matsubara employs the notion *shiyō*, the Japanese rendering of the German *Aufheben* and English "sublation," a problematic notion in dialectical philosophy. I render it here simply as "uplift."

12. Iizawa Tadasu, "Shūkyō mokeya," *Daihōrin* 54:7 (July 1987): 130–31.

13. Matsunami Kōdō, "Mizuko-rei no tatari kaiketsuhō," *Daihōrin* 54:7 (July 1987): 146–47.

14. Ochiai Seiko, "Mizuko kuyō to reikon-kyō," in *Onna no sei to chūzetsu: yūsei hogohō no haikei*, Shakai Hyōronsha Henshūbu eds. (Shakai Hyōronsha, 1983), 68.

15. Ibid., 61–64 (slightly abridged).

16. Ibid., 65–66.

17. Ibid., 67–68.

18. Ibid., 68–69.

19. *Mizuko kuyō no hōhō*, a promotional sheet published by Hashimoto Tetsuma and Shiunzan Jizō-ji. See Appendix.

20. Herbert E. Plutschow, "The Fear of Evil Spirits in Japanese Culture," *Transactions of the Asiatic Society of Japan*, 3d series, 18 (1983): 139; see also the discussion in his *Chaos and Cosmos: Ritual in Early and Medieval Japanese Literature* (Leiden: E.J. Brill, 1990). It is significant that Japanese instances are prominent in the entry on "exorcism" by Geoffrey Parrinder, in *The Encyclopedia of Religion*, Mircea Eliade, ed., 5 (New York: Macmillan Publishing Co., 1987): 225–33.

21. Domyo Miura, *The Forgotten Child: An Ancient Eastern Answer to a Modern Problem* (Henley-on-Thames: Aidan Ellis, 1983), 31.

22. Ibid., 34–35.

23. On this see Margaret Lock's important essay "Protests of a Good Wife and Wise Mother: The Medicalization of Distress in Japan," in *Health, Illness, and Medical Care in Japan: Cultural and Social Dimensions*, Edward Norbeck and Margaret Lock, eds. (Honolulu: University of Hawaii Press, 1987), 130–57.

24. Miura, *The Forgotten Child*, p. 35.

25. Ibid., 44.

CHAPTER 11
A RATIONAL, NATIONAL FAMILY

1. Donald Keene, trans., *Essays in Idleness: The Tsurezuregusa of Kenkō* (New York: Columbia University Press, 1967), 64. Emphasis is mine.

2. George Lakoff and Mark Johnson, *Metaphors We Live By* (Chicago: University of Chicago Press, 1980), 40. See also their *More Than Cool Reason: A Field Guide to Poetic Metaphor* (Chicago: University of Chicago Press, 1989).

3. Hyman Rodman, Betty Sarvis, and Joy Walker Bonar, *The Abortion Question* (New York: Columbia University Press, 1987), 30.

4. John Boswell, *The Kindness of Strangers: The Abandonment of Children in Western Europe from Late Antiquity to the Renaissance* (New York: Pantheon Books, 1988), 431–32.

5. Jacques Donzelot, *The Policing of Families*, 10. A work that makes important use of Donzelot's studies is Jeffrey Minson's, *Genealogies of Morals: Nietzsche, Foucault, Donzelot, and the Eccentricity of Ethics* (New York: St. Martin's Press, 1985).

6. Matsuo Bashō, "Nozarashi kikō," in *Nihon koten bungaku taikei: Bashō bunshū*, Sugiura Shōichirō et al., eds., 37 (Iwanami Shoten, 1959), 35–44. Translated by Makoto Ueda in his *Matsuo Bashō* (Tokyo and New York: Kodansha International Ltd., 1970), 126.

7. This preference agrees with a contemporary pattern whereby desperate Japanese mothers driven to commit suicide often kill their children rather than leave them motherless. Compassion is the key factor.

8. Aristotle *Politics*, VII.16, and Plato *Republic* V:460. See Michael Tooley, *Abortion and Infanticide* (Oxford: Clarendon Press, 1983), 60.

9. Cooper, *They Came to Japan*, 60.

10. Ibid., 62–63.

11. Robert Nisbet, entry on "Abortion," in his *Prejudices: A Philosophical Dictionary* (Cambridge, Mass.: Harvard University Press, 1982), 1.

12. Honda Masako, "'Arau onna' kō: kodomo no sei to shi o megutte," *Gendai shisō* 11:10 (October 1983): 132–42.

13. Kenneth K. S. Ch'en, *Buddhism in China: A Historical Survey* (Princeton: Princeton University Press, 1964).

14. I owe information on this to Stephen F. Teiser.

15. Hashimoto Mitsuru, "Fuan no shakai," 43–44. I am grateful to Betsy Scheiner for directing me to this work.

16. Ibid., 50.

17. Robert N. Bellah, Richard Madsen, William M. Sullivan, Ann Swindler, and Steven M. Tipton, *Habits of the Heart: Individualism and Commitment in American Life* (Berkeley: University of California Press, 1985), 37. The internal quotations are from Alexis de Tocqueville, *Democracy in America*, translated by George Lawrence, J. P. Mayer, ed., (New York: Doubleday Anchor 1969), 506.

18. Bellah et al., *Habits of the Heart*, 43.

19. Hashimoto, "Fuan no shakai," 53. An important source for this is Tamamuro Taijō, "Chibyō shūkyō no keifu," *Nihon rekishi* 186 (November 1963): 2–15.

20. As noted earlier, historically a mizuko was not an ancestor.

21. Hashimoto, "Fuan no shakai," 54.

22. Two excellent collections of essays that would for the most part fall within this category are Nihon kazoku keikaku renmei, ed., *Onna no jinken to sei: watakushitachi no sentaku* (Komichi Shobō, 1984) and Nihon kazoku keikaku renmei ed., *Kanashimi o sabakemasu ka?* (Ningen no Kagakusha, 1983).

23. In the earlier discussion of the essays in *Daihōrin*, Matsubara Taidō's position articulated this notion of *hōben*, whereas Fujiyoshi Jikai rejected the notion of "entry-level" Buddhism as a delusion.

CHAPTER 12
CROSSOVERS

1. Robert Aitken, *The Mind of Clover: Essays in Zen Buddhist Ethics* (San Francisco: North Point Press, 1984), 21.

2. Ibid., 22.

3. The provision of a posthumous, Buddhist name for a fetus is, in fact, both recent and controversial in Japan. See Terauchi Daikichi, "Gendai no mizuko Jizō," 92–99.

4. Aitken, *The Mind of Clover*, 21.

5. Sallie Tisdale, "We Do Abortions Here: A Nurse's Story," *Harper's* (October 1987): 66–70.

6. James A. Brundage, *Law, Sex, and Christian Society in Medieval Europe*, 472.

7. Ibid., 491.

8. Jerry Falwell, "Strengthening Families in the Nation," a speech given in Atlanta on 23 March 1982, as printed in Halford Ross Ryan, *American Rhetoric*

from Roosevelt to Reagan: A Collection of Speeches and Critical Essays (Prospect Heights, Ill.: Waveland Press, Inc., 1983), 258.

9. *Los Angeles Times*, March 17, 1989.

10. Robert D. Goldstein, *Mother-Love and Abortion: A Legal Interpretation* (Berkeley: University of California Press, 1988), 71.

11. As noted, to the extent that infanticide still exists in Japan, it clusters around a specialized set of cases—namely those wherein, out of concern for abandoned children, a suicidal mother takes her children with her in death. Even at that, the rate is greatly reduced over what it once had been. See Sasaki Yasuyuki, ed., *Nihon no kogoroshi no kenkyū* (Kōbundō, 1982).

12. Cohen, *"Be Fertile and Increase,"* 135.

13. Ibid., 136.

14. Ibid., 120–21.

15. *New York Times*, October 24, 1987.

16. Nakatani Kinko, "Chūzetsu dataizai no toraekata," in Nihon kazoku keikaku renmei, ed., *Onna no jinken to sei*, 29.

17. Takie Sugiyama Lebra, *Japanese Patterns of Behavior*, 11.

18. Richard Rorty in recent years has been the most articulate advocate of a reappropriation of the American pragmatists, especially in his *Consequences of Pragmatism (Essays: 1972–1980)* (Minneapolis: University of Minnesota Press, 1982) and *Contingency, Irony, and Solidarity* (Cambridge: Cambridge University Press, 1989). But see also Jeffrey Stout's definitions of a "modest pragmatism," questions about some of Rorty's statements, and strong defense of this position as being not relativist in ethics. Stout, *Ethics After Babel*.

19. For a similar assessment of Buddhism and pragmatism, see Kenneth K. Inada and Nolan P. Jacobson, *Buddhism and American Thinkers* (Albany: State University of New York Press, 1984), esp. 76.

20. William Safire, perhaps in this instance more "Japanese" than he realized, advocated the pragmatics of compromise in his "Option 3: 'Pro-Comp,'" *New York Times*, July 6, 1989.

21. Stout, *Ethics after Babel*, 255.

22. Winston Davis, although also critical of it, acknowledges the Buddhists' "silence" as a component in the modern development of Japan. See his important essay, "Buddhism and the Modernization of Japan," *History of Religions* 28:4 (May 1989): 333ff.

CONCLUSION

1. Chalmers Johnson, *MITI and the Japanese Miracle: The Growth of Industrial Policy, 1925–1975* (Stanford: Stanford University Press, 1982).

2. Thomas P. Rohlen, *For Harmony and Strength: Japanese White-Collar Organization in Anthropological Perspective* (Berkeley: University of California Press, 1974).

3. Ronald Dore, *Taking Japan Seriously: A Confucian Perspective on Leading Economic Issues* (Stanford: Stanford University Press, 1984).

4. Merry White, *The Japanese Educational Challenge*.

5. David H. Bayley, *Forces of Order: Police Behavior in Japan and the United States* (Berkeley: University of California Press, 1976).

6. J. Mark Ramseyer and Minoru Nakazato, "The Rational Litigant: Settlement Amounts and Verdict Rates in Japan," *Journal of Legal Studies* 18:2 (June 1989), 263–90.

7. John Owen Haley, *Authority without Power: Law and the Japanese Paradox* (New York: Oxford University Press, 1991), 133.

8. A contemporary pragmatism with social solidarity as a basic component is well articulated by Richard Rorty in, for instance, his *Contingency, Irony, and Solidarity.*

9. Although I have not myself seen the results, I have been told that research by Elizabeth Harrison and Bardwell Smith, employing questionnaires to register the response of persons involved in mizuko kuyō, tends to show positive results.

10. As Richard Rorty demonstrated, even our notions of "rationality" are totally dependent on metaphorical language. See his *Philosophy and the Mirror of Nature* (Princeton: Princeton University Press, 1979).

11. Mary Gordon, "Abortion: How Do We Really Choose?" in her *Good Boys and Dead Girls and Other Essays* (New York: Viking, 1991). 147.

12. There appears to be a growing resistance within the Japanese women's movement itself to the dependence on chemical methods of every type. Conversation with Kozy K. Amemiya, August 6, 1991.

13. Merry White, *The Japanese Educational Challenge*, 191.

14. Bill McKibben, *The End of Nature* (New York: Random House, 1989), 191.

BIBLIOGRAPHY

JAPANESE SOURCES

(Unless otherwise indicated, all works are published in Tokyo.)

Ariyoshi, Sawako. *Kōkotsu no hito*. Shinchōsha, 1972.

Chiba Tokuji and Ōtsu Tadao. *Mabiki to mizuko: kosodate no fuōkuroa*. Nōsangyōson Bunka Kyōkai, 1983.

Fujiyoshi Jikai. "Bukkyō ni okeru reikon sūhai ni tsuite." *Daihōrin* 54:7 (July 1987).

Fukazawa Shichirō. "Michinoku no ningyōtachi." *Chūō kōron* (1979).

Fukunaga Katsumi. *Bukkyō igaku jiten*. Yōzankaku, Shuppan, 1990.

Futaba Kenkō. *Kodai bukkyō shisō-shi kenkyū: nihon kodai ni okeru ritsuryō bukkyō oyobi han-ritsuryō bukkyō no kenkyū*. Kyoto: Nagata Bunshōdō, 1962.

Gorai Shigeru. *Ishi no shūkyō*. Kadokawa, 1988.

Haga Noboru. *Bakumatsu kokugaku no tenkai*. Hanawa Shobō, 1963.

Haga Noboru and Matsumoto Sannosuke, eds. *Nihon shisō taikei: Kokugaku undō no shisō*. Iwanami Shoten, 1971.

Hanayama Shōyū. "Hontō no shinkō o motsu." *Daihōrin* 54:7 (July 1987).

Hashimoto Mineo. *"Ukiyo" no shisō*. Kodansha, 1975.

Hashimoto Mitsuru. "Fuan no shakai ni motomeru shūkyō: mizuko kuyō." *Gendai shakai-gaku* 13:1 (1987).

Hayami Tasuku. *Jizō shinkō*. Hanawa Shobō, 1975.

Hiro Sachiya. "*Hotoke* o shinjite ikiru." *Daihōrin* 54:7 (July 1987).

―――. "Mizu to hi, soshite chi." *Risō* 614 (July 1984): 83–88.

Honda Masako. "'Arau onna' kō: kodomo no sei to shi o megutte." *Gendai shisō* 11:10 (October 1983): 132–42.

Ihara Saikaku. *Kōshoku gonin onna; kōshoku ichidai onna*. Edited by Higashi Akio. Shogakkan, 1985.

Iizawa Tadasu. "Shūkyō mokeya." *Daihōrin* 54:7 (July 1987).

Imai Jun. "Kinsei bukkyō no mondaiten." *Nihon shisō-shi kōza: kinsei no shisō*. Edited by Furukawa Tetsushi and Ishida Ichirō. Vol. 1. Yūzankaku Shuppan, 1976.

Imai Jun and Ozawa Tomio, eds. *Nihon shisō ronsō-shi*. Perikansha, 1979.

Ishida Mizumaro. *Jigoku*. Kyoto: Hōzōkan, 1985.

Iwai Hiroshi. "Nihonjin to mizu no shinsō-shinri." *Risō* 614 (July 1984): 89–99.

Kanaoka Shūyū. *Satori no himitsu: rishugyō*. Chikuma Shobō, 1965.

Kano Masanao. *Senzen "ie" no shisō*. Sōbunsha, 1983.

Kashiwahara Yūsen and Fujii Manabu, eds. *Nihon shisō taikei: kinsei bukkyō no shisō*. Iwanami Shoten, 1973.

Kimura Hiroshi, "Mabiki no jizō ema." *Minkan* 269 (July 1965): 82–83.

Kuroda Hideo. *Kyōkai no chūsei; shōchō no chūsei*. Tōkyō Daigaku Shuppankai, 1986.

LaFleur, William R. "Haikyo ni tatsu risei: sengo gorisei ronsō ni okeru Watsuji Tetsurō no isō." *Sengo nihon no seishinshi: sono saikentō*. Edited by Tetsuo Najita, Maeda Ai, and Kamishima Jirō. Iwanami Shoten, 1988: 112–44.

Manabe Kōsai. *Jizō bosatsu no kenkyū*. Kyoto: Sanmitsudō Shoten, 1960.

———. *Jizōson no kenkyū*. Kyoto: Fuzanbō Shoten, 1960.

Matsubara Taidō. "Tatari o ikasu." *Daihōrin* 54:7 (July 1987).

Matsumoto Sannosuke. "Bakumatsu kokugaku no shisōshiteki igi: shu toshite seijishisō no sokumen ni tsuite." *Nihon shisō taikei: kokugaku undō no shisō*. Edited by Haga Noboru and Matsumoto Sannosuke. Iwanami Shoten, 1971: 633–61.

Matsunami Kōdō. "Mizuko-rei no tatari kaiketsuhō." *Daihōrin* 54:7 (July 1987).

Matsuo Bashō. "Nozarashi kikō." *Nihon koten bungaku taikei: Bashō bunshū*. Edited by Sugiura Shōichirō. Vol. 37. Iwanami shoten, 1959: 35–44.

Matsushima Ken. *Jizō bosatsu-zō*. Shibundō, 1986.

Miyata Noboru. "Sei-shinkō no shomondai." *Gendai shūkyō* 1 and 2 (summer 1975): 114–26.

Miyoshi Tomokazu. *Musashino no jizō-son*. Yūhō Shoten, 1972.

"Mizuko kuyō no hōhō." Hashimoto Tetsuma and Shiunzan Jizō-ji, 1984.

Moriya, Katsuhisa. "Jizō-e." *Edo jidai no minkan shikō*. Edited by Haga Noboru, Miyata Noboru, and Moriya Katsuhisa. Yūzankaku Shuppan, 1984: 96–97.

Moriyama Shōshin. *Tachikawa jakyō to sono shakaiteki haikei no kenkyū*. Rokuyaen, 1965.

Nakatani Kinko. "Chūzetsu, dataizai no toraekata." *Onna no jinken to sei: watakushitachi no sentaku*. Edited by Nihon Kazoku Keikaku Renmei. Komichi Shobō, 1984: 28–39.

Nihon Kazoku Keikaku Renmei, ed. *Kanashimi o sabakemasu ka?* Ningen no Kagakusha, 1983.

Nihon Kazoku Keikaku Renmei, ed. *Onna no jinken to sei: watakushitachi no sentaku*. Komichi Shobō, 1984.

Ochiai Seiko. "Mizuko kuyō to reikon-kyō." *Onna no sei to chūzetsu: yūsei hogohō no haikei*. Edited by Shakai Hyōronsha Henshūbu. Shakai Hyōronsha, 1983.

Ogura Yasushi. "Ojizōsan to kodomo: hitotsu no bunka henyō." *Hikaku bungaku kenkyū*, 48:74–94.

Onshi-Zaidan-boshi-aiikukai, ed. *Nihon san-iku shūzoku shiryō-shūsei*. Dai'ichi Hoki Shuppan, 1975.

Ōta Tenrei. *Datai kinshi to yūsei hogohō*. Keieisha Kagaku Kyōkai, 1967.

———. "Mizuko kuyō no zaiaku." *Chūzetsu wa satsujin de wa nai*. Ningen no Kagakusha, 1983: 48–52.

"Rei no tatari aru ka?" Unsigned editorial. *Daihōrin* 54:7 (July 1987): 92.

Sakabe Megumi. *Kamen no kaishakugaku*. Tōkyō Daigaku Shuppankai, 1976.

Sakamoto Tarō et al., eds. *Nihon koten bungaku taikei: Nihonshoki*. Iwanami Shoten, 1967.

Sakurai Tokutarō, ed. *Jizō shinkō*. Yūzankaku Shuppan, 1983.

Sasaki Yasuyuki, ed. *Nihon no kogoroshi no kenkyū*. Kōbundō, 1982.

Takahashi Bonsen. *Nihon jinkō-shi no kenkyū*. Sanyūsha, 1941–1962.

Takeda Chōshū. *Sosen sūhai*. Kyoto: Keiraku-ji Shoten, 1982.

Tamamuro Taijō. "Chibyō shūkyō no keifu." *Nihon rekishi* 186 (November, 1963): 2–15.

——. *Nihon bukkyō-shi: kinsei kindai hen*. Kyoto: Hōzōkan, 1950.

——. *Sōshiki bukkyō*. Daihōrinkaku, 1963.

Tanaka Gen. *Kodai nihonjin no sekai: bukkyō juyō no zentei*. Yoshikawa Kōbunkan, 1972.

Terauchi Daikichi. "Gendai no mizuko jizō." *Jizōsama nyūmon*. Edited by Daihōrin-Henshūbu. Daihōrinkaku, 1984: 92–93.

Tsuboi Hirobumi. *Ie to josei: kurashi to bunka-shi*. Shogakkan, 1985.

Uesato Shunsei. *Edo shoseki-shō-shi*. Meicho Kankōkai, 1965.

Wagatsuma Hiroshi. *Nihonjin to amerikajin: koka ga ōchigai*. Nesuko, 1985.

Watanabe Shōkō. *Nihon no bukkyō*. Iwanami Shoten, 1958.

Watsuji Tetsurō. " 'Kiku to katana' ni tsuite." *Watsuji Tetsurō Zenshū*. Edited by Abe Yoshinari et al. Vol. 3. Iwanami Shoten, 1977: 355–67.

——. "Sakoku: nihon no higeki." *Watsuji Tetsurō Zenshū*. Edited by Abe Yoshinari et al. Vol. 15. Iwanami Shoten, 1978.

Yanagida Kunio. "Kokyō nanajū-nen." *Teihon Yanagida Kunio shū*. Supplementary vol 3. Chikuma Shobō, 1964.

Yokoi Kiyoshi. *Mato to ena: chūseijin no sei to shi*. Heibonsha, 1988.

Yuasa Yasuo. *Nihonjin no Shūkyō-ishiki*. Meicho Kankōkai, 1958.

WESTERN-LANGUAGE SOURCES

Aitken, Robert. *The Mind of Clover: Essays in Zen Buddhist Ethics*. San Francisco: North Point Press, 1984.

Ariyoshi, Sawako. *The Twilight Years*. Translated by Mildred Tahara. Tokyo: Kodansha International, 1984.

Arntzen, Sonja. *Ikkyū and the Crazy Cloud Anthology: A Zen Poet of Medieval Japan*. Tokyo: University of Tokyo Press, 1986.

Aston, W. G., trans. *Nihongi: Chronicles of Japan from the Earliest Times to A.D. 697*. Rutland, Vt.: Charles E. Tuttle, 1972.

Bachelard, Gaston. *Water and Dreams: An Essay on the Imagination of Water*. Translated by Edith R. Farrell. Dallas: The Pegasus Foundation, 1983.

Bardsley, Jan. *Writing for the New Woman of Taishō Japan: Hiratsuka Raichō and the Seitō Journal, 1911–1916*. Ph.D. diss., University of California, Los Angeles, 1989.

Bataille, Georges. *The Accursed Share: An Essay on General Economy*. Vol. 1. Translated by Robert Hurley. New York: Zone Books, 1988.

——. *"Visions of Excess: Selected Writings 1927–1939*. Edited by Allan Stoekl. Minneapolis: University of Minnesota Press, 1985.

Bayley, David H. *Forces of Order: Police Behavior in Japan and the United States*. Berkeley: University of California Press, 1976.

Bellah, Robert N., Richard Madsen, William M. Sullivan, Ann Swindler, and Steven M. Tipton. *Habits of the Heart: Individualism and Commitment in American Life*. Berkeley: University of California Press, 1985.

Benedict, Ruth. *The Chrysanthemum and the Sword: Patterns of Japanese Culture*. Boston: Houghton Mifflin Co., 1946.

Bloss, Lowell. "The Buddha and the Nâga: A Study in Buddhist Folk Religiosity." *History of Religions* 13:1 (August 1973): 36–53.

Borgen, Robert. *Sugiwara no Michizane and the Early Heian Court*. Cambridge, Mass.: Harvard University Press, 1986.

Boswell, John. *The Kindness of Strangers: The Abandonment of Children in Western Europe from Late Antiquity to the Renaissance*. New York: Pantheon Books, 1988.

Brooks, Anne Page. "'Mizuko Kuyō' and Japanese Buddhism." *Japanese Journal of Religious Studies* 8:3–4 (September–December 1981): 119–47.

Brundage, James A. *Law, Sex, and Christian Society in Medieval Europe*. Chicago: University of Chicago Press, 1987.

Buckley, Sandra. "Body Politics: Abortion Law Reform." *The Japanese Trajectory: Modernization and Beyond*. Edited by Gavan McCormack and Yoshio Sugimoto. Cambridge: Cambridge University Press, 1988: 205–17.

Burch, Thomas K. "Induced Abortion in Japan under Eugenic Protection Law of 1948." *Eugenics Quarterly* 2:3 (September 1955).

Ch'en, Kenneth K. S. *Buddhism in China: A Historical Survey*. Princeton: Princeton University Press, 1964.

Cohen, Jeremy. *"Be Fruitful and Increase, Fill the Earth and Master It": The Ancient and Medieval Career of a Biblical Text*. Ithaca, N.Y.: Cornell University Press, 1989.

Coleman, Samuel. *Family Planning in Japanese Society: Traditional Birth Control in a Modern Urban Culture*. Princeton: Princeton University Press, 1983.

Collcutt, Martin. "Buddhism: The Threat of Eradication." *Japan in Transition: From Tokugawa to Meiji*. Edited by Marius B. Jansen and Gilbert Rozman. Princeton: Princeton University Press, 1986: 143–67.

Cooper, Michael. *They Came to Japan: An Anthology of European Reports on Japan, 1543–1640*. Berkeley: University of California Press, 1965.

Czaja, Michael. *Gods of Myth and Stone: Phallicism in Japanese Folk Religion*. New York: Weatherhill, 1974.

Davis, Winston. "Buddhism and the Modernization of Japan." *History of Religions* 28:4 (May 1989): 304–39.

Dazai, Osamu. *Return to Tsugaru: Travels of a Purple Tramp*. Translated by James Westerhoven. Tokyo and New York: Kodansha International, 1985.

De Vos, George A. "The Relation of Guilt toward Parents to Achievement and Arranged Marriage among the Japanese." *Psychiatry* 23 (1960): 287–301.

———. *Socialization for Achievement: Essays on the Cultural Psychology of the Japanese*. Berkeley: University of California Press, 1973.

Donzelot, Jacques. *The Policing of Families*. Translated by Robert Hurley. New York: Pantheon Books, 1979.

Dore, Ronald. *Taking Japan Seriously: A Confucian Perspective on Leading Economic Issues*. Stanford: Stanford University Press, 1984.

Dower, John W. *War Without Mercy: Race and Power in the Pacific War*. New York: Pantheon Books, 1986.

Dykstra, Yoshiko Kurata. "Jizō, the Most Merciful: Tales from *Jizō Bosatsu Reigenki.*" *Monumenta Nipponica* 33:2 (Summer 1978): 179–200.

Edwards, Walter. *Modern Japan through Its Weddings: Gender, Person, and Society in Ritual Portrayal.* Stanford: Stanford University Press, 1989.

Eliade, Mircea. *Patterns in Comparative Religion.* Translated by Rosemary Sheed. New York: Sheed and Ward, 1958.

———. *Rites and Symbols of Initiation: The Mysteries of Birth and Rebirth.* New York: Harper and Row, 1958.

Endo Shusaku. *Silence.* Translated by William Johnston. Tokyo: Kodansha International, 1969.

Eng, Robert Y., and Thomas C. Smith. "Peasant Families and Population Control in Eighteenth-Century Japan." *Journal of Interdisciplinary History* 6:3 (winter 1976): 423.

Evans-Wentz, W. Y., ed. *The Tibetan Book of the Dead.* New York: Oxford University Press, 1960.

Falwell, Jerry. "Strengthening Families in the Nation." Speech given in Atlanta, 23 March 1982. *American Rhetoric from Roosevelt to Reagan: A Collection of Speeches and Critical Essays.* Edited by Halford Ross Ryan. Prospect Heights, Ill.: Waveland Press, Inc., 1983.

Gennep, Arnold van. *The Rites of Passage.* Chicago: University of Chicago Press, 1960.

Girardot, N. J. *Myth and Meaning in Early Taoism.* Berkeley: University of California Press, 1983.

Gluck, Carol. *Japan's Modern Myths: Ideology in the Late Meiji Period.* Princeton: Princeton University Press, 1985.

Goldstein, Robert D. *Mother-Love and Abortion: A Legal Interpretation.* Berkeley: University of California Press, 1988.

Gombrich, Richard F. *Precept and Practice: Traditional Buddhism in the Rural Highlands of Ceylon.* Oxford: Clarendon Press, 1971.

Gombrich, Richard F., and Gananath Obeyesekere. *Buddhism Transformed: Religious Change in Sri Lanka.* Princeton: Princeton University Press, 1988.

Gordon, Mary. "Abortion: How Do We Really Choose?" *Good Boys and Dead Girls and Other Essays.* New York: Viking, 1991.

Haley, John Owen. *Authority without Power: Law and the Japanese Paradox.* New York: Oxford University Press, 1991.

———. "Sheathing the Sword of Justice in Japan: An Essay on Law Without Sanctions," *The Journal of Japanese Studies* 8:2 (summer 1982): 265–81.

Hall, David L., and Roger T. Ames. *Thinking through Confucius.* Albany: State University of New York Press, 1987.

Hane, Mikiso. *Modern Japan: A Historical Survey.* Boulder, Colo.: Westview Press, 1986.

Hanley, Susan B., and Kozo Yamamura. *Economic and Demographic Change in Pre-Industrial Japan, 1600–1868.* Princeton: Princeton University Press, 1977.

Hardacre, Helen. *Kurozumikyō and the New Religions of Japan.* Princeton: Princeton University Press, 1986.

Harootunian, H. D. *Things Seen and Unseen: Discourse and Ideology in Tokugawa Nativism.* Chicago: University of Chicago Press, 1988.

Havens, Thomas. "War and Women in Japan, 1937–1945." *American Historical Review* 80:4 (October 1975): 916–20.

Hayami, Akira. "The Population at the Beginning of the Tokugawa Period." *Keio Economic Studies* 4 (1966–1967).

———. "Population Changes." *Japan in Transition: From Tokugawa to Meiji.* Edited by Marius B. Jansen and Gilbert Rozman. Princeton: Princeton University Press, 1986.

Hearn, Lafcadio. *Glimpses of Unfamiliar Japan.* 2 vols. Boston: Houghton Mifflin Co., 1894.

Hoffer, Peter C., and N.E.H. Hull. *Murdering Mothers: Infanticide in England and New England 1558–1803.* New York: New York University Press, 1981.

Hori, Ichiro. *Folk Religion in Japan: Continuity and Change.* Chicago: University of Chicago Press, 1968.

Hoshino, Eiki, and Takeda Dosho. "Indebtedness and Comfort: The Undercurrents of *Mizuko Kuyō* in Contemporary Japan." *Japanese Journal of Religious Studies* 14:4 (December 1987): 305–20.

Hurvitz, Leon, trans. *Scripture of the Lotus Blossom of the Fine Dharma (The Lotus Sutra).* New York: Columbia University Press, 1976.

Ihara, Saikaku. *The Life of an Amorous Woman and Other Writings.* Translated by Ivan Morris. New York: New Directions, 1963.

———. *Some Final Words of Advice.* Translated by Peter Nosco. Rutland, Vt.: Charles E. Tuttle, 1980.

———. *The Great Mirror of Male Love.* Translated by Paul Gordon Schalow. Stanford: Stanford University Press, 1990.

Inada, Kenneth K., and Nolan P. Jacobson. *Buddhism and American Thinkers.* Albany: State University of New York Press, 1984.

Institute of Population Studies of Chulalongkorn University. *Thailand's Continuing Fertility Decline.* Paper no. 40. Bangkok: Professional Publishing Co., n.d.

Jannetta, Ann Bowman. *Epidemics and Mortality in Early Modern Japan.* Princeton: Princeton University Press, 1987.

Johnson, Chalmers. *MITI and the Japanese Miracle: The Growth of Industrial Policy, 1925–1975.* Stanford: Stanford University Press, 1982.

Kaempfer, Engelbert. *The History of Japan Together with a Description of the Kingdom of Siam 1690–1692.* Translated by J. G. Scheuzer. 3 vols. Glasgow: James MacLehose and Sons, 1906.

Keene, Donald, trans. *Essays in Idleness: The Tsurezuregusa of Kenkō.* New York: Columbia University Press, 1967.

Kelly, William W. *Deference and Defiance in Nineteenth-Century Japan.* Princeton: Princeton University Press, 1985.

Ketelaar, James Edward. *Of Heretics and Martyrs in Meiji Japan: Buddhism and Its Persecution.* Princeton: Princeton University Press, 1990.

Kiernan, V. G. *The Lords of Human Kind: Black Man, Yellow Man, and White Man in an Age of Empire.* New York: Columbia University Press, 1969.

Kitagawa, Joseph M. *On Understanding Japanese Religion.* Princeton: Princeton University Press, 1987.

————. *Religion in Japanese History*. New York: Columbia University Press, 1966.

Koschmann, J. Victor. *The Mito Ideology: Discourse, Reform, and Insurrection in Late Tokugawa Japan, 1790–1864*. Berkeley: University of California Press, 1987.

LaFleur, William R. *Buddhism: A Cultural Perspective*. Englewood Cliffs, N.J.: Prentice-Hall, 1988.

————. "Contestation and Consensus: The Morality of Abortion in Japan." *Philosophy East and West* 40:4 (October 1990): 529–42.

————. "Hungry Ghosts and Hungry People: Somaticity and Rationality in Medieval Japan." *Fragments for a History of the Human Body*. Edited by Michel Feyer with Ramona Nadaff and Nadia Tazi. Vol. 1. New York: Zone Books, 1989: 270–303.

————. *The Karma of Words: Buddhism and the Literary Arts in Medieval Japan*. Berkeley: University of California Press, 1983.

————. "Zen and the Art of Dealing with Zen and the [Literary] Arts." *Journal of Japanese Studies* 11:1 (winter 1985): 152–69.

Lakoff, George, and Mark Johnson. *Metaphors We Live By*. Chicago: University of Chicago Press, 1980.

Lakoff, George, and Mark Turner. *More Than Cool Reason: A Field Guide to Poetic Metaphor*. Chicago: University of Chicago Press, 1989.

Lau, D. C., trans. *Tao Te Ching*. Baltimore: Penguin Books, 1963.

Leach, E. R. "Pulleyar and the Lord Buddha: An Aspect of Religious Syncretism in Ceylon." *Psychoanalysis and the Psychoanalytic Review* 49:2 (1962): 80–102.

Lebra, Takie Sugiyama. *Japanese Patterns of Behavior*. Honolulu: University of Hawaii Press, 1976.

Le Goff, Jacques. *The Birth of Purgatory*. Translated by Arthur Goldhammer. Chicago: University of Chicago Press, 1981.

Lidin, Olof G. *The Life of Ogyū Sorai, A Tokugawa Confucian Philosopher*. Copenhagen: The Scandinavian Institute of Asian Studies Monograph Series, no. 19, 1973.

Ling, T. O. "Buddhist Factors in Population Growth and Control: A Survey Based on Thailand and Ceylon." *Population Studies* 23:1 (March 1969): 53–60.

Lock, Margaret. "Protests of a Good Wife and Wise Mother: The Medicalization of Distress in Japan." Edward Norbeck and Margaret Lock, eds. *Health, Illness, and Medical Care in Japan: Cultural and Social Dimensions*. Honolulu: University of Hawaii Press, 1987: 130–57.

McCooey, Christopher. "Abortion: Last Resort, First Choice." *Intersect* 1:7 (July 1985): 9–11, 40.

McEwen, J. R. *The Political Writings of Ogyū Sorai*. Cambridge: Cambridge University Press, 1969.

McKibben, Bill. *The End of Nature*. New York: Random House, 1989.

Malalasekera, G. P., et al. eds., *Encyclopedia of Buddhism*. Vol. 1. Ceylon: The Government Press, n.d.

Malthus, Thomas Robert. *An Essay on the Principle of Population and a Summary View of the Principle of Population.* Edited by Anthony Flew. New York: Penguin Books, 1979.

Maruyama, Masao. *Studies in the Intellectual History of Tokugawa Japan.* Translated by Mikiso Hane. Princeton: Princeton University Press, 1974.

Mause, Lloyd de. "The Evolution of Childhood." *The History of Childhood.* London: Souvenir Press, 1976: 1–74.

Miles, John A., Jr. "Jain and Judeo-Christian Respect for Life." *Journal of the American Academy of Religion* 44:30 (1976): 453–57.

Mills, D. E., trans. *A Collection of Tales from Uji: A Study and Translation of Uji Shūi Monogatari.* Cambridge: Cambridge University Press, 1970.

Minson, Jeffrey. *Genealogies of Morals: Nietzsche, Foucault, Donzelot, and the Eccentricity of Ethics.* New York: St. Martin's Press, 1985.

Miura Domyo. *The Forgotten Child: An Ancient Eastern Answer to a Modern Problem.* Henley-on-Thames: Aidan Ellis, 1983.

Morris, Herbert. *On Guilt and Innocence: Essays in Legal Philosophy and Moral Psychology.* Berkeley: University of California Press, 1976.

Morris, Herbert, ed. *Guilt and Shame.* Belmont, Calif.: Wadsworth Publishing Co., 1971.

Murasaki Shikibu. *The Tale of Genji.* Translated by Edward G. Seidensticker. Vol 1. New York: Alfred A. Knopf, 1977.

Mus, Paul. *La lumière sur les six voies: tableau de la transmigration bouddhiques.* Paris: Travaux et Mémoires de l'Institut d'Ethnologie, 1939.

Najita, Tetsuo. *Visions of Virtue in Tokugawa Japan: The Kaitokudō Merchant Academy of Osaka.* Chicago: University of Chicago Press, 1987.

Nakamura, James I., and Matao Miyamoto. "Social Structure and Population Change: A Comparative Study of Tokugawa Japan and Ch'ing China." *Economic Development and Cultural Change.* 30:2 (1982).

Nippo jisho [Vocabulario de Lingoa de Iapam, orig. 1603]. Reprinted. Iwanami Shoten, 1960.

Nisbet, Robert. *Prejudices: A Philosophical Dictionary.* Cambridge, Mass.: Harvard University Press, 1982.

Noonan, John T., Jr. "An Almost Absolute Value in History." *The Morality of Abortion: Legal and Historical Perspectives.* Edited by Noonan. Cambridge, Mass.: Harvard University Press, 1970.

Norman, E. H. *Origins of the Modern Japanese State: Selected Writings of E. H. Norman.* Edited by John W. Dower. New York: Pantheon Books, 1975.

Nosco, Peter. *Remembering Paradise: Nativism and Nostalgia in Eighteenth-Century Japan.* Cambridge, Mass.: Harvard University Press, 1990.

Ohnuki-Tierney, Emiko. *Illness and Culture in Contemporary Japan: An Anthropological View.* Cambridge: Cambridge University Press, 1984.

Ooms, Herman. *Charismatic Bureaucrat: A Political Biography of Matsudaira Sadanobu, 1758–1829.* Chicago: University of Chicago Press, 1975.

———. "The Religion of the Household: A Case Study of Ancestor Worship in Japan." *Contemporary Religions in Japan.* 8:3–4 (1967): 201–303.

———. *Tokugawa Ideology: Early Constructs, 1570–1680.* Princeton: Princeton University Press, 1985.

Pagels, Elaine. *Adam, Eve, and the Serpent.* New York: Random House, 1988.

Parrinder, Geoffrey. "Exorcism." *The Encyclopedia of Religion.* Edited by Mircea Eliade. Vol. 5. New York: Macmillan Publishing Co., 1987: 225–33.

Pelzel, John C. "Human Nature in the Japanese Myths." *Personality in Japanese History.* Edited by A. M. Craig and D. H. Shively. Berkeley: University of California Press, 1970.

Philippi, Donald L., trans. *Kojiki.* Tokyo: University of Tokyo Press, 1968.

Piers, Gerhard, and Milton B. Singer. "Shame." *Guilt and Shame.* Edited by Herbert Morris. Belmont, Calif.: Wadsworth Publishing Co., 1971: 147–54.

Plath, David W. "Where the Family of God Is the Family: The Role of the Dead in Japanese Households." *American Anthropologist* 66 (1964): 300–317.

Plutschow, H. E. *Chaos and Cosmos: Ritual in Early and Medieval Japanese Literature.* Leiden: E. J. Brill, 1990.

———. "The Fear of Evil Spirits in Japanese Culture." *Transactions of the Asiatic Society of Japan.* 3d series, vol. 18 (1983): 139.

Pratt, James Bissett. *The Pilgrimage of Buddhism and a Buddhist Pilgrimage.* New York: The Macmillan Co., 1928.

Ramseyer, J. Mark, and Minoru Nakazato. "The Rational Litigant: Settlement Amounts and Verdict Rates in Japan." *Journal of Legal Studies* 18:2 (June 1989): 263–90.

Robertson, Jennifer. "Sexy Rice: Plant, Gender, Farm Manuals, and Grass-roots Nativism." *Monumenta Nipponica* 39:3 (Autumn 1984): 234–60.

Rodman, Hyman, Betty Sarvis, and Joy Walker Bonar. *The Abortion Question.* New York: Columbia University Press, 1987.

Rohlen, Thomas P. *For Harmony and Strength: Japanese White-Collar Organization in Anthropological Perspective.* Berkeley: University of California Press, 1974.

Rorty, Richard. *Consequences of Pragmatism (Essays: 1972–1980).* Minneapolis: University of Minnesota Press, 1982.

———. *Contingency, Irony, and Solidarity.* Cambridge: Cambridge University Press, 1989.

———. *Philosophy and the Mirror of Nature.* Princeton: Princeton University Press, 1979.

Rozman, Gilbert. *Urban Networks in Ch'ing China and Tokugawa Japan.* Princeton: Princeton University Press, 1977.

Safire, William. "Option 3: 'Pro-Comp.'" *New York Times* (July 6, 1989).

Sanford, James H. "The Abominable Skull Ritual." *Monumenta Nipponica* 46:1 (spring 1991): 1–2.

———. *Zen-Man Ikkyū.* Chico, Calif.: Scholars Press, 1981.

Sievers, Sharon L. *Flowers in Salt: The Beginnings of Feminist Consciousness in Modern Japan.* Stanford: Stanford University Press, 1983.

Smith, Bardwell. "Buddhism and Abortion in Contemporary Japan: *Mizuko Kuyō* and the Confrontation with Death." *Japanese Journal of Religious Studies* 15:1 (March 1988): 3–24.

Smith, Robert J. *Ancestor Worship in Contemporary Japan.* Stanford: Stanford University Press, 1974.

Smith, Robert J. "Something Old, Something New—Tradition and Culture in the Study of Japan." *The Journal of Asian Studies* 48:4 (November 1989): 715–23.

Smith, Robert J., and Ella Lury Wiswell. *The Women of Suye Mura*. Chicago: University of Chicago Press, 1982.

Smith, Thomas C. *Nakahara: Family Farming and Population in a Japanese Village, 1717–1830*. Stanford: Stanford University Press, 1977.

Stout, Jeffrey. *Ethics after Babel: The Languages of Morals and Their Discontents*. Boston: Beacon Press, 1988.

Tachibana, Shundo. *The Ethics of Buddhism*. London: Curzon Press, 1926.

Tambiah, S. J. *Buddhism and the Spirit Cults in North-east Thailand*. Cambridge: Cambridge University Press, 1970.

Taylor, Gabrielle. *Pride, Shame, and Guilt: Emotions of Self-Assessment*. Oxford: Clarendon Press, 1985.

Teiser, Stephen F. *The Ghost Festival in Medieval China*. Princeton: Princeton University Press, 1988.

Tisdale, Sallie. "We Do Abortions Here: A Nurse's Story." *Harper's* (October 1987): 66–70.

Toby, Ronald P. *State and Diplomacy in Early Modern Japan: Asia in the Development of the Tokugawa Bakufu*. Princeton: Princeton University Press, 1984.

Tocqueville, Alexis de. *Democracy in America*. Translated by George Lawrence. Edited by J. P. Mayer. New York: Doubleday Anchor, 1969.

Tooley, Michael. *Abortion and Infanticide*. Oxford: Clarendon Press, 1983.

Turner, Victor. *The Ritual Process: Structure and Anti-Structure*. Chicago: Aldine, 1969.

Ueda, Makoto. *Matsuo Bashō*. Tokyo: Kodansha International, 1970.

Visser, M. W. de. *The Bodhisattva Ti-Tsang (Jizō) in China and Japan*. Berlin: Oesterheld and Co., 1914.

Vlastos, Stephen. *Peasant Protests and Uprisings in Tokugawa Japan*. Berkeley: University of California Press, 1986.

Wagatsuma, Hiroshi, and Arthur Rosett. "The Implications of Apology: Law and Culture in Japan and the United States." *Law and Society Review* 20:1 (1986): 461–97.

Walthall, Anne. *Social Protest and Popular Culture in Eighteenth-Century Japan*. Tucson: University of Arizona Press, 1986.

Warren, Henry Clarke. *Buddhism in Translations*. New York: Atheneum, 1969.

Watson, Burton, trans. *Ryōkan: Zen Monk-Poet of Japan*. New York: Columbia University Press, 1977.

Weinstein, Stanley. "Rennyo and the Shinshū Revival." *Japan in the Muromachi Age*. Edited by John Whitney Hall and Toyoda Takeshi. Berkeley: University of California Press, 1977: 331–58.

Welbon, Guy Richard. *The Buddhist Nirvana and Its Western Interpreters*. Chicago: University of Chicago Press, 1968.

White, Merry. *The Japanese Educational Challenge: A Commitment to Children*. New York: The Free Press, 1987.

Wong, David B. *Moral Relativity*. Berkeley: University of California Press, 1984.

Yosano Akiko. "Never Let Them Kill You, Brother!" *Modern Japanese Poetry*. Translated by James Kirkup. St. Lucia: University of Queensland Press, 1978.

INDEX

abandonment, 38, 135, 180–83
abortion: anxiety about, 51, 126–28, 166–67, 187–90, 204; criminalized, 120, 122, 126, 128, 132, 161, 168, 206; and Japan as "abortion heaven," 136, 164, 170, 187, 206; legalized, 4, 129, 135–36, 162, 192, 203–5, 218–19; methods of, 108, 113, 219; in the U.S., xiii, xv, 14, 191, 196, 202–4, 211–12, 216–19
Aitken, Robert, 198–201
aku, 193
Ames, Roger T., 155
Amida, 3, 15, 36, 47, 230n.27
apology, 8, 53, 146–47, 153, 155, 171, 211
argha/aka, 16
Aristotle, 182
Ariyoshi Sawako, 34
Augustine, Saint, 38–39, 43

baby boom, 135
Bachelard, Gaston, 23
bakumatsu, 108
Bataille, Georges, 85, 89
Bayley, David H., 215
Bellah, Robert N., 188
Benedict, Ruth, 151–52
Bhavisyottara-purana, 18
bochi, 6
bodhisattva, 46–50, 53, 56, 123–24, 128, 130, 180, 199, 201
Bonar, Joy Walker, 180
Boswell, John, 180–81
bricolage, moral, 12, 15, 20, 74, 101, 117, 178, 213, 217, 225n.6
brunahatiya, 225n.4
Brundage, James A., 78, 202
Buddhism: celibacy in, 20, 73–74, 81–82, 84, 87, 111–12, 115, 133, 186; clerical order (sangha) of, 84; compassion in, 56, 114, 116, 165, 199–201; cosmology of, 16, 65, 225n.2; funerary, 80–82, 87, 168, 189, 200; precepts of, 10–12, 199; in Sri Lanka, 21, 116–17, 143–44, 207; in Thailand, 116

Caron, François, 184
Chiba Tokuji, 26, 123

Christianity, 17, 38, 41–43, 47, 56–58, 72, 76, 78, 80, 131, 150, 160–61, 180, 183, 196, 198, 204, 207, 210, 216
Chūjō School, 113
Clavell, James, 151
Cohen, Jeremy, 207
Coleman, Samuel, 136, 161, 205
Collcutt, Martin, 73
commercialization, 62, 138–39, 148, 157, 162, 166, 194, 218
condom, 136, 205
Confucianism, 70–71, 80, 82–83, 85–86, 99, 103, 106–7, 113, 178–179, 230n.4, 232n.33
conservativism, political, 156, 189, 192–96, 217
constitutional rights, 212
contraception, 39, 115–17, 132, 136, 186, 192, 204–6, 218; and family planning, 96, 98–99, 116, 122, 136, 179, 183–84, 186, 219; and "the Pill," 136, 186–87, 190, 205, 218, 242n.12
Cooks, Richard, 94

Daihōrin, 116, 163–64, 167, 170–71, 176, 195
dana, 85
danka seido, 72
Dante, 57
Dazai Osamu, 134–35
Divine Comedy, The, 57
Donzelot, Jacques, 121, 181
Dore, Ronald, 215
Dōsōjin, 124
dreams, 152, 171–74, 199, 201

Eliade, Mircea, 23, 31
Endo Shusaku, 160
epidemics, 92–93, 99, 172
Eugenics Protection Law, 135, 161–62

Falwell, Jerry, 203
famine, 92–97, 99, 101–2, 127, 135, 185
fecundity/fecundism, xvi, 18, 20, 87–88, 112, 115, 120, 130, 134, 161, 170, 178–80, 186, 191, 206–10, 218–20

fetus: "return" of, 26–28, 37, 99, 106, 185; status of, 24, 28- 29, 148, 196, 199–200
Feuerbach, Ludwig, 208
Fire Sermon, 17, 19
folk religion, 36, 51, 80, 124, 194, 213
Francis Xavier, Saint, 40–42, 94, 184
Fujiyoshi Jikai, 163–64, 240n.23
fuse, 85

Ganesha, 75
Ganges River, 22
Gluck, Carol, 121
Goldstein, Robert D., 204
Gombrich, Richard F., 21, 144
Gordon, Mary, 177, 217–19
gu, 195
guilt, 4, 10, 65, 100, 126, 130, 145–47, 151–58, 161–64, 185, 192, 195, 197, 200–201, 203, 215, 217, 237n.13

Haga Yaichi, 54
haibutsu kishaku, 105
Haley, John O., 147, 215
Hall, David L., 155
Hanayama Shōyō, 164
Hanley, Susan B., 92, 97
Han-Yü, 83
Hardacre, Helen, 149–50
Harootunian, Harry D., 111–12
Harrison, Elizabeth, 242n.9
Hase-dera Temple, 3–6
Hashimoto Mitsuru, 187–91, 202
Hashimoto Tetsuma, 168
Havens, Thomas R. H., 132
Hayami Akira, 90
Hayami Tasuku, 47, 50
Hearn, Lafcadio, 45
Hiro Sachiya, 17, 165
Honda Masuko, 185
honne and *tatemae*, 131
hotoke, 36

ichinin, 35
Ihara Saikaku, 72–73, 77, 152, 231n.19
Iizawa Tadasu, 166
Ikkyū, 75
infanticide, 38, 40, 45, 51, 65, 94–97, 113, 120, 122–23, 128–29, 135, 162, 178, 180–82, 184–86, 204–6, 208, 241n.11

infant mortality, 29, 37, 39, 218
infertility, 126–27
Iwai Hiroshi, 24
Izanagi and Izanami, 23, 25, 87

Jainism, 117
Jannetta, Ann Bowman, 93
Japan: education in, 40, 79, 197; family in, 40–42, 79–83, 121, 150, 178, 183–84, 197, 205–6, 213; learning from, xv, 215–16; medieval, 16, 33–37, 39, 48–53, 56–58, 74–76, 118, 145; militarism in, 122, 133; otherness of, 214; xenophobia in, 105, 193–94
Jizō, 4–9, 16, 44–51, 53, 59–60, 64–65, 124–26, 130–31, 148, 180, 191; at crossroads, 49, 124; in groups of six, 49, 149; iconography of, 44, 49, 51, 53, 124, 229n.13; and *koyasu Jizō*, 127, 129
Jizō-Bosatsu Reigenki, 49
Jizō-kō, 51, 62, 106, 129
Jōdo Shinshū, 138, 167
Johnson, Chalmers, 215
Johnson, Mark, 179
Judeo-Christian values, 41, 43, 117, 151–52, 192, 202, 207, 210

Kaempfer, Engelbert, 89–90, 94
kaeru/kaesu, 40, 44, 185
kaimyō, 27, 199, 240n.3
kami, 26–27, 33, 36, 50, 53–54, 56, 115, 130, 209
kami no ko, 40
Kanaoka Shūyū, 78
kanashimi, 193
Kannon, 3–4, 44, 47–49, 131, 153, 186, 222, 225n.1
Kano Masanao, 121
karma, 18, 49, 128, 162, 164–66, 174–75
kata, 155
Keichū, 86
Ketelaar, James, 72
Kishimojin, 129
Kitagawa, Joseph M., 45, 133
kōban, 121
Kojiki, 23, 25
kokeshi dolls, 51–52
kokoro, 155, 158, 197
Kokugaku, 85–88, 103, 107, 109, 112, 124, 126, 133, 193

Konjaku-Monogatari-shū, 49–50
ku, 193, 195
Kūkai, 46
Kuroda Hideo, 33–37
Kūya, 63

Lakoff, George, 179
Lebra, Takie Sugiyama, 211
leech-child, 23–25
Le Goff, Jacques, 56–57
Liberal-Democratic party, 161, 168
Lidin, Olof G., 70
life, 11, 14–15, 19, 31, 38, 170, 193, 195–96, 213
limbo, 27, 57–58, 65, 193
Ling, T. O., 116
litigation, 147, 157–58, 211, 215
Lotus Sutra, 58, 148, 222

mabiki, 99–102, 105–10, 113–14, 118, 123, 134–35, 178–80, 182–85, 191, 205; *mabiki ema*, 122–23
MacArthur, Gen. Douglas, 136, 152
McKibben, Bill, 219
Malthus, Thomas Robert, 92–93, 99–102, 135, 185
Manabe Kōsai, 64
Marxism, 31, 96, 131, 161, 178, 192
Matsubara Taido, 165
Matsumoto Sannosuke, 86, 107–8
Matsunami Kōdō, 166
Matsuo Bashō, 181–82
Mause, Lloyd de, 97
Meiji emperor, 120
metaphor, 15, 28, 49, 74, 99, 101–2, 179, 213, 217
midwives, 100, 108, 185
Miki Kiyoshi, 72
Miles, John A., 117
miscarriage, 4, 29, 37, 40, 127, 150, 164, 171
Mito Learning, 104–5, 194
Miura Domyo, 173–75
Miyahiro Sadao, 110–12, 114–15, 120, 133
Miyauchi Yoshinaga, 109–10, 133
Miyoshi Kiyoyuki, 83
mizuko, 4, 8, 16, 23–24, 27–29, 37, 45, 127–30, 136–38, 148, 163, 166–69, 171–75, 193, 199–202, 217; mizuko kuyō, 5, 143–46, 148–50, 152, 155–58,

161–62, 164, 185, 187, 190, 214, 242n.9
modernization, 31, 32, 156–57, 169, 192, 195, 200, 241
Morris, Herbert, 154
Motoori Norinaga, 86, 88
musubi no kami, 87

Nakai Chikuzan, 104, 106
Nakatani Kinko, 210–11
Nakazato Minoru, 215
name, posthumous. See *kaimyō*
Nanzan University, 150
National Eugenics Law, 132
Nembutsu-ji, 15–16, 59
neo-Confucianism, 71, 80, 82, 99, 104, 106, 230n.4
neo-Shinto, 70, 80, 86–88, 104, 108, 111–15, 119–20, 133, 161, 179–81, 191–97, 206–9, 212
Nihonshoki, 23, 25
Nippo Jisho, 100
Nisbet, Robert, 42, 177, 184, 197, 213
Nishida Kitarō, 72
Noh, 34
Noonan, John T., 38
nōsho, 112

Obeyesekere, Ganarath, 21
Ochiai Seiko, 167–70, 176, 195
Ogyū Sorai, 84–85, 107, 231n.31, 238n.21
Ohnuki-Tierney, Emiko, 153, 157–58
okina, 34–35
onryō, 55
Ooms, Herman, 71
Ōta Tenrei, 162, 191
Ōtsu Tadao, 26, 123

paganism, 40–43, 204
Perry, Comdr. Matthew, 40, 120
phallicism, 123–26, 130, 207
Plath, David, 32
Plato, 43, 182
Plutschow, Herbert, 172
population, 70, 89–95, 120, 132, 135, 178, 185–86, 194, 217–20; in China, 91, 98; plateau, 91–93, 107, 120, 183, 186
"post-abortion syndrome," 201

pragmatism, 20, 130, 138, 157, 212–17, 241n.18
purgatory, 56–57
Purple Cloud Temple. *See* Shiunzan

Ramseyer, J. Mark, 215
rationality, 71, 84–85, 98–99, 101–2, 128, 130, 156, 178–79, 187, 217, 242n.10
Reagan, Ronald, 203
reikon, 167
Rennyo, 81, 87
reproductivity, xv, 18–20, 70, 78, 86–88, 110–12, 114–15, 120, 123, 126, 132, 179–80, 206–9, 219
resentment, 55–56, 65, 172, 175
ritual, xiii, 5, 10, 15–17, 27–28, 31, 34–35, 40, 55, 85, 131, 143–46, 149–51, 153–58, 189–91, 199–200, 217, 232n.33, 238n.21
Riverbank of Sai. *See* Sai-no-kawara
Robertson, Jennifer, 112
Robertson, Pat, 209
Rodman, Hyman, 180
Roe v. Wade, xiii, 203
Rohlen, Thomas P., 215
rokudō, 48, 58
Rorty, Richard, 198, 241n.18, 242n.10
Rosett, Arthur, 147
RU-486, 218
Russo-Japanese War, 122
Ryōkan, 75, 86, 228n.11

Sado Island, 59
Safire, William, 241n.20
Sai-no-kawara, 58–65, 149, 158, 193, 197, 200
Sakabe Megumi, 226n.15
samurai class, 179–80
Sanford, James, 74–75
Sanger, Margaret, 122
Sarvis, Betty, 180
Satō Nobuhiro, 107
Seichō no Ie, 161, 168–70, 193
Seitō, 122
sexuality: attitudes toward, 19, 73–79, 85–88, 110–12, 115, 124, 126, 133, 202, 207
Shakyamuni, 17, 21, 105, 114–15, 164, 167, 169, 194
shame, 151–52, 154–55, 193, 237n.13
shichi-go-san, 35

shimatsusho, 147
shingaru, 195
Shinran, 164, 168, 170
Shinto, 21, 31–32, 86, 103, 108–12, 124, 126, 133, 135, 150, 161, 168–70
Shiojiri, 24
Shiunzan, 5–6, 8–10, 62, 168–69, 171–73, 176, 201
"slippery slope," 204–6
Smith, Bardwell, 242n.9
Smith, Robert J., 33, 227n.4
Smith, Thomas, 95–98
Stout, Jeffrey, 12, 101, 213
subjectivity, 151, 169, 188, 192
Sugawara Michizane, 55, 172
Suzuki Shigetani, 108–9, 119, 133

Tachikawa School, 74
Takahashi Bonsen, 23–24
Tale of Genji, The, 17
Tamakuro Taijō, 80
Tanaka Gen, 54
Taniguchi Seicho, 161
Tao Te Ching, 19, 44, 198
tatari, 54–55, 110, 126–27, 138, 162–76, 187–91, 193, 195, 197, 201–2, 213; and exorcism, 168, 170, 172, 175, 190, 239n.20; in the U.S., 202–3
Taylor, Gabrielle, 154–55
televangelists, 166
Teresa, Mother, 169
Terry, Randall, 203
Thales, 19
Tibetan Book of the Dead, 58
Tisdale, Sallie, 201
Toby, Ronald, 69
Tocqueville, Alexis de, 188–90
Tokugawa Ieyasu, 70
transmigration. *See* *umarekawari*
tsumi, 193
Tsurezuregusa, 21

Uesato Shunsei, 71
Uji Shūi Monogatari, 50–51
ukiyo, 76
umarekawari, 36, 178, 182

Vilela, Gaspar, 94–96
Visser, Willem Marinus de, 45

Wagatsuma Hiroshi, 144, 147
Wakamori Tarō, 50

war casualities, 122, 134
water: and fertility, 17, 20–22; symbolism
    of, 16–17, 19–21, 23
Watsuji Tetsurō, 69, 72
White, Merry, 215, 219
Wiswell, Ella, 132
women: and circumventions of law, 128–
    30; and Jizō 45, 50–51, 62, 106, 126–
    29, 131, 138; in Meiji period, 120, 123,
    129

wūman ribu, 168, 192–93, 196, 205

yakuza, 166
Yamada Waka, 122
Yamamura Kozo, 92, 97
Yanagida Kunio, 122–24, 235n.8
Yasuda Satsuji, 122
yasukuni, 133, 169–70
Yoshida Kenkō, 21, 177, 180
Yuasa Yasuo, 43–44, 46, 54–56